THE MALAYSIAN KITCHEN

150 Recipes for
Simple Home Cooking

THE MALAYSIAN KITCHEN

CHRISTINA AROKIASAMY

Houghton Mifflin Harcourt
BOSTON NEW YORK 2017

For information about permission to reproduce
selections from this book, write to trade.
permissions@hmhco.com or to Permissions,
Houghton Mifflin Harcourt Publishing Company,
3 Park Avenue, 19th Floor, New York,
New York 10016.

www.hmhco.com

*Library of Congress Cataloging-in-Publication
Data is available.*

ISBN 978-0-544-80999-4 (hbk)

Printed in China
SCP 10 9 8 7 6 5 4 3 2 1

This book is dedicated to my mother
of blessed memory, Rosalind Francis,
for without her I would not be here

CONTENTS

SAMBALS, AROMATIC PASTES, AND DRESSINGS | 39

SOUPS | 65

SALADS | 93

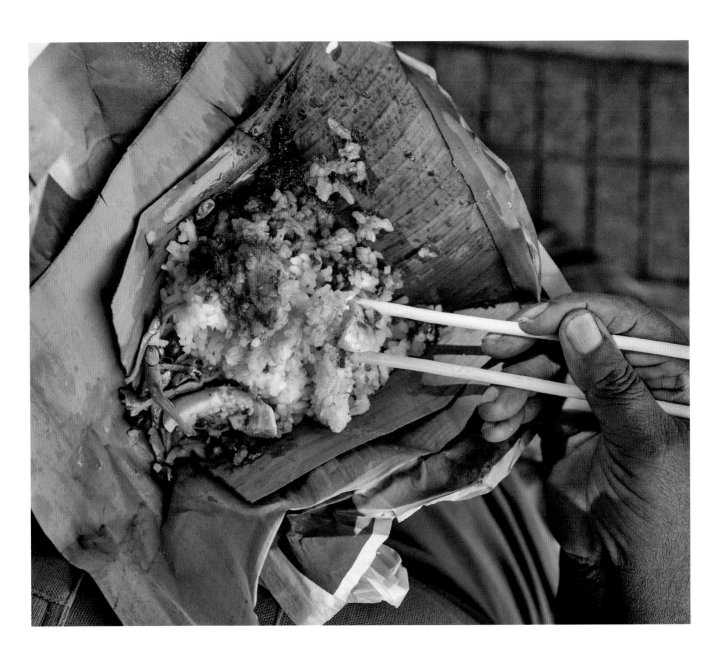

STREET FOOD | 211

MEATS | 247

DESSERTS | 293

INTRODUCTION

I recall 22 years ago, when I migrated to the United States. I invited a few of my neighbors over to my apartment in Hawaii for a simple Malaysian dinner of beef rendang with coconut rice, mango and cashew salad, a bowl of sambal belachan on the side, and a baked pandan custard cake for dessert. I will never forget my neighbors' praise and the way they devoured the dishes with gusto.

And so I agreed to walk my new American friends through a series of cook-along dinners. The six of us would cram ourselves into my tiny kitchen, and I would teach them the under-pinnings of Malaysian cuisine with ingredients that they might never have seen nor heard about.

Although I had a fair collection of cookbooks and had spent loads of time browsing through food magazines to feed my growing interest in upgrading my culinary skills, I had never taught anyone to cook. Before coming to America, my time was spent as a chef in the professional kitchens of Thailand's and Bali's Four Seasons resorts. Any vacation time I had was spent learning in the kitchens of the Wandee Culinary Institute in Thailand, as I wanted so much to embrace the cooking traditions of the neighboring Southeast Asian countries. During my journey, I was often surprised to find similarities to the dishes that I cooked with my mother in our home in Malaysia.

In preparation for my very first cooking class in my little Hawaiian apartment, I placed the "three sisters"—cinnamon, star anise, and cloves—in small bowls on an old bamboo tray alongside fresh lemongrass, galangal, makrut lime leaves, ginger, and other aromatics. Tamarind and colorful bottles of seasoning sauces from my cupboard were neatly arranged on the table. My friends were surprised that even before we began cooking the aromas of the ingredients filled the apartment. After introducing them to the three sisters, I begin to sauté the spices in hot oil to release their flavor. A sweet aroma permeated the kitchen and the entire apartment. "I love cinnamon sprinkled in my hot chocolate and in my desserts," my neighbor Karen commented, "but have never used it in meat dishes. This is incredible." As the beef rendang continued to cook, she inhaled the spices wafting from the pan.

That moment of sharing reminded me what a big part cinnamon played in my own world. I was transported back to Malaysia, where beautiful scents infused my life. My mother was a spice merchant, and my family's colonial home was surrounded by spice trees. I recall that during harvest time, the morning air carried a whiff of spice as the dark almond-shaped cinnamon leaves brushed against my window, delivering a sweet fragrance. I enjoyed watching my mother's seasonal workers with their wrinkled hands skillfully selecting and cutting off the best parts of the bark of the cinnamon trees with special knives. They stacked the moist bark sheets, painstakingly rolled them into long pipes, and left them to dry in the sun. After the pipes had completely dried, the workers cut them into those short sticks that the rest of the world knows as cinnamon. For us, cinnamon was not just a spice; it was a way of life, infused in our food, in our medicine cabinet, and even arranged in vases as decoration. The aromatic brown sticks were sautéed in hot oil to add a savory flavor to our pot of chicken curry or to boost the veggie pilafs and lamb biryanis. Mid-afternoon, several quills of cinnamon were brewed with Ceylon tea leaves, making a long delicious thirst quencher for the hot afternoons. I can clearly remember my father placing ground cinnamon in small glass bottles in his medicine cabinet, so he could later create brews to relieve muscle aches, cold, flu, and stomach upsets and to maintain cardiovascular health.

Our yard was a place where you experienced food with your eyes and your nose before your stomach. Among the cinnamon, mango, and curry leaf trees were plenty of ginger root plants, with their blindingly green leaves and scarlet flowers. We blended fresh ginger with garlic as building blocks to begin most of our Malaysian dishes. Fresh ginger was also dried under the tropical sun and ground into a citrus-scented powder used in marinades, salad dressings, desserts, and tea. The subtle green-tea scent of the pandanus palm pervaded our garden, tinted our rice cakes pale green, and infused our custard with sublime flavors.

Central to all this was the kitchen. Like most Malaysian homes, the kitchen was divided into two areas: The dry kitchen was much like the Western kitchen except that it was rarely used for cooking. Rather it was a place for storing plates and cutlery for day-to-day use. More importantly, it was a home for spices such as coriander seeds, fennel seeds, star anise, turmeric, and chili powders, stored in large bottles along with other pantry ingredients. An old wooden bench made a lovely spot for resting. The wet kitchen was where the women gathered, holding onto the bonds of tradition, and working to create

masterpiece recipes for the family. This part of the kitchen was a hive of activity: the pounding and grinding of spices into a wet paste; the washing and cleaning of aromatics, vegetables, fish, and meat; the enthusiastic chatter and the din from the clanging of utensils. Whenever we cooked a sambal with chilies, red shallots, and shrimp paste, or had a pot of laksa bubbling away at the stove, the spicy scent would announce to passersby and neighbors that lunch or dinner was being prepared. For most Malaysians, this was an invitation to interact with the neighbors and perhaps share some spicy stories or take a glimpse at what was cooking next door. The wet kitchen was where I first learned to cook.

Food has been an important part of my family for generations. My father would often bring friends home unannounced, and my mother was able to magically prepare a variety of dishes to please the guests. I saw her re-purpose everything and create dishes with whatever ingredients she had on hand. My mother, taught me the details of spice grinding, how to work with the ingredients, and how to smell, feel, and taste the food. But she never concerned herself with quantities and cooking times. A touch of this and a dash of that was the way she cooked without ever using measuring cups or spoons.

Hospitality is the most important aspect of Malaysian culture. When guests enter a Malaysian home, they are greeted with generosity. No matter how modest the family income may be, we are taught to share with guests whatever the family is eating. Everything we cooked came from the vendors—the vegetable seller, the fish monger, the fruit man—who traveled the streets each day with their freshest ingredients. Come mid-afternoon, the young Malay boy would shout out his wares carrying a small basket of colorful homemade snacks: everything from a variety of

coconut and rice cakes to banana fritters that we bought and enjoyed with tea. Later in the evening, it was the Indian bread man on a motorcycle overloaded with freshly baked buns, breads, and cakes called *kuih* in all shapes, sizes, and flavors. He, too, patiently negotiated the streets in the housing estates, his old-fashioned trumpet-like horn blaring to catch the attention of hungry residents. After dinner, you could anticipate an old Chinese vendor on his bicycle selling sticky rice dumplings and red bean buns from a bamboo steamer fitted to his bicycle. If that wasn't enough, there were night markets where street after street were filled with all sorts of Malaysian rotis (flatbreads) and *teh tarik* (sweetened tea), peanut pancakes, satays, steamed meat dumplings, sugar cane drinks, and pandan custard pies.

Growing up within the cultural heritage of the main ethnic groups in Malaysia—Indian, Chinese, Nyonya, Malay, and Portuguese—I believe it is the food, and the love for sharing it, that melts our boundaries to unite us.

Although Malaysia is an amalgamation of cultures, the pantry of each ethnic group comes stocked with its own set of ingredients. In a Malay home there is a variety of shrimp pastes and chilies, anchovies and lemongrass, galangal and lime leaves. My mother's Indian kitchen cupboard is filled with cinnamon, cumin, cardamom, dried chilies, mustard seeds, curry, mint, and coconut. My Chinese auntie's kitchen cupboard is stocked with dried lily buds, dried black mushrooms, five-spice powders, and a variety of fermented soy bean sauces. The Nyonya family down the street stocks dried bean curd, candlenuts, sambals, and kalamansi limes.

Unique to the Malaysian way of cooking is the cultures borrowing each other's ingredients to create an endless variation of culinary experience.

It was this culinary tradition and way of life that I missed when I came to the United States. I remember spending time browsing the supermarket aisles for "real" food, as I had never seen so many packaged frozen dinners, or vegetables cut up in plastic bags, in my life. I had never seen artificial "egg beaters," and I could not understand why spices were stored in small glass jars and given only a small section in the supermarkets. This was all new for me.

Eventually, I moved to the Pacific Northwest and my longing to share my cuisine got only deeper. I taught at many culinary schools, colleges, and universities, offering classes in Southeast Asian cuisine. I remember strapping both my young children in the back of the car and telling them we were going to visit Vietnam—which actually meant a drive to Seattle's International District. Back then it took me approximately an hour each way just to buy a few bottles of soy, fish, and oyster sauces and a few packets of rice vermicelli for my cooking class. You might think this insane, especially when I got to class to find only a handful of people had shown up. In the beginning, class payments barely covered the supplies and gas. But I taught with the biggest joy in my heart. The feedback and energy from the students was tremendous and the classes slowly started to fill, not only in the Seattle area but throughout the entire Pacific Northwest. I remember students from the computer class next door waiting outside my class to volunteer to clean the pots. I later learned they were hoping to taste the little bits of *char kway teow* and peanut sauce left in the woks. I moved from basics to the vast and rich repertoire of Malaysian home cooking—although this cuisine remained unknown to many.

People often ask why the flavors they try to replicate from Southeast Asian cookbooks published overseas are not as tasty as the ones they create during my cooking classes. Simply put, cookbooks published in Asia may not work well in American homes because the ingredients have different flavors and potency when grown under different soil conditions. For instance, while a cook in Malaysia might need only one stalk of lemongrass, in America the cook might need five. This principle holds true for virtually every spice. When I began writing this cookbook, my aim was to assemble the kind of dishes that North Americans want to eat and cook, and are also delicious, healthy, exciting, easy to approach, and fulfilling. The book you're holding in your hand is about traveling with your palate, experiencing the simple pleasures of discovering other worlds and cultures, brought to you by an insider from Malaysia so that you make no mistakes in your American kitchen. If you have never sliced lemongrass and galangal to make a spice paste, never squeezed a tamarind for its juice or peeled a ginger root, you may actually find the experience soothing, especially since the ingredients are pleasantly aromatic. But it isn't just the ingredients that reflect a culture. It is also the ways that people cook. This cookbook bridges the gap between the way my grandmothers would cook and the way you, the reader of this book, learned to cook.

You might already be familiar with sambals, satays, *char kway teow*, rendang, roti, and a wide range of fresh aromatics and dry spices that you have tasted in restaurants, but have never prepared them at home. This book changes all that. It provides measurements in familiar terms and tested quantities, with common pantry substitutions where appropriate. I also know that you do not have the time to live in the kitchen. What takes a seasoned Malaysian cook ten minutes to do might take a less experienced cook much longer. So I use quicker methods—for instance, using a blender to make spice paste.

In 2013, I was appointed official Malaysian Food Ambassador to the United States with a mission to educate and introduce Malaysian cuisine throughout America.

As I travelled the country and demonstrated the cuisine in Seattle and Los Angeles, New York and Chicago, San Francisco and Miami, I learned that people everywhere had the same questions. They wanted to know how to create a multitude of flavors, how to prevent noodles from becoming too sticky or mushy while stir-frying, how to adjust a dressing that is too salty or too sweet, how to adjust a spicy curry, how to lock in the flavor of braised Asian dishes, how to pair spices with the main ingredients, or how to prevent a spice from burning and becoming bitter. I have taken time to explain these techniques in the chapters, and hope you will find them useful in your cooking. In 2015, through a television program on the Cooking Channel called *Malaysia Kitchen*, I shared ways to infuse everyday American dishes with layers of flavor, techniques that also appear in the pages of this book.

When cooking, it is important to hit all parts of the palate: sweet, salty, sour, spicy, and savory. These elements should work in harmony. In Southeast Asian cuisine, great emphasis is placed on combining these five flavors—or rasa, a Malay word that points to a perfectly balanced taste. You will learn to incorporate *rasa* into your cooking, even re-training your taste buds to make healthier choices. The Malaysian culture believes that eating meals infused with all these five tastes can provide the body with balance. By contrast, the American diet of the past had focused on three

major tastes: sweet, sour, and salty, which often leaves the diner "unbalanced." Understanding the art of balancing flavors with spices and aromatics is the natural path to greater health.

America, however, has been changing so much in the last few decades. There are now large immigrant communities in every city and town across the country. Now, every supermarket too shows the influence of this immigration, and from every corner of the globe. When people come to live in a new land, they bring their tastes with them, and in turn, a demand for the foods from home.

What used to take me so much time to find in the right kind of grocery is no longer a problem. There are now grocery stores selling the foods from the four corners of the earth in nearly every town and suburb in the United States. Even if it isn't on the shelves of a market close by, there is always the miracle of Internet shopping. Every ingredient I have ever needed can be found online, with just a few keystrokes on the computer.

This is true for you, too. You never need to feel intimidated by the strangeness of an ingredient. It is as close as your laptop. I still think your life can be transformed for the better by the act of exploring an ethnic grocery store, but that is up to you and your level of adventurousness.

Even after all my years in America, every cinnamon stick holds a fragrant story. The recipes in this book have been an important part of my life. My passion for home-cooked meals bursting in divine flavors of spice remains an inheritance of my native land. I am grateful for the chance to share my passion with you, and it is given with feelings of sincere tenderness.

MALAYSIAN HISTORY:
WINDSWEPT SEAS AND WAFTING SCENTS

Open a pantry and you will see on its shelves the history of food and its trade. This is most dramatic with sauces, spices, and herbs. Your small jar of cinnamon, if it could speak, would tell you tales of adventure and travel, war and trade, wealth and hardship. As the global trade in many commodities spread, things that were once impossibly exotic have now become commonplace. Look again at the cinnamon on your pantry shelf; it came originally from the "Spice Islands" of Southeast Asia.

The islands of tropical Southeast Asia, tucked as they are between the Indian Ocean on the west and the South China Sea on the east, were always perfectly situated to be the center and most important trading area in the global spice trade. In fact, these lands stretching from southern Thailand to New Guinea formed one of the oldest and most significant seafaring kingdoms in world history. From Malacca on the Malay Peninsula to the lands east of Java, spices we now consider commonplace were once so rare, so treasured, that they fueled one of the world's first global trading networks.

The Malay Peninsula, lying between the Indian Ocean and the South China Sea, has played an important role geographically, anthropologically, and economically since as early as the 2nd century with the founding of the Langkasuka kingdom, one of the first seafaring kingdoms of Asia. Langkasuka was founded by a settlement of Mon people (of modern-day Burma) who travelled along the narrowest part of the isthmus downward to the West Coast of Malaya. The settlement of the Mons subsequently introduced Hinduism and later Buddhism to the area.

The Malay Peninsula and the Indonesian Archipelago were used as meeting places for traders from across Asia. Indian and Persian merchants followed the monsoon trade winds while the Chinese followed the trade winds of the South China Sea, causing the two great superpowers to converge, meet, and trade goods such as gold, tin, spices, and valuable kinds of woods in Malay harbors. The Ta-che (or western Asians) exported camphor, woods, spices such as cloves and cardamom, pearls, perfumes, ivory, coral, and cotton in exchange for porcelain, silk, sugar, iron, and rice. This active trade marked the first wave of globalization in Southeast Asia.

In the 7th century, one of the world's greatest empires, the Srivijaya kingdom, was a power throughout the islands and peninsulas of Southeast Asia with major seats of power in Palembang, Sumatra (now Indonesia), and Ligor in southern Thailand. Visiting merchants from faraway lands paid homage to the rulers of Srivijaya in return for trade concessions. The subjects of the kingdom were active in trade and shipping, visiting ports in China and even the coast of eastern Africa. Conflicts and competition wore away at Srivijaya power and, by the 9th century, the ports and trading posts throughout the straits, islands, and harbors of Southeast Asia had become more independent. This was also the time that saw the rise of the Angkor Empire in present-day Cambodia, which competed with Srivijaya for trading business from India and China. As the Srivijaya empire weakened during the 12th and 13th centuries, this resulted in large-scale migration of people from mainland Southeast Asia, especially from present-day Vietnam, Thailand, and Burma, to new and thriving port cities located at the straits of the Malay Peninsula and the islands.

By the time Marco Polo sailed past the southern tip of the Malay Peninsula in 1292, the straits of Malacca provided a safer route for merchants. No trading post was as important as Malacca. The trade winds enabled traders from China, Java, India, Arabia, and Persia to barter and store their merchandise in narrow townhouses situated along the Malacca River (the present day culinary mecca called Jonker Street), for trade to customers arriving later. As trade grew, so did intermarriages between the Malay and Chinese, particularly in the higher social classes. Rich Javanese, Indians, Arabs, and Persians also established themselves permanently here, playing an integral role in the rise of Malacca.

The Chinese created a flourishing pepper export trade, the first global spice trading network, during the 13th century. Through the pepper trade, many Muslim traders traveled from North Africa, the Middle East, and India, leading to the introduction of Islam to the islands and peninsulas of Southeast Asia, including modern Malaysia, Indonesia, southern Philippines, and southern Thailand.

Malaccan prosperity was entirely based on trade. At the end of the 15th century, hundreds of merchants from all over flocked together every year in Malacca, which became the center of inter-Asian trade, a busy Eastern market like a rich and colorful bazaar under the blazing tropical sun. This made an indelible impression on the Portuguese who were first to arrive in port

in the early 16th century, marking the beginning of European colonial expansion and the coming of the second great wave of globalization. It took the Portuguese explorers little time to realize that whoever controlled the sea controlled the wealth of the land behind it, and they soon seized control of Malacca. Moving quickly to consolidate their gains, the Portuguese built a fort called A Famosa primarily to protect their fleet and to expand their domination over the spice trade. This was the first opportunity for Europeans to connect to the trading networks of Southeast Asia.

The spice trade was behind the creation of the world's first corporations. To take advantage of the riches in Southeast Asia and the weakening in the economic power of the Portuguese, the Dutch formed the United East India Company and the British formed the Honourable East India Company in the 18th century. These privately owned national corporations led rapidly to the colonial conquest and domination of Southeast Asia. The Portuguese city-state of Malacca fell to the Dutch, who controlled the area for two centuries before being defeated by the British in 1824. The Dutch took over Indonesia, while the British conquered Burma, India, Singapore, and Malaysia.

However, in 1941, the Imperial Japanese Army invaded Malaysia. The occupation was an attempt to liberate the colonies but brought much hardship upon the locals. The Japanese occupation ended when the British defeated them in 1945.

The third great wave of globalization came after the end of World War II, when the subjects of this colonial rule began to agitate for independence. Beginning in the late 1950s, colonies began to be granted their independence worldwide; Malaysia, for example, became an independent nation in 1957. People around the world began to travel to the lands of those who once colonized them, seeking opportunities both economic and political and bringing their traditions and cuisines along with them.

Today, Malaysia is a melting pot of culinary cultures rooted in spice trade from China, Thailand, India, and Indonesia, as well as the more recent colonial influence from the Portuguese, Dutch, and British. These cultures that make up the cuisine of my tropical homeland Malaysia have allowed me the opportunity to share this flavor journey with America.

The great markers of cultural exchange in world history have been religion, language, and food. As an example, think of the Indian traders who expanded their influence to Southeast Asia, bringing with them riches from the West, including India, Persia, Turkey, and the Arab lands. Their most important commodity was spices, especially those that came originally from the Eastern Mediterranean. In the early days, Indian vendors sold their pilafs, fluffy rotis, grilled kebabs, and curries to homes along streets in Malaysia, carrying their wares in two baskets on either end of bamboo poles slung across their shoulders. These old traditions have left an indelible mark on the renowned cuisine of Malaysia. But trade always goes in two directions. The Indians who settled there were also inventive enough to use tropical fruits and greens, scented herbs and aromatic rhizomes, and the sauces from China in their cooking. Many plants, such as tamarind, were so popular they were then brought back to India and cultivated widely.

Throughout this book, I have delighted in telling tales such as these, stories of cultural sharing as seen in ordinary kitchens. I have tried to tell you some of the stories that our humble jar of cinnamon has been eager to share. Allow me the honor.

STOCKING YOUR PANTRY

Most of the following ingredients will be at least somewhat familiar to you, while others might be completely new and possibly very exotic. Embarking on this exploration will empower you to add Southeast Asian ingredients to your pantry and then to use them as the foundation of your cooking.

For the most part, spices, bottled sauces, and dry ingredients do not need refrigeration. The trick is to keep them within reach while keeping your work space clear. In my kitchen, I have a deep cabinet with a pull-out shelf conveniently located next to my stove with all the seasonings and sauces easily accessible. If you store most of your spices in clean airtight bottles at room temperature away from sunlight, they will retain their flavor for quite some time, even as long as 6 months in some cases. On the other hand, fresh aromatics such as ginger, galangal, lemongrass, and cilantro certainly need to be stored in the refrigerator. Small sandwich bags work well. Refrigerated, aromatics are usually only good for 2 weeks at the most. However, longer storage is possible if you keep the bag in the freezer.

CANDLENUTS

Native to Malaysia and Indonesia, the candlenut tree produces small white flowers that grow in clusters at the end of the branch. The fruits from the flowers are called candlenuts because they can be used as candles owing to their high oil content. The nuts, known as *buah keras* in Malay and *biji kemiri* in Indonesian, are cream colored and rich tasting after cooking. The candlenuts you find in Asian groceries have already had their outer shells removed and can be used directly in cooking. Alternatively, you can use macadamia nuts instead. Candlenuts must never be eaten raw because they are toxic when raw; instead, they must be cooked and are often pounded into a spice paste first. They especially add texture and a delicate flavor to seafood dishes. They turn rancid quickly, so store them in an airtight container.

CARDAMOM

Cardamom pods are from a shrub in the ginger family that is native to India. The pods are harvested when green, just before they open, then sorted by hand and dried on mats under the sun until they lighten in color. Cracking the green pods unveils the fragrant black seeds inside.

The whole pods keep their flavor the longest, but the hulled seeds work just as well. They can be lightly pounded or ground to a fine powder to add aroma and infuse flavor in rice, curries, tea, and desserts. Be careful if you are shopping for whole pods, because the white pods that are sometimes sold are bleached and not as aromatic. You may also find smaller and darker pods; these are another variety from India with nearly the same flavor. If you cannot find either pods or seeds, use the dried powder instead.

CHILI PEPPERS

Peppers are a huge grouping of fruits from a single type of capsicum. From this genus come all the varieties of peppers we know, from sweet bell peppers to fiery hot bird's-eye chilies to ornamental capsicum shrubs. Along with potatoes, tomatoes, and eggplants, they are all members of the nightshade family. Capsicums are native to Central America, so chili peppers were unknown to Southeast Asia until the Portuguese traders brought them to the region in the later part of the 16th century. Before chili peppers, black peppercorns were used to provide that tingling pungency or "heat" in Asian cooking. The sensation we call heat comes from *capsaicin,* and its power is measured by the use of Scoville heat units. As a rule of the thumb, the smaller the chili, the hotter it is, and most of its power lies in its seeds, which contain 80 percent of the capsaicin. To make the heat milder and bring out the flavor of the pepper itself, remove the seeds before cooking. Some chilies are sold dried and some fresh. You may use them interchangeably when recipes call for dried chilies.

FRESH CHILIES

Any variety of chilies can be used in recipes calling for fresh chilies. Local cooks in Malaysia rarely seed chilies, as the seeds are where most of the flavor is concentrated, but feel free to do so if you prefer milder heat. In Malaysian cooking chilies are typically ground into a paste which can be stored in bottles in the refrigerator for 1 week. Whole chilies can be frozen in airtight bags for 3 months or more.

BIRD'S-EYE | Very small and narrow chilies about 2 inches in length, with 50,000 to 100,000 Scoville heat units, bird's-eye chilies contain lots of seeds and are very hot. They can be both green and red. In Malaysia, they are called *chili padi*. Because they are so commonly used in Thai food, they are also sold as Thai chilies, and are commonly available in supermarkets and most Asian markets.

JALAPEÑO | Fleshy and available in both green and red, jalapeños range from mild to medium heat, and are commonly found in most supermarkets. When the recipes in this book call for fresh chilies, for instance when making Sambal Ulek (page 44) or Sambal Belachan (page 43), use this variety.

DRIED CHILIES

In Malaysian cuisine, all manner of dried chilies are commonly used in sambals and spice pastes. To use them, cut away the stem and soak them in hot water until softened, then grind into a paste in a food processor. Or whole dried chilies can be ground into a powder, without soaking, using a spice grinder. Do not freeze chili powder.

DE ARBOL | Spanish for "tree chili," de arbol chilies have a smoky flavor with a hint of nuttiness. A bright red color when mature, the peppers are 2 to 3 inches long and have a heat level of 15,000 to 30,000 Scoville units.

JAPONES | Bright red with pods about 3 inches in length, Japones (which is Spanish for "Japanese" and pronounced ja-pon-aaas) are aromatic, smoky, and peppery in flavor. I normally like to fry them in oil and then reserve the chili oil, which is great for adding instant heat to noodle dishes and soups. Japones are popular in Southeastern Asian cuisine because they do not have complex flavor profiles, allowing for better balance when used with cilantro, garlic, and lemongrass. They have Scoville heat between 15,000 and 30,000 units. The dried spice cayenne comes from a long thin dried chili that is very similar to Japones peppers.

NEW MEXICO OR ANAHEIM (OFTEN LABELED AS CALIFORNIA) | This mild variety of pepper with large dark red pods about 6 inches in length carries a smoky flavor. The Anaheim name comes from a farmer named Emilio Ortega who brought the seeds to the Anaheim, California, area in the early 1900s. The heat of Anaheims typically ranges from 500 to 2,500 on the Scoville scale.

POWDERED AND GROUND CHILIES

CHILI POWDER | Asian chili powder, such as Baba's brand, comes in bottles or packets and is found in Asian stores and online. It is made with a combination of ground chilies that works well in Southeast Asian recipes. But this is not to be confused with either the Mexican-style brownish chili powder or the trademark spice blend used in chili con carne and commonly sold in general supermarkets. In my cooking classes, I have learned that many people dislike chili-based dishes because they are afraid the "hot" will take control of the other flavors. Using Asian chili powders will find you a friend, not a competitor.

GROUND CHILIES | I like to cook with my own home-ground dried chilies because they lend a variety of heat based on personal preference. Chilies' characteristics may be sharp, hot, or mild, and the color red or brown. And grinding your own means you can use different chilies to suit your taste. For instance, if you're not a fan of spicy foods, this would be a perfect opportunity to grind

up some milder dried California chilies. On the other hand, if you like it hot, use cayenne, Japones, or de arbol. Remember, you can always add more, but you can't take it out once it's in the pot.

To make your own ground chilies, fill a spice grinder with as many dried chilies as it will hold. Grind the chilies into a fine powder; the texture should be similar to finely ground black pepper. Set aside in a bowl. Repeat until all the chilies are ground. Sift the ground chilies through a fine sieve to remove the coarse bits and transfer to an airtight glass jar. Use within 6 months for the flavor, although the heat lasts a lot longer.

When ground chilies are called for in my recipes, I sometimes use store-bought cayenne, known for its pungent flavor and bright red color.

PAPRIKA | The plant we know as paprika came originally from Central America (as did all the other chilies). Cultivated in Turkey, it became popular throughout eastern Europe, where it got the name paprika, meaning "little pepper." The most common form is a bright red powder made from the dried Hungarian sweet peppers, which, when cooked, releases a savory sweet-hot flavor. Hotter varieties are similar to ground cayenne. You may also find smoked paprika in some shops, which is made by roasting or smoking the fresh peppers. These varieties are good for spice rubs, especially for seafood.

You can use just a few dashes of paprika to add that characteristic chili flavor without heat; it is great on eggs or in salad dressings. In Malaysian cuisine, paprika is blended with ginger-garlic paste, some chili flakes, salt, and oil to make a lovely marinade for barbecues and roasts. Since paprika becomes bitter with age, always purchase it in small quantities.

CINNAMON

Cinnamon is a small evergreen tree indigenous to Sri Lanka, although today you will find it cultivated on the many Spice Islands of the Malay Archipelago. Cinnamon trees are part of the laurel family, as are avocados, and they often grow up to 30 feet in height. Commercial cinnamon is obtained by removing the inner and outer bark of the tree. The inner bark curls naturally into quills to form cylinders, often called "cinnamon sticks"—or *kayu manis,* in Malaysian, literally meaning "sweet wood." When these sticks are toasted and ground, they form the powder we know as cinnamon.

Add several sticks of cinnamon to your sugar container and the sugar will pick up hints of its flavor, then use the fragrant sugar for a subtle cinnamon effect in baking. Adding a stick or two to a gentle tea is a zero-calorie change of pace. Or put a stick into a bottle of ice water for a refreshing lift.

When cooking, it is better to add cinnamon sticks directly to hot oil to draw out the flavors (whereas ground cinnamon would burn). One particularly great combination is cinnamon partnered with star anise, which adds amazing flavor to meat dishes. Ground cinnamon, however, is the best option for sprinkling on your morning coffee, toast, or oatmeal. Try doubling the amount you might normally use in recipes for baked goods, sprinkling it on baked sweet potatoes, or adding it to spicy chili-based dishes and curries for authentic Spice Islands flavor.

Cinnamon also has health-imparting qualities. It contains compounds called *saponins,* which bind to cholesterol and help it to be excreted from the body when necessary, and contains the compound MHCP (methylhydroxychalcone polymer), which causes cells to absorb glucose faster and convert it more easily into energy. It is thought to cut heart-threatening triglycerides and low-density lipoprotein (LDL) cholesterol. Cinnamon is also a time-honored digestive aid and a warming, circulatory tonic that increases blood flow throughout the body.

CLOVES

The aromatic clove is the unopened flower bud of an evergreen, pyramid-shaped tree in the myrtle family. Native to the islands of Southeast Asia, the tree can reach up to 50 feet in height. When sun-dried, the buds turn brownish black. The oil of cloves, called *eugenol,* is used as a topical anesthetic, and features in the *kretek* cigarettes of Indonesia. Eugenol is also a principal ingredient in ointments used for muscular pain. Because eugenol is so strong, the amount of cloves one uses in cooking should be very sparing.

Cloves have a sweet, earthy, and peppery taste that goes well with most meat dishes. Just a few cloves added to a cup of coffee impart a delightful additional aroma. In many Malaysian curries, 4 or 5 whole cloves are lightly fried in oil and used with other spices before the main ingredients are added. Cloves pair well with cinnamon and star anise. Because the flavor fades rather quickly once ground, whole cloves are preferred. But if you are grinding cloves into a powder for use in spice rubs or in your baking, grind only small quantities as needed.

COCONUT MILK AND CREAM

Wherever they are grown, coconuts are an extremely valuable ingredient in the local cuisine. The fresh meat is used in a huge variety of dishes, and the liquid is an important part of cooking throughout Southeast Asia.

Clockwise from left: lemongrass, ginger, curry leaves, chili peppers, cilantro, galangal, makrut lime leaves, shallots, garlic

Thailand exports canned coconut milk that is found in supermarkets across America. When you purchase coconut milk, shake the can before opening to fully mix the small amount of cream on the top with the runnier milk. (If a recipe calls for coconut cream, purchase a can of coconut *cream* instead of coconut milk). Once the can is opened and if you have any leftovers, transfer the coconut cream or milk to an airtight container and refrigerate for 4 days or freeze for up to 3 months.

COOKING SAUCES

The Malaysian cook is never far from a shelf of cooking sauces to add to stir-fries, soups, stews, and braised one-pot dishes as needed. Here are a few of the important ones.

FISH SAUCE | This fermented sauce was first developed in Vietnam as a byproduct of the fermentation and storage of fish. It is used to add the element of saltiness required in many Southeast Asian dishes. Fish sauce is made from fish too small to be eaten and often taken from the nets of large catches. The fish are placed in large containers and covered with a mass quantity of sea salt (about 40 percent of their weight), which flavors and preserves the fish. The resulting highly concentrated sauce is filtered several times, strained, and bottled for the market. Fish sauce is sold in many grades, and there are many fine brands on sale at Asian markets. My personal favorite is the brand called Golden Boy. It is a high-quality, transparent golden-brown liquid with a sheen that has a pleasant scent and tastes great in your food.

KICAP MANIS (SWEET SOY SAUCE) | A much-loved seasoning in Malaysian cooking, kicap manis comes from the same Cantonese word that gave us the English word ketchup. It is a dark, thickened soy sauce, sweetened with palm sugar, with a distinct molasses-like flavor and honey-like consistency. Malaysian and Indonesian brands will also add star anise and garlic for an enticing sweet-salty taste. If you cannot find bottles of kicap manis, adding brown sugar to regular soy sauce will get close to the flavor. Use it to achieve a rich complex flavor in your food, especially as a marinade for meats or in braised dishes—even a tablespoon will make a difference. A good-quality brand is ABC Kecap Manis, which is sold in dark bottles in most Asian grocery stores.

OYSTER SAUCE | Deep brown and concentrated, the taste of oyster sauce is salty and slightly sweet with an umami undertone of oysters and mushrooms. The sauce is a combination of oysters, sugar, salt, wheat flour, cornstarch, caramel, and filtered water that is boiled until thickened. The sauce is filtered several times, bottled while still hot, and vacuum packed. It is commonly used in Chinese restaurants as a condiment with steamed *gai lan* (Chinese broccoli). A good-quality oyster sauce should be dark brown and velvety in consistency. Use it to instantly add flavor when stir-frying vegetables, meat, or noodles. The sauce also makes a delicious marinade.

SOY SAUCE | To make soy sauce, soybeans are washed, soaked, and cooked in large steel vats. Then, ground wheat, salt, and cultures are added. After several days of fermentation in a controlled environment, the beans are transferred to tanks and covered in brine to ferment for several more months. The mixture is finally filtered, pasteurized, and bottled as soy sauce. What does not turn to sauce is sold in the market as salted beans or yellow bean sauce. There are many varieties of soy sauce, depending on where it is made: Japanese soy sauce is slightly sweeter with a rounder flavor. Chinese soy sauce is saltier and thicker, while Hawaiian shoyu sauce carries a smooth and simple taste with a low acidity. All soy sauces come in a light or dark variety. There are many types of soy sauces in the market and trying new ones can be fun. Some are made with additional roasted rice, others with mushrooms; and some are dark and concentrated to add sweetness and to help caramelize a dish. Make sure to check the ingredients to see that you are getting the real fermented sauce of soybeans with non-GMO beans and not a chemical imitation.

CORIANDER

This plant, native to the Mediterranean, is in the same family as anise, carrots, cumin, and celery. Coriander seeds were brought to Southeast Asia by Indian spice traders and soon they became part of local cuisine. The dried seeds are called coriander, while the leaves are often called by the Spanish name *cilantro*. Coriander, both seeds and leaves, is highly nutritious. The seeds are rich in calcium and beta-carotene and the leaves contain vitamins A, C, and K.

CILANTRO | Cilantro, probably the most commonly used herb in Malaysian cooking, has a distinct aroma and a warm, sweet, and fruity flavor. If you buy it fresh, the roots can be washed and used too, and in fact have the greatest concentration of flavor. But if the roots are unavailable, you can use the stems instead. The leaves are used for flavoring curries and soups, in salads, and for making chutney. When using cilantro, remember to stir it in at the end. If you are going to store cilantro in the refrigerator, be

sure to shake off excess water. Place the cilantro on a paper tower and gently pat dry, then wrap in a fresh paper towel. Cilantro stems and roots will freeze well in airtight bags for 3 months. Cilantro pairs well with mint leaves.

CORIANDER SEEDS | The seeds of the coriander plant are round, yellowish brown in color, and somewhat sweet in taste. They also have a unique, orange-lime aroma. I use coriander in the preparation of curry powders and other spice rubs. To prepare curries at home, add some coriander seeds to hot oil before cooking the rest of the ingredients to release its warm, spicy-aromatic sweet taste. Coriander pairs well with black peppercorns and when mixed with salt it makes an excellent spice rub for meat dishes.

CUMIN

Cumin seeds originated in Egypt and later found their way around the world through the spice route. The seed is the dried fruit of a small slender annual herb that, like coriander, is in the same family as anise, carrots, and celery. The seeds are brown and have a strong, spicy-sweet aroma with a slightly bitter taste. Cumin closely resembles fennel, although the latter seeds are somewhat bigger, lighter in appearance, and with an anise-like flavor. Cumin seeds are part of the distinctive flavor of chili con carne and most Malaysian curries, and also form the basis of commercial chili powder.

Cumin is most commonly sold already ground in major supermarkets but you can find the seeds in most Indian grocery stores. If you buy the whole seeds, you can use them whole or grind them yourself. Simply crush the seeds into powder using a mortar and pestle or, for larger quantities, a spice grinder. Sift and store your

Clockwise from top left: basil,
Vietnamese mint (rau ram), Chinese
chives, curry leaves, mint, cilantro

freshly ground cumin in an airtight glass jar.

To use the whole seeds, lightly toast them in a dry pan to release the aromas, bring out a nutty flavor, and remove the slightly bitter taste they have when raw. The toasted seeds can be added to soups, lentils, curries, and savory rice dishes. Cumin is often paired with coriander and also goes well with seafood and yogurt dishes.

CURRY LEAF

Nearly every Malaysian Indian home has a curry leaf tree in its yard. Widely cultivated in India, the tree was brought to Malaysia by Indian migrants in the 15th century and initially planted in temple grounds. The tree is in the same family as citrus plants, but other than the shape of the leaves, these trees look completely different. Known as *daun kari* in Malaysia, the leaves have a distinctive fragrance similar to anise. Malaysian Indians use the leaves for making curry powders, chutneys, and pickles; the name of the curry spice blend comes from the use of these leaves.

If you walk along the residential areas outside the city, you will notice stripped stems hanging from the curry leaf trees. This is because, in Malaysia, we pluck them straight from the tree before using and therefore they are never stored in the refrigerator.

You can purchase fresh curry leaves packed in plastic bags in most Indian or Southeast Asian grocery stores. Frozen leaves are also available, but I do not recommend using them since the leaves turn black and lose their aroma shortly after defrosting. Wrap curry leaves in cheesecloth or a kitchen towel and they will keep for up to 2 weeks in the refrigerator. For longer storage, I gently fry the leaves in a little warm canola or olive oil and then store both the leaves and oil in an airtight container at room temperature for up

to a month. This way, the oil is already seasoned with the flavor of curry leaf and is delicious even as a salad dressing or in pesto. When cooking, especially for curries, the flavors of the fresh leaves are maximized by frying them in oil with the other spices before the main ingredient is added. They pair well with potatoes, seafood, and meat dishes.

FENNEL

Originating in the Mediterranean, fennel (like coriander and cumin) is in the same family as carrots, celery, and anise. In Europe, the entire plant is used as an herb and vegetable, but in Southeast Asian cooking, only the seeds are used. In Indian customs, it is regarded as a sacred herb. The hay-like plant is often hung over doorways to ward off evil spirits and is believed to keep young people strong and healthy. Indian restaurants will serve fennel seeds, either plain or coated with sugar, as a breath freshener.

The fennel seeds are grayish-green in color and have a sweet, mellow flavor similar to anise seed. They complement seafood particularly well: Take a teaspoon of crushed or whole seeds, add them to hot oil, and allow them to sizzle before adding the seafood. Alternatively, you may pound the fennel seeds into powder, add some sea salt, and use as a spice rub for seafood. Buying whole fennel seeds is worth that effort, because the ground fennel you find in the stores is less sweet and aromatic than the whole seeds.

FENUGREEK

The fenugreek plant is native to western Asia, where it is widely used as a seed grain, a spice, and a vegetable. The seeds are small, hard, and yellowish brown. In Southeast Asia, the dried seeds are used mainly to flavor seafood curries and in lentil soups and to make seasonings for pickles and chutneys. When using it, be sure not to add too much—start with 10 to 15 seeds—as it can overpower the flavors of other spices. Fenugreek seeds have a strong aroma and slightly bitter, nutty taste.

GALANGAL

Galangal, the fragrant ingredient popular in cuisines across Asia, tends to get lumped in with ginger. It makes sense: They're closely related (galangal is sometimes called *blue ginger*), both are rhizomes (knobby, underground stems that sprout roots and shoots), and both have long been thought to have medicinal properties. However, they're wildly different. Though galangal and ginger share some similarities—a pungent umami flavor and slight tang—galangal is mild where ginger is spicy and its culinary purpose is actually the opposite of ginger. The purpose of galangal is to perfume the food and bring delicateness to the dish, imparting a rich aroma somewhat like roses, lime, and honey, rather than adding assertive tangy heat. Like ginger, galangal contains enzymes that help tenderize meat, which is why it's a popular addition to marinades.

Galangal can readily be found in Asian markets in the United States but it tends to be on the mature side. Young galangal is easier to slice, laden with fragrant oils, and colored in pale shades of pink and gold; as the plant ages, it turns a dull beige and becomes more fibrous, making it difficult to slice. Neither young nor mature galangal requires peeling before use. Older galangal also loses much of its prized oils, so you may need to use twice as much for the same effect. Plus, it tends to mold easily, so if your galangal looks spotted and black, toss it out.

Most of the signature dishes in Malaysia, such as beef rendang and satay, include galangal in their favoring paste. You can also add a few thin slices of galangal to soups and stir-fries for a lovely added fragrance and texture. In Malaysia, fresh galangal and its flowers are cut into thin slices and served with a sambal as an appetizer.

Store galangal as you would ginger, wrapped in a paper towel and stored in the vegetable compartment of the fridge. It can last for at least a week or up to 2 weeks, but be sure to check it for mold before using. You can also slice galangal and freeze it in airtight bags for 1 month. Slicing it first makes it effortless to remove the quantity you need without having to thaw the whole rhizome.

GARAM MASALA

There are many spice powders used by Malaysian cooks in Indian-style dishes. In English, we have come to call all of them curry powders, but that is not strictly correct. *Curry* refers to a combination of whole spices such as star anise, cinnamon, cloves, turmeric, coriander seeds, and chilies that is ground to a powder with curry leaf. Garam masala, on the other hand, does not include curry leaf; rather, it is a combination of warm spices (cinnamon, cumin seeds, nutmeg, cloves, cardamom, black peppercorns) blended into a powder. Garam masala is added at the midpoint of cooking to add depth, or a dash at the end of the cooking to give the food a punch. *Masala* simply means "mixture" and *garam* means "heat" in the traditional Ayurvedic medical sense of a body's internal heat or coolness. In this tradition, if your ailment requires heat, garam masala in your food would help to treat it.

GARLIC

Garlic, originating from central Asia, belongs to the same family as onions and leeks, among the first plants ever cultivated by humans. There are many varieties; in general, the smaller the bulb, the stronger the flavor. Garlic that is sold at most Asian grocery stores is smaller, perhaps half the size of the more common varieties, with purple streaks instead of pure white skins. However, any supermarket variety will work just as well for cooking if you use the same number of cloves.

In Southeast Asian cooking, there is sometimes as much garlic used in a recipe (by weight) as onions or shallots. This should give you an idea of its importance. When stir-frying garlic, make sure to fry until it is golden brown, otherwise you'll end up with a raw garlic taste. If you have time, it makes sense to peel several

heads at a time and keep the cloves in an airtight glass jar in the refrigerator. To speed up daily cooking preparation, I also mince enough fresh garlic for 3 days and store that in an airtight glass jar.

GINGER

The rhizome called ginger root, from the same family as turmeric and cardamom, is believed to be native to the Malay Archipelago. It takes several months for a ginger plant to be ready for harvest, which is why it only grows in warm moist climates.

In Malaysian cooking, the fresh root is used most commonly, although it is sometimes dried for storage or pickled. Young ginger, with a thin creamy colored skin with pink edges, can be eaten raw, pickled, or used in marinades. Mature ginger, on the other hand, is beige-brown with a thicker skin. It has a wonderfully sweet, warm, citrus-like aroma. When I call for fresh ginger, use mature ginger. Before slicing or grating, peel off the skin with a potato peeler or paring knife, or use the edge of a spoon.

Ginger has a powerful protein-digesting enzyme called *zingibain,* which makes it a natural meat tenderizer. It has also been studied for its anti-inflammatory and antioxidant properties. When buying fresh ginger, choose a knob that has a firm, fresh, shiny, unwrinkled skin and inspect it for mold at the tips. Wrapped in plastic wrap and stored in the refrigerator, it will keep for up to 10 days. For longer storage (about 3 months), grind the fresh ginger into a paste, place in a glass jar, and freeze.

Outside Asian cuisines, ginger is sold as a dried powder and used primarily in baking (gingerbread, cookies, and so on). The ground ginger can also be added to curry masala blends or spice rubs, although the flavor is quite different from the aromatic zest of fresh ginger. Powdered dried ginger does not keep its flavor for long, so don't buy too much at a time.

LEGUMES

Beans, peas, lentils, and many other legumes may well be the first crops ever cultivated by humans, having been found in 10,000-year-old archeological sites throughout the eastern Mediterranean and Mesopotamia. In Malaysia, the legume used most commonly is the mung bean, a small, round green bean. It is most commonly sold as a yellow-colored split bean with the green hull removed. These split mung beans cook very quickly and do not need to be soaked first.

The red lentils known as *masoor dal* are also widely used in Indian-style Malaysian cooking and are used interchangeably with yellow split lentils, or *toor dal*. The biggest difference though between the two is cooking times: When soaked in water for the same amount of time, red lentils take roughly double the cooking time of yellow. If you plan to eat lentils with roti, you want to make sure they are cooked to the point where each lentil retains its shape and firmness. However, if you're enjoying them with rice, cook the lentils to a mushier stage so that they blend together with the spices, meat, and vegetables.

LEMONGRASS

Lemongrass is the name of perhaps 50 species of a grass that grow naturally throughout Asia, Africa, and Australia. Some species, such as citronella, are used to keep mosquitoes away. The main species used in cooking has bulbs that, when crushed, release a lemony aroma. In Malaysia, it is often planted in backyard gardens and its citrus-like aroma is the secret behind many spice pastes. The distinctive lemon-like flavor is strongest within 6 inches of the base. When shopping for fresh lemongrass, pay attention to the color. The ends of the leaves should be a pale green color. As the leaves turn to a light brown, the flavor at the base begins to fade.

Lemongrass can be finely sliced and added to salads and stir-fries or bruised and chopped for use in soups or stocks, as well as pounded with other fresh seasonings to make a spice paste for curry dishes. Wrap lemongrass in a paper towel and store it in the vegetable compartment of the fridge for up to 2 weeks. To freeze it, first grind it with some water or slice it finely, then place in a container and freeze for up to 3 months. To thaw the amount you require, leave it out at room temperature, use what you need, then freeze the remainder. It will not turn rancid provided you use a clean spoon each time.

MAKRUT LIME LEAF

Makrut lime leaves (also called kaffir lime leaves; see page 191 for more) are forest green in color, short, and shaped like an hourglass; they are a signature aromatic in Malaysia, Indonesia, and Thailand. We add several leaves to soups and to curry pastes, and thinly julienne other leaves to use in salads and stir-fry dishes. The leaves impart a delicate citrus-like aroma and flavor that is unlike that of lemons or limes. Always remove the stem before use; this allows the leaf to better impart its aroma and flavor to the dish. In Malaysia, makrut lime trees are planted abundantly in most home gardens and the leaves are used almost daily in cooking. The fruit has a warty, rough skin and a dark green color. It does not contain any juice but its zest releases an intense flavor when grated and can be added to desserts.

You will find makrut lime leaves in the produce section of Asian grocery stores, often beside the fresh chilies, or in plastic bags in the freezer section. You can freeze them in a freezer bag for up to 2 months. Soak them in water for 5 minutes to thaw before using.

MUSTARD

Mustard seeds have appeared in Sanskrit records dating as far back as 3000 BC In the same family as broccoli, cabbage, and bok choy, there are three types of mustard plants that produce seeds: black mustard; pale yellow or white mustard, which is native to Europe; and the tiny, dark reddish-brown mustard seeds widely used in Asian cooking. In South Asia, mustard seeds are grown as an oil seed, and the oil is used in cooking and to make pickles.

Mustard seeds have a hot and pungent taste and are always cooked in hot oil until they pop to achieve a pleasant nutty and sweet flavor. When frying the seeds, it is helpful to cover the wok or skillet with a spatter screen to keep the mustard seeds from jumping out of the pan. They can then be added to a variety of vegetable and lentil dishes, sauces, or curries. If you want to use them in chutneys and pickles, the seeds should be dry roasted and ground instead. The seeds can also be used in marinades for meat or seafood. Grind about 1 tablespoon mustard seeds into a powder and mix with water to form a paste before adding it to your marinade for a hot sharp taste. For milder flavor, mix the powder in milk.

NUTMEG AND MACE

Nutmeg, native to the Banda Islands of Indonesia, is an evergreen tree, distantly related to the magnolia, that grows up to 60 feet. Known as *buah kemiri* in Malaysia and Indonesia, the tree produces fruit with a firm yellow flesh, which looks much like an unripe peach. Inside the fruit is a nut covered by a shiny brown shell. The nut is called *nutmeg*, while the outer portion of the shell consists of a red lacy web known as *mace*. Nutmeg has a stronger aroma and flavor than mace, although they are often used interchangeably.

Ground nutmeg lacks some of the volatile oils that provide the complete flavor; if you can find the whole nut, available in spice shops, it will keep well for a long time and you can grate it just before using. Use it to make spice paste, to flavor meat dishes, and in desserts. You can also add a few fresh nutmegs (whole or cracked) to a sugar bowl so that the sugar takes on a lovely nutmeg aroma.

PALM SUGAR

The palm sugars from Malaysia (*gula melaka*) and Indonesia (*gula jawa*) come in both disc and cylinder form. Palm sugar is hard, reddish brown, and a little moist, with a sweet, caramel-like flavor. You can buy it at most Asian grocery stores. It is used to impart sweetness but also to calm the intensity of spicy chili dishes and to balance and complement a multitude of flavors in salad dressings.

When palm sugar is used throughout this book, it should always be in liquid form. An effective way to prepare palm sugar is to melt it in a pot as described on page 316. Store the liquid sugar in an airtight glass jar in the refrigerator and use a little at a time in salads, desserts, curries, and braised dishes.

PANDAN LEAVES

The leaves of the daun pandan plant are a beloved aromatic in the Malay Archipelago. It is commonly grown in home gardens throughout Southeast Asia and the Pacific Islands. In addition to cooking, the leaves are used in various handicrafts to make mats and baskets.

The flavor of the leaves is aromatic and sweet, and they are as important to Asian cuisine as vanilla is to Western food. You can use the leaves in several ways: Tie into a knot and add to rice before cooking to provide a fragrance of newly harvested grain; blend or pound and use

the juice to flavor and color cakes and sweets; or wrap around marinated chicken pieces prior to barbecuing. In America, you can buy fresh or frozen leaves, as well as pandan extract, at most Southeast Asian stores. Place the leaves in freezer bags and freeze for up to 3 months. The leaves thaw out quickly under running water.

PEPPERCORNS

The word *pepper* in this case refers to the spice we know as black pepper, a vine that produces small grape-like fruits in bunches. The original species may have come from India, although different varieties grow in abundance in the hot tropical regions of Southeast Asia, from southern China to the Spice Islands. Most high-quality black pepper is grown in Sarawak in East Malaysia.

All peppercorns—green, red, black, and white—come from the same plant. When the pepper berries are formed on the vine, they start out green in color. If allowed to ripen naturally on vines, they mature to a bright red color. If the green, unripe berries are picked and dried under the sun, they turn into black peppercorns. When the shell is removed from the black peppercorns through a tiresome steaming process, you get white peppercorns.

Green peppercorns are used in various curries and soups, and are often stir-fried with seafood dishes. Red peppercorns are sweet and mellow in taste and often used in making Asian pepper powders. Black pepper is used for piquancy in most dishes. Ground white pepper is milder and less aromatic and usually sprinkled on eggs or added to stir-fried rice. Although you might find peppercorns of all colors mixed up in a small pepper mill for its look, it is best not to blend peppercorn varieties, otherwise you complicate the palate and create heat without flavor.

SHALLOTS

Shallots, very closely related to onions and garlic, originated in central Asia thousands of years ago. The shallots sold in Asian grocery stores have a reddish-purple skin and are about 1 inch in size. They are sweeter in flavor and more intense than the larger variety you may find in supermarkets. I prefer shallots over onions for making spice pastes, as they are more aromatic and contain less moisture. In Malaysia, shallots are used daily to make the spicy paste known as *rempah*. They can also be fried in oil until crisp and used as garnish in soups, salads, noodles, and rice dishes (see recipe, page 56). Fresh shallots can be sliced ahead of time and then refrigerated in an airtight container lined with a paper towel to absorb moisture; stored this way, they will stay fresh for up to a week. Whole, unpeeled shallots are best stored in a basket kept in the pantry or, for longer storage, in a cool, dry place.

SHRIMP PASTE

Shrimp paste, made from fermented dried shrimp, is available in block form, in tubs, or in glass jars. I prefer the blocks, which are naturally reddish dark brown in color and are traditional in Malaysian cooking. The strong smell of the paste dissipates when it is mixed with other ingredients.

It's important to note that when you purchase shrimp paste in any form, it is raw. If you are going to add it to other ingredients that are served raw, such as in a salad, you must toast it before using; see pages 116–117 for instructions. If you will be cooking it with other ingredients, however, such as in a spice paste for curry, you do not need to toast it first. The raw paste from the store should be wrapped in thick foil and placed in an airtight bag before refrigerating. Shrimp

paste is available in Southeast Asian stores and online. There is no substitute for this ingredient and it should not be confused with fish sauce.

STAR ANISE

Star anise is the beige flower head of a tree that, like nutmeg, is a member of the magnolia family. Found throughout Southeast Asia, particularly in Malaysia and Sumatra, it is harvested from August to October using hooks attached to a long pole or by shaking the tree's branches. The harvested fruits are dried in the sun until they turn deep reddish brown. Star anise looks like a perfect eight-pointed star, each point containing a shiny brownish-black seed.

It is a popular spice in Chinese food, where it is one of the ingredients in Chinese five-spice blend. It is also the main spice in Vietnamese pho. Star anise releases an aromatic, licorice-sweet taste when cooked. The recipes in this book use star anise in its whole form, not ground. You can add it to meat dishes, soups, and stews for a hearty taste. Always store star anise away from heat, light, and humidity.

TAMARIND

Tamarind fruit looks very much like a peanut pod, but longer, with a thin, hard shell. Inside the pod is a tart, sticky fruit. In provision shops around residential areas in Malaysia, you can find little hills of tamarind left open in buckets or sometimes bundled in plastic bags by the kilos; it is a key ingredient in soups, curries, and stews.

When shopping for tamarind in the United States, you will most likely find it in a jar as ready-to-use concentrated juice or sold in a block form, either with seeds or seedless. The block form is preferable because it is fresh pulp without additives. To use it, the tamarind block must be broken down into liquid form; see page 54 for instructions. The block of pulp may be stored in the refrigerator or freezer for up to one year.

TURMERIC

Part of the same family as ginger and cardamom, turmeric is a rhizome with an intense flavor and vivid yellow color. In fact, it used as a natural coloring in cosmetics and textiles. Hindu and Buddhist monks are known to dye their robes in turmeric, not only because the color is appropriate, but also because it is thought to have antiseptic properties.

Both ground and fresh turmeric is used in Southeast Asian cooking, and it is considered a crown jewel in Malaysian cooking where you'll find it is used in most recipes. If you cannot find fresh turmeric at your local supermarket, you can find it at most Indian grocery stores or health food stores. Ground turmeric (fresh turmeric sun-dried then crushed into a powder) delivers a savory flavor and rose-like aroma to the food while fresh turmeric has a more ginger-like flavor, slightly bitter with the texture of carrot.

The fresh rhizomes can be crushed for their juice and used to produce a lovely yellow color in rice dishes; ground turmeric is added to curries, soups, and rice dishes and sprinkled on meat and seafood before cooking. It is best to use only a small amount, the size of a pea for fresh turmeric or about ½ to 1 teaspoon ground, or food can end up bitter. Take care also not to stain your clothing and skin when cooking with fresh turmeric. I recommend using gloves when working with fresh turmeric.

The active ingredient in turmeric is curcumin, a substance considered to be a potent anti-inflammatory agent and antioxidant, which gives turmeric its bright yellow color. It is thought that turmeric promotes colon and liver function and protects against heart disease (see page 266 for more on the health benefits of turmeric).

PREPARING SPICES

All spices, whether ground, barks, or whole seeds, weaken in flavor and aroma over time. For instance, ground cardamom can lose its flavor in 2 weeks, while whole cinnamon bark may lose its flavor after 6 months. This is because whole spices contain more of the flavorful volatile oils, or natural essential oils, and therefore deteriorate much slower than ground spices. Your spice cabinet may contain some older whole or ground spices. But, before you think of tossing them out, remember these treasures can be refreshed quickly by toasting. Toasting also enhances the flavors of whole spices even when they are new.

TOASTING SPICES

To toast whole or ground spices, place in a dry skillet on your stovetop and warm over medium heat for a few seconds, until they release a fragrant aroma. Once fragrant, remove the spices from the pan and allow to cool. In Malaysian homes, oftentimes this is how local cooks reawaken spices on hand. Whole spices in particular will be easier to grind after toasting. When toasting, you will notice the spices getting slightly darker as their flavors are being enhanced by the gentle heat. To help you judge the color change, you can place some raw spices on a plate next to the stove and compare them to the ones in the pan as you toast them.

TIPS FOR TOASTING WHOLE SPICES | Break heavier or denser spices, such as cinnamon sticks and star anise, into pieces before toasting. Lighter and smaller spices such as cloves, coriander, cardamom, cumin, fennel, and mustard seeds should be toasted separate from denser ones as they require less time to cook. Remember, the spices will continue to cook for a few seconds after being removed from the heat. Put the spices in a dry skillet over low heat and use a wooden spoon to continuously move the spices to avoid burning them. When they appear one shade darker, transfer to a plate and set aside to cool briefly before grinding them.

TIPS FOR TOASTING GROUND SPICES | Commercially processed ground spices are cheaper in cost but lose some of their aromatic properties as the essential oils and volatile compounds oxidize. This can happen during production or just over time. Ground spices are extremely delicate and will burn quickly if you don't pay close attention to them. Toast them in a dry skillet only for a few seconds, until fragrant. Certain spices—like ground turmeric and paprika—are seldom toasted, since the toasting does not enhance them.

GRINDING TOASTED SPICES
It is very easy to grind spices, just as you would grind coffee beans. This little bit of effort goes a long way to making your dishes turn out light, fresh, and fabulous.

To create your own spice blend, begin by placing ground spices and smaller seeds in the spice or coffee grinder and then any heavier ones on top and grind them in batches. This prevents larger spices from getting caught between the blades. Your grinder should be at least half full for best results. The method I provide you will work for a single type of spice—say, coriander seeds—being ground into powder or an assortment of spices blended together.

Throughout this book you will find wonderful opportunities to use whole and ground spices in the recipes. For example, Perfect Peanut Sauce (page 62) uses ground coriander and ground cumin; Split Yellow Lentil Soup with Opo Squash (page 74) uses garam masala; Cabbage Sautéed with Eggs, Turmeric, and Curry Leaves (page 128) uses ground white pepper; Spiced Clarified Butter Rice with Almonds and Cranberries (page 161) uses cloves, star anise, cardamom seeds, and cinnamon sticks; and Spice Island Prawn Curry (page 182) uses coriander seeds and fennel seeds.

My cooking friends are always fascinated with the aromatic journey they take when I twist open one of my many glass jars of spices from my treasured spice cabinet. The secret to spicing is now yours to enjoy.

SPICE CHART

SPICE/AROMATIC	TASTE AND AROMA	VITALITY AND HEALTH	HOW TO USE & PARTNERS TO CREATE FLAVOR
BASIL			
Native to Southeast Asia, with small narrow leaves, purple stems, and a purple-colored flower. The English name for the most common version used in Asian cuisines is "Thai basil" or "Asian sweet basil."	Southeast Asian variations have a stronger flavor and aroma than Italian, with hints of licorice, cinnamon, and mint.	Basil oils and extracts are said to have antioxidant and antibacterial properties. Fresh basil offers a healthy dose of vitamin K, vitamin A, manganese, and magnesium. It stimulates the appetite and helps curb flatulence.	Basil is a key herb in Southeast Asian cooking. It is commonly used in stir-fries, curries, and noodle dishes. It also partners well with chicken, pork, and seafood. Prolonged heat will cause basil's oils to dissipate, along with its flavor. STORAGE Keep for a short time in plastic bags in the refrigerator, or blanch in boiling water and then store in the freezer.
CANDLENUTS			
Soft, oily, cream-colored seeds within a hard-shelled nut that comes from a tropical tree related to the castor-oil plant. Known as *kemiri* in Indonesian and *buahkeras* in Malay.	Pleasant, delicate nutty flavor.	In most areas where it is a native, it has been used as a traditional medicine. The oil can be used sometimes instead of castor oil since it is an irritant and also a purgative.	Must be cooked, since candlenuts are toxic when raw. Ground nuts are used as a thickening agent. You can also shave off slivers, dry roast them in a pan, then add to curries or sprinkle them over the top of rice dishes. Candlenuts' oily consistency makes for a great paste for seafood. STORAGE Store tightly-wrapped in the freezer for up to a year.
CARDAMOM			
Sold in the pods or as whole or ground seeds. The fragrant black seeds are unveiled when the green pods are crushed.	Warm, slightly pungent, and highly aromatic.	Used as a digestive aid since ancient times, known for its properties to aid indigestion and flatulence. A medicinal can be made by macerating seeds in hot water.	Add ground cardamom to infuse flavor in rice, curries, tea, and desserts. Whole pods are best used in recipes with some kind of liquid for the cardamom to infuse. Best to buy whole pods and then grind the seeds as you need them. STORAGE Store in a tightly sealed container in a dark, cool place. Whole pods last approximately one year this way, after which their flavor will dissipate. Ground cardamom keeps its flavor for a few months.
CHILIES, FRESH			
Jalapeño, bird's-eye (also called Thai chili), and serrano are the most commonly used fresh chilies in Malaysian cuisine.	Different varieties range in heat from mild to medium to very hot.	Known for their intense sinus-clearing effect. They are also known to be rich in vitamins A and C, with dried versions higher in vitamin A and fresh version higher in C. Their vibrant colors are suggestive of their high amounts of antioxidant beta-carotene, which supports the cardiovascular system and maintains the health of the skin, eyes, and immune system. Green chilies also contain vitamins B and E and are a good source for iron and potassium. The hotness of chili peppers causes the release of endorphins, which are neurotransmitters in the body that reduce pain and induce euphoria.	Be careful when handling, as chilies contain oils that can burn your skin and especially your eyes. Most commonly used alongside chicken, curries, vegetables, and a variety of sauces. STORAGE Store for up to 2 weeks in the refrigerator or a cool, dark place.

SPICE/AROMATIC	TASTE AND AROMA	VITALITY AND HEALTH	HOW TO USE & PARTNERS TO CREATE FLAVOR
CHILIES, GROUND			
Dried, pulverized fruit of one or more varieties of chili pepper, used to add piquancy or pungency to dishes.	Has a rich and tangy aroma and spicy, musty flavor and adds heat.	Chilies boost metabolism and are full of vitamin C.	Make your own chili powder by filling a spice grinder with as many dried chilies as it can hold. Grind to a fine powder, then sift with a fine sieve. Use de Arbol, New Mexico, or Anaheim chilies interchangeably. Used in soups, curries, and stews or as a spice rub. STORAGE Purchase pre-ground chilies in small quantities. After opening, the flavor will begin to diminish. Store away from heat in a cool, dry place or refrigerate to prevent loss of flavor.
CILANTRO			
The bright green leaves and stems of the coriander plant.	Distinctly pungent, bright flavor, with bold tones of citrus and sage.	Cilantro leaves are packed with nutrients: minerals (copper, iron, zinc, magnesium, calcium, sodium and potassium), vitamin C, vitamin A, B-complex vitamins (which act as antioxidants), carbohydrates, proteins, and dietary fiber. Recent studies have shown that the nutrients and compounds in cilantro can help your body eliminate toxic metals. In addition, cilantro may protect the nervous system from damage, and may be a treatment against depression or anxiety.	A perfect complement to assertive chilies, garlic, and onions. Often combined with coriander, turmeric, garam masala, or cumin to make curries and soups. Always use fresh cilantro, not dried. Add to most cooked foods toward the end of cooking to preserve its color, flavor, and texture. STORAGE Place stems in a glass of water, cover loosely with a plastic bag, and store in the refrigerator. Snip off leaves as you need them and re-cover. Change the water every 2-3 days. Do not wash until you are ready to use it because excess moisture will turn the leaves to green slime. It should last up to a week in the refrigerator. To freeze cilantro, arrange the leaves in a single layer on a cookie sheet and freeze. Once frozen, gather them into a zip-top bag and return to the freezer immediately. Use within 6 months, and do not thaw before using.
CINNAMON			
The inner bark of several trees from the genus Cinnamomum. It was imported to Egypt as early as 2000 BC, and so highly prized among ancient nations that it was regarded as a gift fit for monarchs. Native to Bangladesh, Sri Lanka, India, and Burma.	Pungent yet sweet, woody taste.	Boosts the immune system, regulates blood sugar, acts as an anti-inflammatory, may reduce the risk of certain cancers, helps prevent heart disease, promotes digestive health, and heightens brain activity, including cognitive processing and memory. It also has antibacterial properties.	Best partnered with other spices like star anise. Use to give braised meat dishes such as rendang a deeply-layered flavor. Perfect with apples, pears, sweet potatoes, curries, pilafs, and ice cream. STORAGE Store in a cool, dark area where it will remain dry. Whole sticks of cinnamon will last for 2-3 years; ground cinnamon for 6-12 months.

CLOVES

SPICE/AROMATIC	TASTE AND AROMA	VITALITY AND HEALTH	HOW TO USE & PARTNERS TO CREATE FLAVOR
Cloves are the unopened pink flower buds of the evergreen clove tree. These buds are picked by hand when they start to turn pink, and are dried until they turn brown in color. They have a hard exterior, but their flesh features an oily compound.	The smell of cloves is a combination of earthy, spicy, and slightly sweet, and can be overpowering.	Thought to aid in digestion, have antimicrobial properties, fight against cancer, protect the liver, boost the immune system, control diabetes, preserve bone quality, and contain anti-mutagenic properties. Cloves are known for fighting against oral diseases and headaches, and also display aphrodisiac properties.	The slightly sweet flavor of cloves goes well with meats such as venison or beef, as well as fruits such as apples, oranges, and plums, and with pickled vegetables. You can also grind cloves into a powder for use in spice rubs or in baking. STORAGE Store in an airtight container in a cool, dark, and dry area. Ground cloves will keep for about six months, and whole cloves will stay fresh for about one year. Shelf life can be extended by storing in the refrigerator.

COCONUT

SPICE/AROMATIC	TASTE AND AROMA	VITALITY AND HEALTH	HOW TO USE & PARTNERS TO CREATE FLAVOR
The oval fruit of the coconut palm grows naturally in the tropics, and contains more "water" than other fruits. Young coconuts have a green shell and a white "husk" and are sweeter than mature coconuts. The thick white coconut meat can be grated or used to make coconut milk or cream (available canned). Mature coconuts have firm meat and less water.	Sweet, nutty taste and mild sweet floral scent.	Studies from the *Journal of the American College of Nutrition* show that pure coconut oil is a medium-chain fatty acid composed of lauric acid, believed to inactivate bacteria, yeast, and fungi in the human body, boosting the immune system. In Asia, coconut water is believed to boost energy and endurance, enhancing physical and athletic performance. Coconut milk contains zinc, which is vital in promoting prostate health.	Use coconut milk in combination with stock to add a mellow nutty flavor to soups, curry sauce, or braised dishes. Use coconut cream to tone down a spicy dish. For desserts such as puddings, flan, or cakes, use coconut cream in place of cream. Do not substitute cream for coconut milk in Southeast Asian cuisine, as dairy does not have the ability to enliven spices and aromatics. Coconut pairs well with lemongrass, ginger, garlic, cumin, mustard seeds, coriander, chilies, and turmeric. STORAGE Coconuts can be refrigerated for up to 1 week. Coconut milk and cream can be frozen for up to 1 month.

CORIANDER

SPICE/AROMATIC	TASTE AND AROMA	VITALITY AND HEALTH	HOW TO USE & PARTNERS TO CREATE FLAVOR
The fruits, commonly known as coriander seeds, of the coriander plant (the leaves are commonly called cilantro).	Stems, leaves, and fruit all have a pleasant aromatic odor. Whole seeds have a floral, citrusy, and musky flavor. Ground seeds have a nutty aroma with an earthy scent.	The seeds are filled with dietary fiber (which can help digestion and reduce cholesterol production), fatty acids (which stimulate the digestive process), minerals (iron, copper, calcium, potassium, zinc, and manganese), vitamin C, and B-complex vitamins that act as antioxidants. Used in household medicines to cure colds, seasonal fevers, nausea, vomiting, and stomach disorders.	Coriander seeds are used in the preparation of curry powders and other spice rubs and satay sauce. They can be added to hot oil when preparing Malaysian curries to release their sweet, spicy-aromatic taste. Ground coriander can be used in soups orcurries, and is commonly used alongside rice. STORAGE Store in an airtight container in a cool, dark place away from direct sunlight or heat.

CUMIN

SPICE/AROMATIC	TASTE AND AROMA	VITALITY AND HEALTH	HOW TO USE & PARTNERS TO CREATE FLAVOR
A flowering plant in the family Apiaceae, native from the east Mediterranean to India and used in the cuisines of many different cultures.	Cumin seeds have a warm flavor and a pungent, strong aroma, with a slightly bitter taste. Black cumin, the smaller, darker variety, adds a smoky note to dishes.	The health benefits of cumin include its ability to aid in digestion, insomnia, respiratory disorders, asthma, bronchitis, common cold, lactation, anemia, skin disorders and boils, and to improve immunity.	A common component of curry powder and the spice mixture garam masala. Add to lentils, curries, soups, and savory rice dishes. It also partners well with coriander. STORAGE Replace frequently, as it quickly loses its pungency.

SPICE/AROMATIC	TASTE AND AROMA	VITALITY AND HEALTH	HOW TO USE & PARTNERS TO CREATE FLAVOR
CURRY LEAVES			
Dark green, almond-shaped leaves native to South Asia and Southeast Asia. It is mostly planted in home gardens and plucked fresh for curries. Found in the produce section in Indian or Asian markets.	A distinctive lemon-pepper essence and a subtle savory clove-like taste.	Used as a medicinal plant in traditional Ayurveda and Unani medicine to treat digestive problems and remove fats from the body.

In Indian homes, curry leaf juice is consumed for heartburn, and the leaves applied as a poultice to treat burns and skin eruptions. | For potatoes, lentil dishes, chicken, or fish curries, sauté a few sprigs with ginger, garlic, chilies, cumin, and coriander to create a prolonged flavor experience. Chop and grind the leaves with tamarind, garlic, and salt to create a simple chutney.

STORAGE Wrap the leaves in a damp paper towel and refrigerate in an airtight bag for up to 2 weeks. You may freeze the leaves in an airtight bag, but some flavor will be lost. |
| **CURRY POWDER** | | | |
| Curry powder recipes usually include coriander, turmeric, cumin, chili peppers, and fenugreek. Additional ingredients can include fennel seed, cloves, cinnamon, mustard seeds, and ginger. | Adds golden color and a savory flavor to dishes. | As a spice blend, curry powder has a number of health benefits. Studies have found that turmeric, one of the blend's main spices, may lower the risk of diabetes by controlling blood sugar. Studies also show that consuming curry powder regularly may provide cancer-preventative benefits. | Often used for vegetable curries and frequently paired with coconut milk to make coconut curry. It is also commonly used in Malaysian meat dishes including beef curries, chicken curries, lamb curries, and fish curries.

STORAGE Store in an airtight container in a cool, dark area away from heat. |
| **FENNEL SEEDS** | | | |
| Elongated, light green seeds of the fennel plant used to flavor Indian and Southeast Asian cuisine. Sold in most Indian grocery stores. | Fruity sweet licorice and anise flavors with a bittersweet aroma.

Ground fennel is less sweet, more savory. | Traditionally used as a breath freshener and to aid digestion. A teaspoon can be chewed after every meal. Fennel seeds are a concentrated source of minerals such as copper, iron, zinc, and potassium. | Sauté in hot oil in combination with mustard and cumin seeds to complement fish and seafood. Dry-roast ground fennel seeds combined with pepper, chili, and salt and add to a marinade for grilled meats.

STORAGE Store in a clean airtight container in a cool, dry place. |
| **FENUGREEK** | | | |
| The brown seeds from an annual clover-shaped plant called *Trigonella* (triangular shape), native to South Asia and Southeastern Europe; one of the oldest plants grown for culinary and medical use. | Nutty with a maple-like aroma. | Fenugreek seeds demonstrate significant anti-diabetic effects in clinical studies, with abilities to improve glucose tolerance. In Asia, fenugreek seeds are soaked in water and consumed by diabetic people, which many believe to lower blood sugar. In the Indian system of Ayurveda medicine, fenugreek is recommended as a spice to promote lactation and as an aphrodisiac. | Use a teaspoon of fenugreek seeds along with cumin, fennel, mustard seeds, garlic, ginger, and onions in hot oil for Malaysian curry flavor for seafood or vegetable dishes. Add ground fenugreek to cookies, cakes, chutneys, and jams.

STORAGE Store in a clean airtight container in cool, dry place. |
| **FIVE SPICE POWDER** | | | |
| A blend of Szechuan pepper, star anise, fennel seeds, cloves, and cinnamon used traditionally in Chinese cuisine. | Highly aromatic, not hot, with a concentrated spicy-sweet flavor. The Chinese, when creating the blend, attempted to make an all-encompassing "wonder powder" representing all of the five flavors: sour, bitter, sweet, pungent, and salty. | This powder takes all the essential health benefits of each spice that composes it. | Often used with fatty meats such as pork, duck, or goose. Also used as a spice rub for duck, chicken, pork, and seafood, added to breading for fried foods, or used to enhance stir-fries. Use sparingly.

STORAGE Store in a dry place in a sealed jar. |

SPICE/AROMATIC	TASTE AND AROMA	VITALITY AND HEALTH	HOW TO USE & PARTNERS TO CREATE FLAVOR
GALANGAL			
A rhizome in the ginger family, native to Southeast Asia. Feels woody and solid to the touch but does not appear knotted. Look for pale buttercream-colored galangal with little pink shoots at the end of the root, found in the produce section in Asian markets.	An incredible orange- and pepper-like flavor, with a sweet scent reminiscent of citrus and rose.	Prized for its anti-inflammatory properties, immune boosting abilities, and use in treating sluggish digestion. Galangal is also taken after childbirth for the general well-being of the mother.	Always thoroughly wash galangal before using, but it is not necessary to peel it. Cut thick slices, bruise them, and add to soups or rice dishes for a lovely aroma. Thinly slice and stir-fry to perk up any dish with gingery flavor. Blend with lemongrass, makrut lime leaves, shallots, and turmeric for curry sauce. STORAGE Wrap in a paper towel and refrigerate for 7 days or slice and freeze for up to 3 months.
GARAM MASALA			
A staple of South Asian cuisine, translated literally as "warm spice mix." Though the recipe can vary from household to household, garam masala is a spice blend consisting usually of coriander, peppercorns, cumin, cardamom, nutmeg, mace, and cinnamon.	Cinnamon adds sweetness, nutmeg adds complexity, pepper adds heat, and coriander adds a lemony flavor and texture to the blend.	As a spice mix, garam masala has the many health benefits of the combined spices that comprise it , including boosting immunity, promoting weight loss, helping with digestion, and lowering blood sugar levels.	When used whole, garam masala spices are called khada masala and are added to hot oil before other ingredients. Once added, they will sizzle (the cumin), unfurl (the cinnamon stick) and release their essence into the oil. For the ground version, the spices are gently roasted on a griddle until they release their aroma, then ground together into a powder to use as a finishing spice. The ground spice blend is usually added toward the end of the cooking process, as a garnish. Adds a warm, sweet flavor to curries, chicken, lamb, fish, potatoes, rice pilaf, and breads, and to marinades, salad dressings, vegetable sautés, or soups and stews. Commonly paired with nutmeg, red pepper, or saffron. STORAGE Store in an airtight container for up to 4 months.
GARLIC			
A member of the same family as onions and leeks. A number of varieties that differ in size, color, and pungency.	Garlic has a deeply pungent taste. Southeast Asian garlic has purple streaks and is stronger in flavor than the white-skinned variety.	Some studies suggest that garlic may have cardiovascular benefits and reduce the accumulation of cholesterol. Health benefits increase if you let it sit after it has been chopped or crushed in order to activate healthy enzymes. Garlic helps improve iron metabolism and is a good source of selenium.	Use whole, crushed, or chopped. The easiest way to crush garlic is to place a clove on a board and firmly press down with the flat side of a knife until you squash it to a pulp. The more finely the garlic is crushed, the stronger it will taste in the dish, but slow roasting mellows the flavor. Often cooked to golden-brown in stir-fries, or paired with onion, tomato, or ginger. STORAGE Ideally, garlic should be stored uncovered in a wire mesh basket in a cupboard.

GINGER

SPICE/AROMATIC	TASTE AND AROMA	VITALITY AND HEALTH	HOW TO USE & PARTNERS TO CREATE FLAVOR
A perennial herb with thick knotted rhizome cultivated throughout the tropics. Young ginger, which is whitish-pink and plump, can be found in the produce section of Asian markets. Mature ginger is dry and beige in color, and is commonly sold in Western supermarkets.	When consumed raw, fresh ginger has a distinct hot and pungent taste. Cooked ginger tastes somewhat lemony, with high notes of a sweet citrusy rose-like aroma. Mature ginger has a sweet, warm, and citrus-like aroma.	Used in China and throughout Southeast Asia to treat stomachache, colds, motion sickness, and nausea and to improve digestion. Fresh ginger has strong antioxidant and anti-inflammatory properties. May also protect against carcinogens and defend against cancer.	Always wash and peel ginger before using. Thinly slice and sauté with onions and garlic to liven up any chicken, shrimp, or beef stir-fry dish. Grind into a paste with garlic and add to soups, stir-fries, curries, seafood, vegetables, rice, or noodle dishes. Use juice as a natural meat tenderizer in marinades. The more finely grated, the stronger the flavor. STORAGE Wrap in plastic and refrigerate for 10 days. When grated, freeze for up to 3 months.

LEMONGRASS

SPICE/AROMATIC	TASTE AND AROMA	VITALITY AND HEALTH	HOW TO USE & PARTNERS TO CREATE FLAVOR
A sturdy cream-greenish bulb similar to a miniature leek. In Asian markets, fresh lemongrass is found in the produce section, and grated lemongrass in the freezer section.	The fragrance and flavors in lemongrass are concentrated in the bulb and in the bottom 6 inches of the stalk. Crunchy with a distinctive gingery lemon-like taste and an arousing citrus scent.	In Southeast Asia, used to treat stomachaches and flatulence. Contains vitamin A for the maintenance of healthy skin. In Thailand, lemongrass tea is believed to reduce excess body fat. May help lower cholesterol.	Remove tough outer layers and use the cream-colored bottom 6 inches of the stem and bulb only. Bruise the stalks to impart a lemony scent and delicate oils on stocks and stews, without the acidic bite of lemon. Good with beef, pork, poultry, and seafood. Finely slice into thin rounds to add great crunch to salads and stir-fries. Grind together with galangal, garlic, turmeric, and chilies to form a fragrant paste for curries. STORAGE Wrap in a paper towel and refrigerate for up to 2 weeks. Grind and freeze for 3 months.

MAKRUT (KAFFIR) LIME LEAVES

SPICE/AROMATIC	TASTE AND AROMA	VITALITY AND HEALTH	HOW TO USE & PARTNERS TO CREATE FLAVOR
Dark green, hourglass-shaped leaves. Found fresh or frozen in the vegetable section of Asian markets.	Similar to blended lime, orange, and lemon rind, with a deep citrus aroma.	Volatile oils contain potent antioxidants that are believed to cleanse the blood. The leaves also contain calcium, beta-carotene, and vitamin C.	Makrut lime leaves can be thought of as the "Asian bay leaf," and are often paired with poultry and fish. Blend whole leaves with lemongrass, galangal, garlic, and chilies for curry spice pastes; julienne and add to salads and stir-fries; add 8-10 whole leaves to stocks and stews. STORAGE Store in an airtight bag; refrigerate or freeze for up to 3 months.

MINT

SPICE/AROMATIC	TASTE AND AROMA	VITALITY AND HEALTH	HOW TO USE & PARTNERS TO CREATE FLAVOR
Aromatic, almost exclusively perennial herbs. There are more than 30 species, the two most popular and widely available being peppermint and spearmint.	Cool, refreshing, yet pungent. Its most popular forms, peppermint and spearmint, bear a flavor that is like a cross between pepper and chlorophyll.	The aroma activates salivary glands as well as glands that secrete enzymes, which helps facilitate digestion. The strong and refreshing aroma makes a quick and effective remedy for nausea. Just the smell of crushed mint leaves can help alleviate stomach problems. As a naturally soothing substance, mint can alleviate the inflammation and temperature rise associated with headaches and migraines. It is also effective in clearing up congestion of the nose, throat, and lungs, which relieves respiratory disorders such as asthma or the common cold.	Used in both sweet and savory dishes. Available fresh, as an extract, dried, and in oil forms. Mint complements certain meats such as poultry and lamb, or can be used as a refreshing addition to summer salads or couscous. STORAGE Trim the stems and place in a tall container, and add enough water to cover the cut ends. Cover loosely with a plastic bag and keep in the refrigerator. Change water every 2-3 days.

MUSTARD

SPICE/AROMATIC	TASTE AND AROMA	VITALITY AND HEALTH	HOW TO USE & PARTNERS TO CREATE FLAVOR
The three types of mustard seeds are black, pale yellow or white, and dark reddish brown; the brown variety is commonly used in Malaysian cuisine.	Brown mustard seeds are spherical, medium in size and have a nutty, sweet, and mellow burning flavor. The heat in yellow mustard is released on the tongue, whereas in brown and black mustard the heat is also felt in the nose and eyes. The severity of pungent aroma varies with different mustards. Brown seeds are more pungent than the white or yellow type; black mustard seeds have the highest pungency.	Stimulates the flow of salivary and gastric juices and promotes appetite; enhances digestion and is used as a laxative, diuretic, and to induce vomiting. It is also a treatment for asthma and relieves congestion and coughs. Externally, it is an ingredient in many Ayurvedic medicated oils used as liniment and to treat arthritis and rheumatism.	Cook mustard seeds in hot oil to release their flavor before adding to vegetable or lentil dishes, sauces, and curries. Grind into powder, mix with water to form a paste, and add to marinades. STORAGE Store mustard seeds and ground mustard in an airtight container in a cool, dark place away from direct heat or sunlight. Seeds will store well for up to one year; ground mustard will last for up to six months.

NUTMEG AND MACE

SPICE/AROMATIC	TASTE AND AROMA	VITALITY AND HEALTH	HOW TO USE & PARTNERS TO CREATE FLAVOR
Two different parts of the same fruit, from the nutmeg tree. Nutmeg is the nut; mace is the lacy red web that surrounds the outer shell. Nutmegs are sold without the shell in plastic packets in most health or Asian markets. Grate it before using.	Both nutmeg and mace have a similar flavor: a slightly bittersweet taste of mint and hazelnut that lingers on the top of the palate. The aroma of nutmeg is deeply sweet and aromatic.	Nutmeg is used to stimulate digestion, improve appetite, ease stomachaches, colic, flatulence, and nausea, and treat bad breath. It is a "nervine," or agent that calms and soothes the nerves, believed to reduce tension, stress, and anxiety. In Asia, nutmeg is used for its essential oils in aromatherapy.	Used like pepper in many Malaysian, Indonesian, and Dutch dishes. Grate a little nutmeg into potato dishes or add it to egg dishes, pork, lamb, or chicken stews. Also commonly grated into cake batters or custards. Mace is normally sautéed in hot oil along with coriander, pepper, bay leaf, and cumin seeds, and partners well with chickpeas and legume dishes. You can also use ground mace as a sauce thickener. STORAGE Store whole nutmeg in a clean airtight container in cool, dry place.

ONIONS

SPICE/AROMATIC	TASTE AND AROMA	VITALITY AND HEALTH	HOW TO USE & PARTNERS TO CREATE FLAVOR
Range in size, color, and taste depending on their variety.	Spanish onions are the largest, with brown skin, with a milder, sweet flavor. Yellow onions are hot and pungent. Brown onions are a smaller version of the yellow onion, with an even more pungent flavor. Red onions have a stronger taste, while green onions are fresh and mild. Sweet onions such as Walla Walla can be white or yellow and often have a flattened appearance.	Exhibit antibacterial, antifungal, and anti-parasitic activity. They have been shown to help lower blood pressure and lower glucose levels. Historically have been used to help with asthma.	Arguably the world's most widely-used ingredient Can be used as flavoring or as a vegetable on their own; boiled, fried, grated and sautéed, roasted, or used as the main ingredient in onion soup, onion marmalade, or an onion tart. STORAGE Hang them from a string or raffia rope somewhere cool and dry, or store in a paper bag or a vegetable rack for up to 10 days. Do not keep them in the fridge or they will soften.

PANDAN LEAVES

Fan-shaped sprays of long, narrow, blade-like leaves, commonly used in Southeast Asian cuisine as a flavoring.	Pandan has a nutty, botanical fragrance and a sweet, unique flavor that enhances both sweet and savory dishes.	Pandan leaves are considered to be diuretic and useful for healing various wounds and diseases. Pandan leaves are said to be pain relievers and are used to cure chest pain, headache, fever, arthritis, and earaches.	Use either fresh or dried to enhance the flavor of rice dishes and cakes. Sometimes the leaves are steeped in coconut before being added to a dish. The leaves are also commonly wrapped around chicken and baked. STORAGE Store the leaves whole, in a plastic bag in the freezer.

PAPRIKA

Ground bright red powder from sweet and hot dried peppers.	Ranges in flavor from sweet and mild to pungent and hot. It has distinct earthy undertones.	Loaded with carotenoids, a nutrient that includes vitamin A. It also contains vitamin E and iron, which supports cellular metabolism.	Can be combined with other spices such as garlic powder and cayenne, or used as a spice rub for chicken, fish, or red meat. Can also be used as a seasoning for soups, or for vegetables such as sweet potatoes or carrots. STORAGE Store in a cool dark place for no more than 6 months; refrigerate to prevent loss of color and flavor.

PEPPERCORNS

High-quality pepper is derived from a pungent-smelling vine that grows in the hot tropical regions of Sarawak in East Malaysia. All peppercorns—green, white, and black—come from the same plant.	Black pepper is the strongest in flavor of all pepper varieties, with a slightly hot, spicy taste and a hint of sweetness. Ground white peppercorns are less aromatic and pungent, with a much milder flavor.	Stimulates gastric juices to aid digestion. Historically used as a medicine believed to cure illnesses such as constipation, earaches, gangrene, heart disease, hernia, hoarseness, insect bites, insomnia, joint pain, liver problems, lung disease, and toothaches.	Available whole, coarsely or finely ground, or cracked. Freshly ground delivers more flavor than pre-ground pepper, which quickly loses its taste. Green peppercorns pair well with seafood and are mostly used for stir-fries. STORAGE Store peppercorns in a sealed container in a cool, dry place for up to 1 year. Ground pepper loses flavor after about 4 months.

SESAME SEEDS

Tiny, flat oval seeds with a nutty taste and a delicate crunch. They come in a host of colors, including white, yellow, black and red.	Nutty, slightly sweet flavor. Sesame oil is deep to pale yellow in color, fragrant, with a pleasant odor and taste.	Seeds, oil, leaves, and roots have medicinal value. Sesame oil is rich in vitamin E, but deficient in vitamin A. The seeds are a good source of certain minerals, particularly niacin, folic acid, and tocopherols. Sesame tones the kidney and liver and relaxes the bowel. Additionally, the seeds are thought to alleviate respiratory disorders such as chronic bronchitis, pneumonia, asthma, dry cough, and other lung infections.	A versatile ingredient to use in baked goods such as cakes and cookies, breads, and confections. In Southeast Asian cuisine, they are used in condiments, sauces, soups, salads, and sambals for their texture, body, and nutritional value. STORAGE Their high oil content makes the seeds turn rancid quickly. Store airtight in a cool, dark place for up to 3 months, refrigerate for up to 6 months, or freeze for up to 1 year.

SHALLOTS

Shallots sold in Southeast Asian grocery stores have a reddish-purple skin and are about 1 inch in size, smaller than most U.S. shallots.	Sweet in flavor, with a taste somewhat like a common onion but with a milder flavor.	Shallots contain iron, which contributes to red blood cell health and facilitates metabolism and brain function.	Shallots are generally preferred over onions in Southeast Asian cuisine as they are more aromatic and contain less moisture. Used in Malaysian cuisine to make a spicy paste known as rempah. They are also fried in oil until crisp to use as a garnish. STORAGE Whole shallots can be kept in the pantry. Sliced shallots should be placed in a plastic container lined with paper towels to absorb moisture and stored in the refrigerator.

SPICE/AROMATIC	TASTE AND AROMA	VITALITY AND HEALTH	HOW TO USE & PARTNERS TO CREATE FLAVOR
STAR ANISE			
Woody reddish-brown seed pods shaped like an eight-pointed star, from an evergreen tree in the magnolia family. Sold whole and ground.	Sweet and pungent licorice taste and a sweet aromatic scent similar to anise seeds.	Often included in remedies for indigestion and also in cough mixtures, particularly because of its anise seed flavor. It is believed to be antibacterial and have diuretic properties, and can help relieve abdominal pain, flatulence, and digestive disturbances.	One of the signature flavors of Chinese and Malaysian cuisine. Goes well with pork, chicken, and duck braised dishes or roasts. Add a few whole star anises to stews and soups. Combines well with cinnamon, cloves, and black pepper as a spice rub for grilled meat dishes or marinating meat before stir-frying. STORAGE Store in a clean airtight container in a cool, dry place.
SZECHUAN PEPPER			
Rust-colored peppercorns with hair-thin stems and open ends, native to the Sichuan province of China. They are dried berries and not actually a part of the pepper family.	Warm, pepper-like bouquet with a woodsy and acrid flavor.	The berries prevent flatulence and are anti-spasmodic. The bark and berries are stimulative and used as a blood purifier and digestive.	Associated with dishes native to the Sichuan province of China, which are hotter and spicier than the rest of Chinese cuisine. Often roasted and browned in a wok and served as a condiment to accompany chicken, duck, and pork dishes. It is also commonly paired with star anise and ginger. STORAGE Store in sealed containers away from light.
TAMARIND			
Dense, sticky fruit found inside pods of the tree. Look for it in the produce section in Asian or Mexican markets, sold as 14-ounce blocks wrapped in plastic or as a liquid pulp concentrate from Thailand.	Sour with high notes of a fruity aroma and a flavor like date, apricot, and lemon-lime combined.	In Asia, tamarind pulp is used therapeutically as a laxative. In Indonesia and Malaysia, tamarind is widely used in many aromatherapy spas as a skin scrub; it leaves the skin smooth and supple. Tamarind fruit contains high amounts of ascorbic acid and carotene, which are potent antioxidants.	Use watered-down tamarind as a tangy ingredient for salad dressings, curries, BBQ, sauces (peanut sauce), stews, soups (tom yum and mulligatawny), noodles (pad thai), and chutneys. Add honey and water to create a delicious tamarind drink during summer. In Southeast Asia, tamarind is coated with honey or sugar to be sold as little sweet sour candies in school canteens or tuck shops. STORAGE Can be refrigerated for up to 2 months. Tamarind diluted into tamarind water can be frozen for up to 1 month.
TURMERIC			
A thick rhizome of the ginger family, cultivated extensively in India, Malaysia, and Indonesia. The fresh rhizome is orange-brown on the outside and bright orange inside; also sold as a ground powder. Look for fresh turmeric in Southeast Asian markets.	Pungent and savory, with the unmistakable scent of fresh roses.	Clinical research shows that Turmeric's principal compound, called curcumin, has demonstrated protective anti-tumor effects in skin, epithelial, stomach, lung, and liver cancers. Thought to have significant antioxidant, anti-carcinogenic, and anti-inflammatory effects. In Balinese and Malaysian Indian culture, turmeric powder is mixed with honey and warm water and consumed as a routine cleansing therapy.	Use a pinch of turmeric to add a brilliant yellow color and rose-like aroma to curries, stews, braise dishes, and sauces. A pea size amount of turmeric added to beans, legumes, potatoes, vegetables, seafood, poultry, meat dishes, pickles, and chutneys adds complexity and makes even leftovers taste lively. The main ingredient in curry powders, chicken bouillon, and an all-purpose spice that goes well with any other spice, aromatic, or herb. Do not use more than ½ teaspoon for 4 servings or your food will taste bitter. STORAGE Store ground turmeric in a clean airtight container in a cool, dry place; refrigerate fresh turmeric.

SAMBALS,
AROMATIC PASTES,
AND DRESSINGS

Sambals are the salsas of Malaysian cuisine. Generally prepared in small quantities, they graciously adorn Malaysian dinner tables of families among all walks of life and promise to offer a burst of flavor upon the palate. It is because of its valued status that Malaysians will not hesitate to declare, "What's a meal without sambal belachan?" These dishes are not mere condiments but small treasures that Malaysians can't live without.

It's believed that sambals originated in Indonesia, but their many variations are cherished all over Asia. Malaysia alone prides itself in having more than 100 different sambals. Although sambals may seem demanding to prepare, most are actually simple to make once you know the secrets.

All sambals begin with chilies and salt, and the variety of flavors is created with a wide selection of secondary ingredients. These can include shallots, garlic, palm sugar, lemongrass, green mangoes, vinegar, peanuts, lime juice, and shrimp paste, and any change in the ingredients gives it a new name. For example, if you add belachan (shrimp paste), it is sambal belachan; if you add vinegar and garlic, it is sambal ulek (sometimes spelled oelek); when the mixture is fried in coconut or peanut oil, it is the famous sambal tumis. Lastly, if the mixture is flavored with sweet soy sauce, it's sambal kicap (from which English got the word ketchup), which can then be used either as a condiment or cooking sauce. From the freshness of red jalapeños that provide a tingle on the tongue to the full-blown spicy explosion of Thai bird's-eye chilies, sambals also vary in spiciness depending on the type of chili used. There are seemingly endless regional variations, and Malaysian chefs often use these as a base or rempah (spice paste) to cook with or flavor other favorite dishes.

Another beauty reflected in Malaysia's multicultural cuisine is the blending of spices, contributed by immigrants from India. The Indian style of preparing spices involves frying spices, such as cinnamon, clove, and star anise, in oil. The infused oils with a single note of flavor are then combined with locally grown aromatics from the Malaysian soil—lemongrass, purple shallots, galangal, and turmeric—to create a symphony of fresh and vibrant flavors in a single spice paste. The fresh spice paste elevates main ingredients, whether meats, potatoes, noodles, or seafood, and has become the building block of Malaysian cuisine.

The Rendang Spice Paste (page 58), Laksa Spice Paste (page 61), and Ginger, Garlic, and Cilantro Paste (page 53) are examples of these concentrated pastes, which are used to begin a dish. The pastes also make excellent marinades for grilled foods. I consider them my prescription for well-being given their amazing health benefits as referenced on page 266 to 268. The pastes are easily stored in jars in your refrigerator as a time-saving convenience.

This chapter also features some dipping sauces and dressings. Across Malaysia, tropical coconut, tart fruity tamarind, zesty limes, and earthy ground spices are ingredients that bring food to life. They come together in condiments

that take American favorites such as grilled meats and tossed green salads to new heights. Even the creamy and nutty taste of peanut butter is taken to a whole new level of enjoyment: In Perfect Peanut Sauce (page 62), chilies, palm sugar, and coconut milk are added to peanuts to make a silky, sweet, and savory sauce that is perfect with noodles and grilled chicken, or as a dip for your favorite vegetables. For something tangy and sweet, the freshness of Tamarind Ginger Chutney (page 53) is incomparable to store-bought chutneys, and so incredibly easy to make. The perfect dipping sauce for roasted

vegetables or seafood is the Sweet Chili Dipping Sauce on page 45.

Nearly every visit to the market, I pick up fresh cilantro, mint, and green onions as they are the necessary ingredients for everyday cooking. When these herbs are combined with limes and tamarind, the flavors are vivacious and enhance everything they touch. That is why they are perfect used in dressings for vegetable or fruit salads. Try the Cilantro Mint Vinaigrette on page 48 and Spicy Avocado-Tamarind Dressing on page 46 and you will find endless uses for these lively dressings.

SAMBAL BELACHAN

Sambal belachan, an uncooked sambal made from fresh red chilies, shallots, shrimp paste, and fresh lime juice, is a staple on the Malaysian table. The mere mention of sambal belachan will get any Malaysian salivating, and without it, we would not feel the meal was complete. We enjoy the sambal as a dipping sauce that goes well with almost anything—steaks, fish, rice, noodles, and vegetables. It can also be used to begin your stir-fried dishes.

Belachan refers to a paste made from tiny dried shrimp, and this shrimp paste is the key ingredient in the sambal. Although it does have a rather strong pungent smell, the shrimp flavor delicately dissipates into the background, creating the fifth flavor—or umami—that is complex and lingers for a long time. In Malaysia, sambal belachan is made fresh daily the old-fashioned way, using a stone mortar and pestle. Although that is charming and traditional, this recipe is easier to make using an electric mini chopper or food processor. You can reduce the number of chilies for less spiciness. MAKES 1 CUP

8 fresh red jalapeño chilies, chopped

5 shallots, peeled and left whole

1 tablespoon shrimp paste, toasted (see page 116)

1½ teaspoons salt

1½ teaspoons sugar

2½ tablespoons fresh lime juice

1. Combine the chilies, shallots, shrimp paste, salt, and sugar in a food processor. Blend until smooth. The paste should be light orange when well blended.

2. Transfer the sambal to a bowl, add the lime juice, and mix well. Serve at room temperature. Leftover sambal can be stored in the refrigerator for up to 4 days.

CLOCKWISE FROM TOP LEFT: Sweet Chili Dipping Sauce (page 45), Sambal Ulek (page 44), Sambal Belachan, and Sweet Soy and Shallot Sambal (page 45)

SAMBAL ULEK

One of my favorite condiments is sambal ulek (sometimes spelled sambal oelek). Bright orange and tangy sweet in flavor and aroma, it is made with fresh red jalapeños blended with shallots and gently cooked with vinegar, salt, and sugar to create a perfectly balanced taste. The word *ulek* comes from the Javanese word *oelek,* meaning "grinding," in this case referring to the twisting way of grinding chilies using a mortar and pestle. My mother was well-known for her sambal ulek, which she made with the old stone mortar that was our family's heirloom. This is largely my mother's beloved recipe, but I do use the convenience of a food processor. It is important to seed the chilies for a pleasantly sweet and gentle tasting sambal. You might want to wear gloves when handling chilies, but if you prefer to use bare hands, try soaking your fingers in a bowl of milk afterwards to soothe them.

Since sambal ulek is used in so many recipes throughout this book, it's worth doubling the recipe and making it ahead of time. The cooked sambal will store well in the refrigerator or you may freeze it for up to a year. The sambal is not only welcome when served in a small bowl on the table, but you can also use it in many creative ways in your cooking—and not just Malaysian cooking: Toss a spoonful into soups or pasta sauces, add a bit to your marinades, especially for chicken, or use a little to begin a stir-fry. It can even be used as spread for sandwiches in place of mustard! MAKES 1 CUP

10 fresh red jalapeño chilies, seeded and chopped

 5 shallots, peeled and left whole

 5 cloves garlic, peeled and left whole

¼ cup peanut oil

¼ cup rice wine vinegar

1½ teaspoons salt, or to taste

1½ teaspoons sugar, or to taste

1. Combine the chilies, shallots, and garlic in a food processor and blend until smooth. The paste should be light orange and smooth.

2. Heat the oil slightly in a skillet over low heat. Add the chili mixture before the oil gets too hot to prevent splattering. Using a wooden spoon, gently swirl the mixture into the oil to combine thoroughly. Bring to a soft boil and cook, stirring occasionally, for about 10 minutes.

3. Stir in the vinegar, salt, and sugar and cook until the sambal sizzles slightly around the edges. Taste and add more sugar if you prefer it sweet, or salt if you like the tangy flavor to arise. Remove from the heat.

4. Transfer the sambal to an airtight container. Serve at room temperature. Leftover sambal can be refrigerated for up to 4 days.

SWEET SOY AND SHALLOT SAMBAL

This sambal, which is not too spicy, is excellent for adding complexity, sweetness, and hearty flavors to fried rice, fried chicken or grilled meats, and soups. Shallots are preferred over onions as they are more aromatic, not pungent, and contain less moisture. Also, the smaller the shallots, the sweeter the taste. When browning, try not to stir too often, so they brown evenly and stay crispy. MAKES ABOUT 1 CUP

¼ cup extra-virgin olive oil

1 cup thinly sliced shallots

¼ cup kicap manis (sweet soy sauce; see page 16)

1 tablespoon fresh lime juice

1. Heat a wok or deep skillet over medium heat and add the oil. Carefully toss in the shallots and stir once to combine. Fry the shallots, stirring occasionally with a wooden spatula or spoon, for about 10 minutes. The shallots will bubble as they give off moisture. Allow the shallots to cook until golden brown, stirring once or twice only, for an additional 10 minutes.

2. Transfer the shallots and oil to a bowl and add the kicap manis and lime juice. Stir well to combine. Transfer to a glass jar, seal, and store in the refrigerator for up to 1 week. Let it come to room temperature (but do not heat it in the microwave) before serving.

SWEET CHILI DIPPING SAUCE

This versatile sauce is a great-tasting dressing that showcases sweet, sour, salty, and spicy flavors. It works well with salads, like the ones beginning on page 93, and with grilled chicken, fish, lamb chops, French fries, and sunny-side-up eggs. I always have a small jar of it in my refrigerator (the vinegar acts as a natural preservative, preventing the mint from discoloring). MAKES 1 CUP

⅓ cup liquid palm sugar (see pages 315–316)

⅓ cup rice vinegar

2½ tablespoons fish sauce

4 cloves garlic, minced

Leaves from 3 sprigs fresh mint, cut into chiffonade

Leaves from 3 sprigs cilantro, chopped

2 fresh red chilies, chopped

2 fresh green bird's-eye chilies, chopped (optional, for more heat)

Combine all the ingredients in a bowl and whisk well. Store in an airtight container in the refrigerator for up to 4 days.

SPICY AVOCADO-TAMARIND DRESSING

Throughout Southeast Asia, tamarind pulp is used abundantly in salad dressings, curries, relishes, and sweets. (It's also an ingredient in Worcestershire sauce and other Western meat condiments.) Cooks in Malaysia use tamarind in dressings because of its tangy flavor and also because it helps prevent foods like avocado and apple from discoloring. This dressing is quite tasty over romaine, raw spinach, tomatoes, mushrooms, sweet peppers, cucumber, tofu, or eggs for a plate of lively flavors. I keep a small batch of it in a glass jar in my refrigerator and use it as my go-to salad vinaigrette or as a dipping sauce for spring rolls; it will keep for up to 4 days. Its great strength is that each fresh ingredient speaks for itself. As an added bonus, the healthy dressing is packed with vitamins A, B, and C, thiamine, calcium, iron, and fiber. Tamarind itself can lower cholesterol, promote a healthy heart, help the body digest food, and is a good source of antioxidants that fight against cancer. What more can you ask?

MAKES 1½ CUPS

½ or 1 small ripe avocado, pitted

¼ cup Tamarind Water (page 54)

¼ cup honey

3 tablespoons fish sauce

3½ tablespoons rice vinegar

2 cloves garlic, peeled and left whole

1 fresh green jalapeño chili, cut in half and seeded

2 fresh red bird's eye chilies, cut in half and seeded

Place all the ingredients in a food processor and blend to a smooth sauce. Transfer to an airtight container and refrigerate. The dressing will keep for up to 4 days in the refrigerator.

PINEAPPLE SAMBAL TUMIS

Juicy pineapple and fresh lime spiced with red chilies together create a burst of tropical flavors. This refreshing and light sambal is perfect with grilled or fried fish—especially good in the summer. You can add a dollop to everyday salads, along with chopped cucumber, diced pineapple, and romaine with a sprinkle of cilantro to provide a new twist. The shrimp paste (belachan) provides the fifth flavor, or umami. Without it, the sambal would lack depth and the complex flavor that makes it so appealing. I came to truly love this sambal during my childhood. My mother would make large batches every week and share it with our relatives and friends. Her philosophy was to make food that was good and simple, and to serve it creatively with a warm heart. SERVES 4

2 cups diced fresh pineapple

1 Roma tomato, chopped

6 fresh red jalapeño chilies, chopped

2 teaspoons raw shrimp paste

2 tablespoons fresh lime juice

1½ teaspoons salt

¼ cup peanut oil

1. Combine the pineapple, tomato, chilies, shrimp paste, lime juice, and salt in a food processor and pulse several times until the chilies are finely processed.

2. Heat the oil in a skillet over low heat. Add the sambal before the oil gets too hot to prevent splattering. Using a wooden spoon, gently swirl the sambal into the oil to combine it thoroughly. Bring to a soft boil and cook until the oils separate onto the surface and the raw shrimp paste is cooked off, stirring occasionally, about 10 minutes.

3. Serve at room temperature. Leftover sambal can be stored in an airtight container in the refrigerator for up to 1 week.

CILANTRO MINT VINAIGRETTE

One of the most inviting sections of any market the world over is the herb section. It evokes the feelings of a stroll through a fragrant garden. Cilantro and mint, so essential in Malaysian cooking, are usually laid out neatly in large bins for unmatched freshness. Cilantro lends a spicy, citrusy, and pungent flavor. I have found that the lightness of this vinaigrette perfectly lifts the flavor of meat, so it makes a great rub for grilled lamb chops, as a fresher alternative to commercially sold mint jellies. It is also wonderful drizzled on any grilled white fish.

MAKES ABOUT 1½ CUPS

2 cups fresh cilantro leaves, chopped

1 cup fresh mint leaves, stemmed

3 green onions (white and green parts), chopped

4 cloves garlic, peeled, and left whole

1 fresh green chili, stemmed

Juice of 2 fresh limes

2 tablespoons sugar

1½ teaspoons salt, or to taste

½ teaspoon freshly ground black pepper

¼ cup rice vinegar

¼ cup extra-virgin olive oil

Place all the ingredients except the oil in a food processor and blend until smooth. With the motor running, add the oil in a slow stream through the opening at the top of the food processor and blend until smooth. Serve at room temperature or chilled. The vinegar and lime will help the vinaigrette stay emulsified. The vinaigrette keeps for up to 4 days in an airtight container in the refrigerator.

PINEAPPLE ACHAR

When it comes to pickles, pineapple is one of my favorite ingredients, both sweet and acidic. A quick and easy recipe, this pickle, or *achar* as we say in Malaysia, makes a refreshing and colorful statement when served with curries or barbecued meats. Each bite yields a different flavor on the tongue, sometimes a combination of sweet and tart and sometimes the cool taste of cucumber, depending on what is on your fork. The other great thing about this relish is that it stimulates a healthy appetite and aids digestion. SERVES 4

2 tablespoons rice wine vinegar

2 tablespoons fresh lime juice

1 tablespoon palm sugar or brown sugar

½ teaspoon salt

½ pineapple, peeled, cored, and cut into ½-inch cubes

1 medium English cucumber, peeled, seeded, and diced

2 small shallots, thinly sliced

1 fresh red jalapeño chili, cut in half and sliced

1. Combine the vinegar, lime juice, sugar, and salt in a bowl and whisk well until the sugar and salt are dissolved.

2. In a separate bowl, combine the pineapple, cucumber, shallots, and chili. Pour the vinegar mixture over the pineapple and toss well. Allow the achar to sit for about 5 minutes for the natural juices from the pineapple and cucumber to infuse into the dressing. Serve warm or cold with grilled dishes and curries.

USING A MORTAR AND PESTLE

In the outdoor wet kitchen of my childhood home, our old stone mortar (*batu*) and pestle (*lesong*) sat quietly, acting as the head cook among old hand-hammered woks and cast iron pots. My mother's handed-down mortar was the center of her universe and she would always refer to the stones as *mother* (mortar) and *child* (pestle). I watched her over the years, rolling chilies between her hands to release the seeds, gently removing the outer layer of the shallots, tenderly peeling the garlic, and patiently slicing the lemongrass. When she was ready to pulverize them into a paste, she gripped the pestle firmly in one hand and pounded the ingredients in a confident rhythm.

In my kitchen, I have mortars and pestles in various shapes and sizes for different purposes that I have acquired in my travels throughout Southeast Asia. You can purchase your own in most Asian markets in the U.S. A heavy stone or granite set from Malaysia or Thailand is perfect for making condiments and curry pastes, especially if the recipe contains a lot of fresh chilies, garlic, aromatics, and shallots. This sort of stone mortar is also suited for crushing fresh ginger, turmeric, galangal, and lemongrass. At home, this is the type I use most often as it can pulverize fibrous roots and hard seeds in no time.

On occasion, I also use a larger and fairly shallow mortar that I purchased in Bali. Made out of volcanic stone, this porous mortar is ideal for grinding coconut and releasing the oil in candlenuts, peanuts, and cashews, lightly bruising cardamom pods to remove the seeds for grinding, pounding mustard, coriander and cumin seeds to a delightfully aromatic powder, and making the perfect guacamole and chunky sambals. After many years of valiant use, I know that this particular volcanic mortar will eventually wear away and split in half.

Then there is the bright sunset-colored wood mortar and pestle which sits artfully on my countertop. This beauty absorbs and holds flavors; as such, these wooden ones tend to be useful for bruising papayas, long beans, and tomatoes ever so gently, the perfect technique for making green papaya salad. Wood mortars are also great for grinding rice into powder. However, as with all wood products, these must be dried properly between uses to prevent mold from forming, and seasoned with coconut oil every so often. (Although there are varnished wooden mortars and pestles available, the varnish adds its flavor to your food, so they are better for decoration purposes.)

While so many cultures around the world use mortars and pestles, each particular design is appropriate for a particular use. For instance, the Mexican mortar and pestle, or *molcajete*, is better for grinding rather than pounding. The fibrous roots and aromatics used in Southeast Asian cuisine are meant to be pounded to a paste, not crushed, so for this purpose the deep heavy stone mortar is appropriate. My ideal stone mortar is 4½ inches deep and 6 inches in diameter and my pestle 8½ inches long. Too small a bowl makes it difficult to pound your curry paste ingredients into a smooth paste since there's so little room for things to move around, and the pieces will pop out of the bowl.

USING A MORTAR AND PESTLE

In most of the recipes in this book, I have suggested using a food processor for its convenience. However, there is such beauty in the mortar and pestle: beauty in appearance, beauty in its music, and beauty in the job it does. Here is how to go the old-fashioned way and use the "mother and child" yourself:

Hold the mortar firmly in place with one hand while holding the pestle firmly in your other hand. Begin by crushing the ingredients on the side of the mortar to shred the fibers. When the pestle strikes the sides of the mortar, the sound is more high pitched and treble. Once crushed, bring the ingredients to the bottom and pound firmly with short strokes. This produces a resonant bass sound like a drum, which is what you want to hear in order to pulverize the ingredients. Once the ingredients are well crushed, you can begin to use a circular grinding motion to break them down further into a smooth paste. Once you are skilled, you will soon realize what delightful music the mortar and pestle produces, mixing the treble and bass sounds in a steady rhythm.

GRINDING SEEDS

Toasted seeds such as sesame, cumin, coriander, cloves, cinnamon, star anise, mustard, and peppercorns should be allowed to cool before grinding. Place them in a deep stone mortar. Grind these spice seeds in small amounts, no more than 2 tablespoons at a time. Using the pestle, pound lightly at first to crack open the seeds, with one hand covering half the mortar to prevent the spices from popping out. Then, gradually increase the force of the pestle to break them up into a coarse powder. Finally, use a circular grinding motion to bring them into a fine powder.

GRINDING REMPAH OR SPICE PASTE

The act of cutting fibrous ingredients will not release their full range of essential oils. It is better to pound the ingredients to create a greater depth of flavor. When working with lemongrass, trim and slice it with a sharp knife then cut the stalk into thin rounds to break up the lengthwise fibers. Thinly slice galangal and finely slice makrut lime leaves. If using dried chilies, they must first be reconstituted in hot water; these chilies provide some moisture which helps binds the spice paste. If you are in a rush, you can chop the ingredients in a food processor prior to pounding them together.

Always pound one or two ingredients at a time, moving from most fibrous to the softest and wettest. When each batch is done, remove the ingredients from the mortar before proceeding with the next. There is no need to rinse the mortar, just continue with the next ingredient. Herbs are reduced quickly when pounded with a sturdy, straight up-and-down motion. When all the ingredients have been crushed, place them back into the mortar together and pound until smooth and well blended. Using a mortar and pestle melds the ingredients into one, yielding an immensely aromatic paste that a food processor can never achieve.

After using, rinse the stone mortar and pestle with warm water and wipe the bowl dry.

GINGER, GARLIC, AND CILANTRO PASTE

When cooking Malaysian food, you will notice that most meat, rice, and seafood dishes use plenty of healthy aromatics. The trio of fresh ginger, garlic, and cilantro, ground into a paste, is the secret foundation that provides depth and aroma to many dishes. Preparing it in advance is a terrific time saver, because you won't have to peel the garlic and grind the ginger for each use. You only need to use a few tablespoons of this paste to start your cooking: Add to marinades, soups, stir-fries, or braised meat and seafood dishes. I even add it to canned marinara sauces to bring them alive. This essential paste keeps well in your refrigerator for at least a week or, to extend its shelf life, you can freeze it in small containers or in ice cube trays. MAKES ABOUT 1 CUP

2 pieces (5 inches each) fresh ginger, peeled and chopped (about 1 cup)

½ cup whole peeled garlic cloves

½ cup cilantro, chopped

¼ cup water

Combine the ginger, garlic, cilantro, and water in a food processor. Blend into an aromatic paste, scraping down the sides of the bowl as often as needed. Transfer the paste to an airtight glass jar. Store in the refrigerator for 1 week or in the freezer for up to 3 months.

TAMARIND GINGER CHUTNEY

When friends come for dinner at my home, they are usually greeted with white wine and a platter of fresh fruits and vegetables and this spritely chutney. I have made and served countless batches since it is so easy to pair with other savory appetizers. The complex flavors are memorable, including the sweet tang from the tamarind, the lively aroma and gentle spice of the ginger, and a hint of piquancy from the chili peppers. If there is any left over, I use it to marinate steak or chops. The natural acids in tamarind make it an excellent meat tenderizer, and when pan-fried in a cast iron skillet, chops become tender, sweet, and tangy. SERVES 4

6 tablespoons store-bought tamarind concentrate

1 cup water

1 piece (1 inch) fresh ginger, peeled and shredded

5 tablespoons brown sugar, or to taste

½ teaspoon salt

¼ teaspoon ground cumin

¼ teaspoon chili powder or cayenne

Combine all the ingredients in a medium saucepan and bring it to a soft boil over medium heat. Cook until thick and reduced by half, about 20 minutes. Remove from the heat and serve at room temperature.

TAMARIND WATER

The tamarind tree is more than just an ornamental tree that provides shade from the scorching tropical sun; its seed pod is widely used in cooking throughout Southeast Asia. Whenever I return home to Malaysia, I enjoy plucking the gnarled tamarind pods from the trees; I savor the fruity, soft, brown pulp inside by coating it in sugar to make a natural sweet and sour candy. Tamarind is most commonly sold in a block of pulp. To use the block in cooking, you need to transform it into tamarind water by squeezing the pulp in water, as you would squeeze a sponge, which separates the seeds from the fibers (although some tamarind pulp is sold in seedless form). Strain the liquid and you have tamarind water.

Tamarind in block form or liquid concentrate is sold at most ethnic groceries (Latin American, Asian, Middle Eastern, etc.), and even in some major supermarkets. Brands from Thailand are best suited for the recipes in this book. An entire block of tamarind pulp will make 4½ cups tamarind water (add 4½ cups water), which you can easily freeze for later use. If you're purchasing the liquid concentrate, just add 1 cup water to ¼ cup concentrate to make tamarind water. For most of the recipes in this book, I use about 1 cup. MAKES 4 CUPS

3½ ouncesblock tamarind pulp

4½ cups hot water

1. Place the block of tamarind in a bowl. Add the water and allow the tamarind to sit for 5 minutes to soften.

2. Using your fingers, squeeze the tamarind block (like you would squeeze a sponge) until the pulp separates from the seed and dissolves in the water. Strain the tamarind water into a medium bowl. Discard the seeds and any pulp that has not dissolved. The strained tamarind liquid should be reddish brown in color.

3. Transfer the tamarind water to an airtight canning bottle or jar. Store in the refrigerator for up to 1 week or in the freezer for up to 6 months.

4. To use small quantities of your tamarind liquid, simply allow it to thaw on a countertop and remove the amount you require with a clean, dry spoon. Freeze the remainder. The tamarind liquid contains natural acids that prevent it from turning rancid; as such it can be thawed and frozen again provided a clean dry spoon is used each time.

GREEN CHILI, VINEGAR, AND LIME SAMBAL

This sambal is excellent as a spread for sandwiches as it enlivens the main ingredients tucked between the bread, especially turkey, chicken, or cheese. You may use any kind of hot green peppers, so try serrano chilies instead of jalapeño if you prefer more heat.

The secret to making this sambal is to let it simmer over low heat, stirring only once or twice, to allow the chilies to release their moisture. Ultimately, the oil will separate and appear on the surface. When you taste the sambal at this point, you will notice the chilies are not as intense and the vinegar is less tart. The color has changed from bright green to sage green. Use this change in color, and the oil separating onto the surface, as your guide to determine that the sambal is cooked and it is time to add the fresh lime juice. MAKES 1 CUP

10 fresh green jalapeño chilies, seeded and chopped

10 cloves garlic, peeled and left whole

5 shallots, peeled and left whole

¼ cup peanut oil or coconut oil

¼ cup rice wine vinegar

2 tablespoons brown sugar, or to taste

1½ teaspoons salt, or to taste

2 tablespoons fresh lime juice

1. Combine the chilies, garlic, and shallots in a food processor and blend until smooth. The paste should be light green when well blended.

2. Heat the oil in a skillet over low heat. Add the chili mixture before the oil gets too hot to prevent splattering. Using a wooden spoon, gently swirl the chili mixture in the oil to combine thoroughly. Bring the sambal to a soft boil and cook for about 10 minutes, stirring only once or twice.

3. Add the vinegar, brown sugar, and salt and mix well. Cook until the sambal sizzles slightly around the edges and the oils have separated onto the surface, 15 to 20 minutes. Add the lime juice. Taste and add more sugar if you prefer it sweet, or salt if you like its tangy flavor. Remove from the heat.

4. Serve at room temperature, or transfer to an airtight container and store in the refrigerator for up to 4 days.

FRIED GARLIC IN OIL

I love the simplicity of fried garlic in oil, a staple in the Malaysian kitchen, as it goes with virtually anything. I normally make double batches since I find myself using plenty of the crispy garlic and oil to garnish my stir-fried rice and noodle dishes. Adding just a teaspoon to any salad dressing, marinade, or hot noodle soup will lend an instant kick of flavor.

MAKES ABOUT 1 CUP

½ cup extra-virgin olive oil or peanut oil
4 to 5 heads garlic, minced (about 1 cup)

1. Place a wok or deep skillet over medium heat and add the oil. Carefully toss the garlic in the oil and stir once to combine. Fry the garlic until it is golden brown, about 10 minutes, stirring occasionally with a wooden spatula to prevent the garlic from burning. Let cool slightly.

2. Transfer the fried garlic and the oil to a glass jar, seal, and store in the refrigerator for up to 2 weeks.

3. For each use, let the oil come to room temperature (but do not microwave it) to maintain the garlic's flavor and texture.

FRIED SHALLOTS IN OIL

These bring depth and complexity to noodle soups, salad dressings, stir-fried rice or vegetables. I prefer to make larger batches, for which you can double this recipe, or you can simply make them when you need them. It is important to cook the shallots slowly until they release all their moisture. Only then can they turn golden brown. You can store the crispy shallots and the flavorful oil separately or in one containe. MAKES ABOUT ½ CUP

1 teaspoon salt
1 cup water
½ pound shallots
1 cup peanut oil or extra-virgin olive oil

1. Combine the salt and water in a medium bowl. Add the shallots and soak for 5 minutes to soften the skin and make peeling easier. The salt water will also help remove moisture from the shallots. Drain the shallots then dry them thoroughly on paper towels or a clean dish-cloth. Peel and thinly slice.

2. Place a wok or skillet over medium-high heat. When the wok is hot, add the oil. Add the shallots and fry until golden brown and crisp, about 15 to 20 minutes. Remove the shallots with a slotted spoon and allow to cool on a paper towel.

3. Store the shallots with one-quarter of the oil in an airtight container in the refrigerator for up to 3 months

Fried Garlic in Oil (left) and Fried Shallots in Oil

RENDANG SPICE PASTE

Rendang has been called the national dish of Malaysia. The extremely aromatic spice paste is made from fresh lemongrass, chilies, galangal, and coconut cream. Besides being used to make Beef Rendang (page 261), it is a quick and easy way to add plenty of flavor to a variety of dishes. I use the fragrant paste to marinate chicken, and flank, rib eye, or tri-tip steak prior to grilling to perfection. You can also use the paste to start braised dishes. The lemongrass and galangal (a member of the ginger family) naturally tenderize the meat while the coconut cream creates that "melt in your mouth" flavor.

Because it is so easy to make in the food processor, I normally make a double batch to keep on hand. Fresh lemongrass is lovely here, but you can use frozen for convenience: Asian markets sell chopped frozen lemongrass in clear plastic containers. The frozen version is exceptionally fragrant and imparts a stronger citrusy flavor since this particular lemongrass is grown in Southeast Asia. MAKES 2 CUPS

1 cup coconut cream

5 shallots, peeled and quartered

3 stalks fresh lemongrass, outer layers discarded, minced; or ¼ cup chopped frozen lemongrass

1 piece (3 inches) unpeeled fresh galangal, chopped

6 cloves garlic, peeled and left whole

5 candlenuts or macadamia nuts

2 tablespoons Sambal Ulek (page 44 or store-bought) or chili powder

1 tablespoon ground coriander

½ teaspoon ground turmeric

Salt to taste

Place all the ingredients in a food processor and blend until velvety smooth. You will end with a fragrant light-orange spice paste. Transfer to a glass jar, seal, and store in the refrigerator for up to 1 week, or in the freezer for up to 6 months.

SOUTHEAST ASIAN ROASTED CHILI PASTE

This paste gets its bite from the dried red chilies and shallots and its delicate sweetness from palm sugar and sweet soy sauce. Stir it into salad dressings and soups, and use as the final ingredient in stir-fries, to add an authentic Southeast Asian touch. MAKES 1½ CUPS

½ cup whole dried red chilies de arbol

4 small shallots, peeled and halved

10 cloves garlic, peeled and left whole

6 tablespoons vegetable oil

10 tablespoons liquid palm sugar (see pages 315-316) or brown sugar

2 tablespoons kicap manis (sweet soy sauce; see page 16)

½ cup Tamarind Water (page 54)

2 teaspoons salt

1 teaspoon toasted shrimp paste (optional; see page 116)

1. Combine the chilies, shallots, and garlic in a heavy skillet over medium heat and cook until the garlic turns golden brown, turning the cloves frequently so they do not burn, 10 to 12 minutes. Remove from the heat and set aside to cool.

2. Transfer the chili mixture to a food processor and grind it. With the food processor running, slowly add 3 tablespoons of the oil in a steady stream through the opening in the lid. Process until pureed. You may need to scrape down the sides of the bowl every so often.

3. Heat the remaining 3 tablespoons oil in a wok or skillet over medium heat. Add the blended chili paste and cook, stirring frequently, until the oil separates onto the top, about 15 minutes.

4. Add the palm sugar, kicap manis, tamarind water, and salt. Reduce the heat to low and cook until the paste appears deep red, about 3 minutes. Add the shrimp paste and cook for an additional 1 minute. At this point, the chili paste should appear thick like jam with a little oil on top, and taste sweet, spicy, salty, and a little sour.

5. Remove from the heat and let cool. Transfer the chili paste to an airtight glass jar. Store the paste in the refrigerator for 1 month or in the freezer for 6 months.

LAKSA SPICE PASTE

In Malaysian cuisine, laksa is the magic wand that flavors a large number of dishes, including fish, chicken, noodles, and aromatic cooking stocks. It is a classic mix of fresh citrusy lemongrass, rose-scented galangal, garlic, ginger, and turmeric, all of it bound together by peanut oil. You'll find that once you have made your laksa paste, much of the time-consuming part of your cooking is already done. For instance, by just adding coconut milk and water, you have a sensational broth for simmering fresh tofu and your choice of protein (chicken, seafood, and so forth.) Laksa can also be used as a marinade before grilling or baking any kind of fish, added to stir-fries, or, like many sambals, used as a spread in sandwiches. This may become a mainstay in your kitchen. MAKES 1 CUP

2 stalks lemongrass, outer layers discarded, thinly sliced

1 medium onion or 6 shallots, chopped

4 cloves garlic, peeled and left whole

1 piece (1 inch) unpeeled fresh galangal, chopped

1 piece (1 inch) fresh ginger, peeled and sliced

3 tablespoons Sambal Ulek (page 44 or store-bought)

6 macadamia nuts or 2 tablespoons cashews

½ teaspoon ground cumin

½ teaspoon ground turmeric

1 cup water

½ cup peanut oil

2 teaspoons salt, or to taste

1. Add the lemongrass, onion, garlic, galangal, ginger, sambal ulek, and nuts to a blender and blend. Next add the cumin, turmeric, and water and blend until smooth.

2. Heat the oil in a deep saucepan over medium heat. When hot, add the spice paste and stir-fry until aromatic and the oil separates onto the surface, about 15 minutes.

3. Stir in the salt, taste, and add more if needed. Bring to a boil, then remove from the heat. Store in an airtight container in the refrigerator for up to 1 month, or freeze for up to 6 months.

PERFECT PEANUT SAUCE

In Malaysia, hunting for a good peanut sauce can be a serious pursuit. The best peanut sauce is, without a doubt, made by a satay man, a street peddler who specializes in spiced, grilled meat threaded onto bamboo skewers and grilled over charcoal flames.

I start with raw peanuts and roast until golden. If you really need to save time, you could buy unsalted roasted peanuts. However, the aroma of peanuts roasting in the oven is heavenly and also provides an unmatched nutty taste. Use the kicap manis as your color guide to gauge the correct golden color of the peanuts. The finished peanut sauce will be yellowish orange in color due to the red chilies; the flavor will be semi-sweet and the texture never gooey! Enjoy the sauce as a dip, pour it over salad, or use it to stir-fry chicken for a quick weeknight meal. MAKES 4 CUPS

3 cups (1 pound) unsalted shelled raw peanuts

7 cloves garlic, peeled and left whole

6 fresh red bird's-eye chilies, chopped

1 piece (3 inches) unpeeled fresh galangal, sliced

1 piece (3 inches) unpeeled fresh turmeric, chopped; or ½ teaspoon ground turmeric

2 cups coconut milk

2 cups water

¼ teaspoon ground coriander

¼ teaspoon ground cumin

4 makrut lime leaves, torn

3 tablespoons liquid palm sugar (see pages 315–316)

Juice of 1 lime

¼ cup kicap manis (sweet soy sauce; see page 16)

½ teaspoon salt, or to taste

1. Preheat the oven to 350°F. Spread the nuts on a baking sheet and roast until golden brown, about 15 minutes. Transfer to a plate to cool.

2. Put the peanuts in a food processor and blend for about 20 seconds, until finely ground. Add the garlic, chilies, galangal, and turmeric and grind until smooth, adding a little water at a time if needed to facilitate blending.

3. Transfer the paste to a heavy pot or Dutch oven and add the coconut milk, water, coriander, cumin, and lime leaves. Bring to a boil, then lower the heat and simmer, uncovered, for about 10 minutes, stirring frequently to prevent the coconut milk from burning and sticking on the bottom.

4. Add the palm sugar, lime juice, kicap manis, and salt. Bring to a boil, then lower the heat and simmer, uncovered, stirring periodically, until a little oil separates onto the surface, about 5 minutes. Serve hot, or refrigerate for up to 4 days or freeze for up to 1 month.

MALAYSIAN TOMATO SAMBAL

Tomatoes and chilies, so important to Malaysian cooking, are not native to Southeast Asia. In fact, they only arrived with the Portuguese traders about 500 years ago. This shows how versatile and open to new ideas the cooks of Malaysia can be. This tomato sambal, a marvelous condiment, is usually the color of red salsa and the consistency of sweet chutney. The sweetness and piquancy comes from the lime along with chunks of tomato in each bite. At home, this sambal complements fried eggs, grilled beef or chicken, or tacos, just as a Latin salsa might. It can also make a perfect topping for an exotic bruschetta or as a dip for blue corn tortilla chips. Once you make a sufficient quantity, you will go to this sambal before going back to store-bought salsa or other commercial condiments. MAKES 1 CUP

¼ cup extra-virgin olive oil or coconut oil

2 teaspoons minced garlic

6 Roma tomatoes, seeded and chopped

3 to 4 fresh red jalapeño chilies, chopped

1 teaspoon raw shrimp paste

1 teaspoon salt, or to taste

2 tablespoons sugar

1 tablespoon fresh lime juice

1. Heat the oil in a deep sauté pan over medium heat. Add the garlic and cook, stirring occasionally to prevent the garlic from burning, until golden brown in color, about 2 minutes.

2. Meanwhile, place the tomatoes, chilies, and shrimp paste in a food processor and pulse into a salsa-like consistency.

3. Once the garlic is brown, add the tomato mixture, and then season with salt and sugar. Taste and add more salt if needed; you want a balance of sweet, sour, and salty flavors. If the sambal is too spicy, you can tone it down with sugar. Allow the tomato mixture to cook until the oil separates onto the top, the shrimp paste aroma has dissipated, and the sambal bulk is reduced, about 15 minutes.

4. Add the lime juice, stir well, and remove from the heat. Serve warm. Any leftovers can be refrigerated in an airtight container for up to 1 week.

SOUPS

If you enjoy your soups layered with flavor, healthy, and perfectly spiced, then this chapter is going to be an adventure for all your senses and a pleasure for your palate. There are two major styles of soup in Malaysia: a clear-broth style and a more robust lentil-based soup. Soups are an essential part of a complete Malaysian meal and rarely eaten as a separate course, but you might want to serve the heartier soups on their own with bread as a light lunch or dinner.

The soups are incredibly easy to put together if you have the ingredients. As in all Malaysian cooking, the essential technique is to cook the ingredients in stages in order to layer flavors as the ingredients release their enticing oils and aromas. The rich flavors first come from garlic, onions or shallots, galangal, ginger, lemongrass, and other aromatics like makrut lime leaves or spices, which are infused into the stock, until they release their fragrant oils. Then, the next layer of main ingredients: Fish, noodles, and healthy vegetables are added to absorb the wonderful flavors of the soup, so when you bite into the fish or noodles, they are packed with flavor.

A broth-based soup is flavored primarily with fresh aromatics, while a thicker or creamy soup relies on dried spice seeds. When a soup calls for a creamy consistency, you make a fresh spice paste by blending the aromatic ingredients until they reach the consistency of applesauce. Then the spice paste is cooked until the fragrant oils come to the top and separate, at which point coconut milk or stock is added. This method is excellent for squash and root-like vegetables, such as the Butternut Squash Soup on page 86.

The gardens of Malaysia are integral in the making of soups. As a child, I would go out to our family garden and cut a few stalks of lemongrass, pick a few makrut lime leaves,

and dig up a few earthy gingers and knobs of galangal, and bring them to my mother for cooking. When the leaves of the makrut are pressed together between your palms, sweet citrus notes of orange, lime, and cloves are released, which are imparted to soups. These aromatic soups are seen in Malaysian home cooking as especially healthful. Research supports Malaysian cooking in this regard. For instance, consuming lemongrass is known to significantly sustain healthy levels of triglycerides and is believed to reduce the LDL ("bad") cholesterol in the body.

Another great thing about Malaysian soups is that you can customize them according to your own preferences. You can skip the fish and add something else: chicken, shrimp, scallops, squid, mussels, tofu, or a combination. You can vary the vegetables, especially green leafy ones.

Clear broth soups may be the easier recipes in this chapter, and I have included a variety, such as Golden Pompono and Shiitake Soup (page 82), Pork Meatball Soup with Daikon (page 83), Malaccan-Portuguese Spicy Halibut Soup (page 85), and Simple Malaysian Chicken Soup (page 90). The lovely thing about clear soups is that you can freeze them and serve them another day, making them very convenient.

The full-bodied soups made with lentils or dense vegetables are often served alongside

main dishes, but they can be stand-alone meals by themselves. The flavors come from the use of dried spices such as chilies and whole spices, mustard seeds, and cumin seeds. For fuller flavors, the whole spices are tempered in hot oil to extract their volatile oils (compounds that give spices their characteristic flavors and aromas), and then added at the end of the cooking process, as in Yellow Lentil Soup with Cauliflower and Spinach (page 72). A modest amount of ground spices is better for less intense flavor that allows the other ingredients to shine, as in Red Lentil and Chickpea Soup with Mint (page 69) and Red Lentil and Rice Soup (page 70).

Most Malaysian style soups are well-balanced, low in calories, and as satisfying as they are nutritious! Who can doubt the rich healthfulness of such ingredients as kale, bok choy, spinach, cauliflower? And fresh fish like salmon, tilapia, or pompano, or the great variety of lentils and beans? By using these simple techniques presented in this chapter, you will be able to enjoy the health-giving properties of these foods prepared in the Malaysian style. As the Malaysian saying goes, "Soup helps the rice go down."

RED LENTIL AND CHICKPEA SOUP WITH MINT

I feel so fortunate to have had two mothers in my life, both of whom I considered to be great cooks: My biological mother who brought me into this world and taught me about the world of spices; and then my second mother, Philomena, who helped raise me after my mother died and taught me the traditions of cooking. This recipe was Philomena's specialty. We nicknamed the soup *pudina sambar* ("mint lentils") because we used home-grown mint from our garden.

The recipe uses red lentils for their savory flavor, which differs subtly from the nuttier flavor of green lentils, although either one can be used. To complete the soup, rub the mint between your fingers to release its aromatic oils before sprinkling it over the soup. SERVES 6

1½ cups red lentils (*masoor dal*)

3 tablespoons virgin coconut oil

1 yellow onion, finely chopped

4 cloves garlic, minced

2 tablespoons tomato paste

1 large tomato, chopped

1½ tablespoons paprika

½ cup dried chickpeas, soaked overnight and drained; or 1 cup drained canned chickpeas

6 cups water or vegetable stock

1 teaspoon salt, or to taste

1 teaspoon dried mint leaves; or 3 sprigs fresh mint leaves, roughly chopped

1. Wash the lentils by gently rubbing them with your fingers in a bowl under cold running water until the water runs clear. (The running water allows debris, such as tiny stones or outer skin, to float to the top instead of sinking to the bottom with the lentils.) Drain the lentils.

2. Heat the oil in a deep pot over medium heat. When the oil is hot, add the onion and garlic and cook, stirring, until softened but not brown, about 10 minutes.

3. Stir in the tomato paste, tomato, and paprika and cook for a minute to infuse the flavors. You will have a thick tomato mixture.

4. Add the lentils and chickpeas and mix well. Slowly pour in the water or stock and bring the lentils to a boil, uncovered. Skim off any foam that may appear on the surface during the cooking process. Lower the heat to medium-low, cover the pot, and cook, stirring intermittently to ensure that the lentils do not stick to the bottom of the pan, until the lentils have completely broken down and are tender when pressed between your fingers and the chickpeas are tender, 35 to 40 minutes.

5. Add salt to taste. Cook for about another 10 minutes, stirring occasionally; if the soup appears too thick, add a little water.

6. Rub the mint between your fingers. Add the mint, stir the lentils well, and serve.

RED LENTIL AND RICE SOUP

This is another of those thick and hearty soups the Indians of Malaysia love to cook. Nothing fancy, just a bowl of deeply flavored, simple, and nourishing food. The combination of red lentils and basmati rice cooked with the earthiness of paprika and garlic provides layers of savory flavor to the soup. Because onion, garlic, tomato paste, fresh tomato, and paprika form the flavorful base, you will want to make sure this mixture is browned properly; also be sure to use good virgin coconut oil or extra-virgin olive oil, and don't skimp on the quantity. After that, it's all very straightforward, as the lentils and rice are added to the pot and cooked until very soft and creamy. For faster cooking time you could soak the lentils overnight in warm water, although I personally don't fuss with that. SERVES 6

1½ cups red lentils (*masoor dal*)

¼ cup white basmati rice

¼ cup virgin coconut oil or extra-virgin olive oil

2 tablespoons unsalted butter

1 yellow onion, finely chopped

4 cloves garlic, minced

2 tablespoons tomato paste

1 large tomato, chopped

1½ tablespoons paprika

6 cups chicken stock or water

½ teaspoon salt, or to taste

½ teaspoon freshly ground black pepper

1 fresh jalapeño chili, sliced

1. Wash the lentils and rice together by gently rubbing them with your fingers in a bowl under cold running water until the water runs clear. (The running water allows debris, such as tiny stones or outer skin, to float to the top instead of sinking to the bottom with the lentils.) Drain the lentils.

2. Heat the oil and butter in a deep pot over medium heat. Add the onion and garlic and cook, stirring, until softened but not brown, about 10 minutes.

3. Stir in the tomato paste, tomato, and paprika. Cook, stirring, for about 1 minute to infuse the flavors.

4. Add the lentils and rice and mix well. Add the stock or water and bring to a boil, uncovered. Skim off any foam that may appear on the surface during the cooking process. Lower the heat, cover the pot, and cook, stirring intermittently, until the lentils and rice are cooked, about 35 minutes.

5. Season with the salt to taste and add the pepper. Cook for about another 10 minutes, stirring occasionally; if the soup appears too thick, add a little water. Serve garnished with the jalapeño.

FISH AND RICE VERMICELLI SOUP WITH LEMONGRASS

This very simple soup is served at small mom-and-pop-style restaurants and street stalls in Malaysia's larger cities. Malaysians love to add rice noodles to their soups—just as pasta is added to Italian minestrone—to make them more satisfying. You could use any sort of white fish, but a strong-flavored fish, such as striped bass, is best. The lovely citrus flavor and calming aroma comes from the galangal, lemongrass, and makrut lime leaves, a combination I call my "culinary spa." Since I make this soup on a regular basis, for convenience, I soak the dried rice vermicelli noodles in warm water to soften them, then drain and store in small individual airtight bags in the refrigerator so that they are at the ready and I have one less thing to do. SERVES 4 TO 6

7 cups seafood stock

1 piece (6 inches) unpeeled fresh galangal, thinly sliced

10 makrut lime leaves, stemmed

6 stalks lemongrass, outer layers discarded, cut into 4-inch strips

2 shallots, peeled and cut in half

1 pound any white fish (such as striped bass or pomfret), cut into 1- by 4-inch pieces

½ cup rice vermicelli, soaked in hot water for 20 minutes until soft and drained

1 large tomato, quartered

1½ tablespoons fish sauce, or to taste

1 teaspoon Sambal Belachan (page 43) or store-bought roasted chili paste (optional)

½ cup fresh cilantro leaves

1. In a large pot, bring the stock just to a boil over medium heat. Add the galangal, lime leaves, lemongrass, and shallots. Cover and cook, stirring occasionally, until fragrant, about 30 minutes.

2. Once all the aromatics are infused into the stock, add the fish, vermicelli, and tomato, reduce the heat to low, and cook until the fish is cooked through, about 10 minutes. Stir in the fish sauce, sambal (if using), and cilantro. Taste, and if the soup is not salty enough add more fish sauce. Serve immediately.

YELLOW LENTIL SOUP
WITH CAULIFLOWER AND SPINACH

This *dal,* or lentil dish, originated in Brickfields, Kuala Lumpur, a town famous for producing bricks and clay pots and, consequently, for authentic Indian clay-pot cooking. Even though it is soft and creamy, the soup is not made with cream, as is sometimes done in Indian restaurants in the U.S. (If you omit the small amount of butter stirred in at the end, it is vegan as well as gluten-free.) Oil infused with cumin and black mustard seed is added to complete the dal with robust flavor. While I have suggested cauliflower and spinach, you could also use potatoes, fresh pumpkin, butternut squash, or eggplant for great variations. This hearty soup is delicious with brown rice, naan, pita, or whole-wheat bread. SERVES 4

LENTILS

- 1 cup split yellow lentils (*toor dal*)
- 4 cloves garlic, peeled and left whole
- ½ yellow onion, minced
- ½ teaspoon ground turmeric
- 5 cups water
- 8 ounces cauliflower, chopped into bite-size pieces
- 4 ounces fresh spinach leaves
- 1 teaspoon salt, or to taste

SPICE-INFUSED OIL (*TADKA*)

- 2 tablespoons virgin coconut oil
- ½ teaspoon cumin seeds
- ¼ teaspoon black mustard seeds
- 2 sprigs fresh curry leaves, stemmed and coarsely chopped
- 1 teaspoon unsalted butter (optional)

1. Prepare the lentils: Wash the lentils by gently rubbing them with your fingers in a bowl under cold running water until the water runs clear. (The running water allows debris, such as tiny stones or outer skin, to float to the top instead of sinking to the bottom with the lentils.) Drain the lentils.

2. Combine the lentils, garlic, onion, turmeric, and water in a large, deep pot. Bring to a boil, partially covered, over medium heat. Skim off any foam that may appear on the surface during the cooking process. Cook until the lentils are very soft when pressed between your fingers and have a pureed texture, about 40 minutes.

3. Add the cauliflower and spinach and season with salt. Stir gently, cover, and cook until the cauliflower is tender, about 3 minutes. Taste and add more salt if needed. Keep the lentils over low heat while infusing the oil.

4. Infuse the oil: Heat the coconut oil in a small skillet over medium heat. Once the oil is hot, add the cumin seeds, mustard seeds, and curry leaves and immediately cover with a splatter screen, or partially cover with a lid with 1 inch open for the steam to release, to keep the mustard seeds from popping out of the pan. When you hear the mustard seeds popping, after a few seconds, turn off the heat. Immediately pour the hot spice-infused oil over the lentils.

5. Add the butter if desired, and stir well to combine all the flavors. Serve immediately.

COOK'S TIP | When cooking lentils, add a dash of oil (either coconut oil or olive oil) to the water. This lentil-cooking tradition helps to keep the lentils from spilling over during the rapid simmering.

SPLIT YELLOW LENTIL SOUP WITH OPO SQUASH

Opo squash, available in most Asian and health food stores, is light green with a long cylindrical shape, similar to a zucchini. (In fact, if you can't find opo, you can use zucchini here instead.) Before cooking, peel the outer green layer. The flesh has a lovely sponge-like texture, which makes opo excellent in soups since it absorbs all the flavors of the delicious broth. You may like to try the recipe with brown lentils, French green lentils, or split red lentils, as each variety produces its own unique flavor and texture. SERVES 4

LENTILS

- 1 cup split yellow lentils (*toor dal*)
- 5 cups water
- 1 yellow onion, finely chopped
- 4 cloves garlic, minced
- 1 medium opo squash, peeled and diced
- 1 cup chickpeas, soaked overnight and drained; or 1 ½ cups drained canned chickpeas
- ½ teaspoon ground turmeric

SPICE-INFUSED OIL (*TADKA*)

- 3 tablespoons clarified butter (ghee) or extra-virgin olive oil
- ¼ yellow onion, diced
- ½ teaspoon cumin seeds
- ½ teaspoon black mustard seeds
- ½ teaspoon chili powder
- ½ teaspoon garam masala

    Salt to taste
    A few sprigs cilantro, for garnish

1. Prepare the lentils: Wash the lentils by gently rubbing them with your fingers in a bowl under cold running water until the water runs clear. (The running water allows debris to float to the top instead of sinking to the bottom with the lentils.) Drain the lentils.

2. Place the lentils in a deep pot with the water, onion, garlic, squash, chickpeas, and turmeric. Bring to a boil, uncovered. Skim off any foam that may appear on the surface during the cooking process. Lower the heat and allow the lentils to simmer, stirring intermittently, until very soft with a puree-like texture, about 40 minutes.

3. Infuse the oil: Heat the butter or oil in a small skillet over medium heat. Add the onion and cook until brown, about 3 minutes. Add the cumin, mustard seeds, chili powder, and garam masala and immediately cover with a splatter screen, or partially cover with a lid to keep the mustard seeds from popping out of the pan. When the mustard seeds began to pop, turn off the heat. Immediately pour all the spice-infused oil into the lentil soup. Mix the infused oil and lentils well to combine the flavors. Add salt to taste. Cook, stirring, for another minute. Serve garnished with the cilantro.

CULINARY DIVERSITY IN MALAYSIA

The uniqueness of Malaysian dishes comes from the blend of cross-cultural borrowing as waves of different ethnic groups converged and interacted on the Malay Peninsula. The original people of the peninsula are known as Orang Asli (literally, "original people") who now dwell in the rural interior. The Orang Asli consist of many tribes, each with its own language and culture, who depend on the bounty of the rain forest to sustain themselves. Over the years, Southeast Asian, Indian, Persian, Chinese, North African, Portuguese, Dutch, and British peoples arrived, each contributing their own culinary traditions. While each culture retained some original identity in its cooking, a Malaysian cuisine also evolved as people embraced new ingredients and learned techniques from their neighbors. The four major ethnic categories that constitute Malaysia's main population are Indian, Chinese, Malay, and Peranakan; hence there is a saying, "You taste Asia in Malaysia."

MALAY

For generations the many cultures we now know as Malay lived a simple life, dwelling along the coast and riverbanks. Fish were abundant, rice was grown in verdant green paddy fields, and wild and cultivated fruits and vegetables were available year-round due to the tropical climate. The people lived in traditional *kampung* (village) settlements set in neatly raked yards that were shaded by coconut, banana, and papaya trees, with chickens roaming freely, pecking their way around a variety of herbs and coconut pulp. A traditional meal included rice with fresh or salted fish, raw fruits, and vegetable and herb platters called *ulam,* served with pungent dipping sauces made with fermented shrimp paste and anchovies. The slow and laidback village life of the Malays was reflected in their traditional cooking methods of wrapping fish in banana leaves and cooking the pouches over a low fire to retain all the natural flavors. Walk through a rustic Malay village today and you might see fish spread out on weathered tables drying in the sun waiting to add a touch of salinity to rice and vegetable dishes.

Over time, a number of changes transformed how Malay people cooked and ate. People from Thailand, to the north, introduced the rhizomes ginger, galangal, lemongrass, and fresh turmeric; fruits such as tamarind and limes; and aromatics including shallots and fragrant makrut lime leaves. These ingredients, often present in Thai food, became part of Malay cooking repertoire. In residential areas, one can recognize a Malay home by the variety of fresh aromatics grown in the garden and the delicious aroma of lemongrass wafting from the kitchen at dusk.

From Indonesia, the Sumatran influence of richly spiced dishes cooked in coconut milk was revised with the addition of aromatics and pandan to create the dish called *rendang.* And the Javanese contribution of grilling spiced meats—satay—is now classified as a national dish loved by everyone.

CHINESE

China itself is an amazingly diverse society, with different languages, cultures, and cuisines; settlers from various regions of China made their cuisine an indispensable part of Malaysian culinary culture. In the late 19th century, people from the southern provinces of Guangdong and Fujian arrived and settled in the major trading ports of Penang, Malacca, Kuala Lumpur, Ipoh, and Taiping to work in the tin mining industry. With their settlement came woks, noodles, fermented bean curd, and sauces.

From the region of Guangdong, the Cantonese cooking techniques of steaming, stir-frying, barbecuing, braising, and soup making became part of the Malaysian culture. While working under the British, the Cantonese blended Western sauces like tomato ketchup and Worcestershire with their seasonings to create exciting sauces for steak and chops. During a night visit to Petaling Street, Kuala Lumpur's Chinatown, from a distance you can easily spot a white cloud of smoke rising above the red tarpaulin awnings, enveloping you in the sweet spiced aroma of barbecue roasted pork.

From the Fujian region, the Hakka and Hokkien people introduced simple cooking techniques to highlight the original flavors of the ingredients. Their ingenious use of local ingredients elevated their common dishes to a tastier level. The Chinese borrowed curry leaves from the Malaysian Indian neighbors to create dishes like coconut-butter prawns, kam heong clams, and chili prawns. They transformed their Hokkien noodles, *char kway teow*, and oyster omelets with a touch of Malay condiments and chili powder. The famous steamed Hainanese chicken rice was transformed by adding local aromatics. These flavorful dishes made the island of Penang a destination for the best street food in Asia.

INDIAN

Indian traders were working the ports of Malaya as early as the 9th century. As Malacca grew into an important trading port, many Indian traders began settling there in the 15th century and integrated into the local society.

However, it was not until the 19th century, under the influence of the British colonists, that Indians from Tamil Nadu and Kerala in South India came in large numbers to make Malaya (now Malaysia) their home. They were commissioned to work in schools, on rubber estates, and at building the railways. They brought with them clay cooking pots, rice, lentils, curry leaves, and mustard seeds so that they could cook and eat as they did back home. Their traditional dishes involved the tempering of spice seeds with onions and chilies in hot oil to produce heavily spiced vegetarian dishes eaten on banana leaves and served at the temples. The popularity of this cuisine grew beyond the temple walls and the cooking style was modified using less spice and adding meat and seafood to the menu. Today, dishes such as lamb korma, butter chicken masala, tamarind fish curry, and cabbage with curry leaves are served smorgasbord style at the famous "banana leaf" restaurants throughout the country.

With the arrival of South Indians also came the arrival of Indian Muslims known as Mamaks. Unlike the Hindu Indians who set up restaurants, the Mamaks started selling their cuisines in residential areas, carrying their baskets filled with vibrant curries made with fresh turmeric and coconut milk, which is now called *nasi kandar,* and noodles cooked with bean curd, curry powder, and soy sauces called *mamak mee goreng.* Their salads, called *pasembur,* were made with tropical fruits and sprouts drenched with peanut sauce seasoned with palm sugar and Malay sambal. These novel creations, not found in India, were easily accepted by the various cultures owing to the familiarity of ingredients. Due to the popularity of their cuisine, they began operating affordable and unpretentious food stalls to create a casual dining atmosphere seven days a week. One of my favorite dishes is roti canai, a paper-thin flatbread that is grilled until golden and crisp and accompanied by curry. Roti canai is a beloved Malaysian breakfast and one of the most spectacular contributions of the Mamaks.

The North Indians, mainly Gujaratis and Punjabis Sikhs, arrived later in Malaysia, some to fulfill the security needs of the country, others to set up trade in the textile and food industries. They introduced Northern Indian cuisine which consisted of pilafs, yogurt, lentil dishes, naans or breads, and tandoori, meats lightly seasoned with yogurt and spices and cooked in clay ovens.

BABA-NYONYA

One cuisine in particular that showcases Malaysia's fusion at its best is the food of the Babas (men) and Nyonyas (women) who reside in Penang, Malacca, and Singapore. The Babas and Nyonyas, also known as Peranakan, are the children of early Chinese settlers who came to live in Malacca in the 15th century and took wealthy Malay women as their wives.

Baba-Nyonya cuisine blended typical Chinese ingredients—bean curd, soy sauce, fermented soy beans, sesame seeds, dried lily buds, mushrooms—with Malay herbs, rhizomes, and aromatics to create delicious Peranakan, or fusion, cuisine. Unlike the Malays, the Babas and Nyonyas included pork in their cuisine and used the Chinese method of braising to emphasize the fragrance and complex flavors of herbs and spices. In the kitchen, Nyonyas were taught to cook from scratch—to extract tamarind water and coconut milk and create fresh spice pastes with candlenuts, turmeric, chilies, lemongrass, galangal, and shrimp paste using the traditional mortar and pestle for grinding.

The Baba-Nyonya lifestyle embraced a formal colonial-inspired way of living where the Nyonyas ran the entire household like a five-star hotel, with intricate porcelain dinner plates and matching silverware gracing the table. Even in the kitchen, the Nyonya women wore Malay-style silk voile *kebayas* (an embroidered batik sarong and blouse) while they trained their daughters to cook everything from scratch as part of their education.

Today, a walk along Jonker Street in Malacca can still bestow you a taste of Peranakan cuisine. The classical Eastern- and Western-designed homes built during the Dutch occupation, which boast colorful ceramic tiles and Chinese blackwood furniture, will greet you as you sit down to enjoy curry kapitan, *babi pongteh* (pork spareribs in cinnamon-nutmeg sauce), or Nyonya laksa at one of the Baba house restaurants that are unique to the Malay Peninsular region, but slowly fading away.

PORTUGUESE

The Portuguese were the first European colonists to come to Southeast Asia for the spice trade. Long after their empire collapsed, their legacy of culinary and religious traditions is far greater than their ruins. Portuguese soldiers bearing such names as Sequiera, Aranjo, Pinto, Diaz, and Da Silva cherished the traditions of their European lineage. Today, their descendants live in a community called the Portuguese Settlement in Malacca near the beach.

One of the most valuable contributions of Portuguese trade is the introduction of chilies to the region. Portuguese cooks used chilies and vinegar to flavor meat and seafood, and such spicy dishes were called *debal* (a variant on the Portuguese word for devil, *diabo*). The Portuguese used soy sauce, oyster sauce, and sour tamarind to transform traditional stews into fusion dishes. They brought with them European desserts such as flan, which was then made using tropical bananas and coconut.

In Malacca, lemongrass, shallots, and shrimp paste are combined with chilies and vinegar from Portugal to make the highly seasoned dipping sauces called *chinchalok*. Other Portuguese influences like tomatoes, sweet peppers, chilies, and vinegar lend a light Mediterranean touch to Indian curries.

THE MODERN MULTICULTURAL MALAYSIAN KITCHEN

Through a combination of spices and aromatics, Malaysian cuisine continues to combine the best of Malay, Chinese, Indian, Baba-Nyonya, and Portuguese cooking styles to produce a unique palate of flavors that is like no other. It truly is a culinary experience to be able to taste the influences of so many cultures in a single cuisine. As my dear teacher Datuk Dr. Wong Lai Sum would say, "When you eat Malaysian food, you taste many cultures in a spoonful."

GOLDEN POMPANO AND SHIITAKE SOUP

I make this light and delicious fish soup regularly in the cool autumn months. Much of the flavor comes from the somewhat sweet and buttery-soft golden pompano fish, delicate opo squash, and woody shiitake mushrooms. Golden pompano can be found in most Asian fish markets and premium fish markets; I have the vendors at my local seafood markets clean and cut the fish into steaks, making it easy to cook at home. The pompano pairs beautifully with opo squash, an Asian squash that's used much like zucchini; if you cannot find either pompano or opo, you may use halibut and zucchini instead. SERVES 4 TO 6

2 tablespoons peanut oil

4 cloves garlic, minced

1 piece (2 inches) fresh ginger, peeled and julienned

12 shiitake mushrooms (about 1 cup), cleaned with a damp cloth

½ small opo squash, peeled and diced

3 cups seafood stock

½ teaspoon ground black pepper

1½ pounds golden pompano or halibut, cut into 3-inch pieces

1½ tablespoons soy sauce, or to taste

2 tablespoons chopped fresh cilantro, for garnish

Fried Shallots (page 56), for garnish (optional)

1. Heat the oil in a 3-quart saucepan or soup pot over medium heat. Test if the oil is hot by adding a pinch of garlic; it should sizzle slightly. When the oil is ready, add all the minced garlic and stir-fry for a few seconds, until light golden. Add the ginger and cook, stirring, until the ginger sizzles and becomes fragrant, about 1 minute.

2. Add the mushrooms and squash and cook, stirring, for another 2 minutes.

3. Add the stock and pepper and bring to a boil, covered. Reduce the heat and simmer until the mushrooms are soft and the pepper has infused its flavor into the soup, about 4 minutes.

4. Add the fish and soy sauce. Reduce the heat to low, cover, and simmer until the fish is opaque and cooked through, about 10 minutes.

5. Taste the soup for saltiness and add additional soy sauce if needed. Remove from the heat, garnish with the cilantro, and ladle into bowls. Sprinkle with fried shallots, if desired, just before serving.

PORK MEATBALL SOUP WITH DAIKON

This is a Malaccan-style Portuguese soup that is eaten with rice. The blend of daikon and shiitake mushrooms provides an umami flavor that brings savory richness to the soup as it slowly simmers. *Daikon* literally means "large root," and it resembles a huge white carrot. It has a slightly sweet taste and a texture similar to that of turnips. In Chinese restaurants, when they list "white radish," this is what they mean. When cooked in a soup, it softens in texture and blends well with other ingredients. At the market, I try to always pick the smallest daikon, as they are juicier and firmer. If you prefer, you may substitute chopped uncooked chicken for the meatballs. SERVES 4 TO 6

2 tablespoons peanut oil

6 cloves garlic, minced

2 whole star anise

3 whole cloves

1 tomato, quartered

8 shiitake mushrooms (about 1 cup), cleaned with a damp cloth

1 small daikon, peeled and diced (about 2 cups)

4 cups chicken stock

1 pound ground pork

½ teaspoon ground white pepper

1½ tablespoons soy sauce, or to taste

2 green onions (white and green parts), chopped

Fried Shallots (page 56), for garnish (optional)

1. Heat the oil in a 3-quart saucepan or soup pot over medium heat. Test if the oil is hot by adding a pinch of garlic; it should sizzle slightly. When the oil is ready, add all the minced garlic, the star anise, and cloves and stir-fry for a few seconds until the garlic is light golden and the spices are fragrant.

2. Add the tomato, mushrooms, and daikon and stir well to coat with the spiced oil. Cook until the tomato softens, 10 to 15 minutes. Add the stock, cover, and bring to a boil.

3. Meanwhile, mix together the pork, white pepper, and soy sauce in a medium bowl. Take about 1½ tablespoon and form into a ball using the palms of your hands. (Rubbing a little oil on your hands will help make it easier to form the meatballs.) Repeat to make about 15 meatballs, setting them on a plate as you work.

4. When the stock comes to a boil, gently drop in the meatballs. Reduce the heat to low and cook until the meatballs float to the top, about 15 minutes. Taste the soup for saltiness and add a little soy sauce if desired.

5. Remove from the heat, garnish with the green onions, and ladle the soup into bowls. Sprinkle with the fried shallots, if using, just before serving.

MALACCAN-PORTUGUESE SPICY HALIBUT SOUP

Malacca is my favorite place for seafood. Besides its popular historical attractions, hospitable people, and cozy hotels, I adore the Kampung Portugis (Portuguese Settlement) district in Ujong Pasir, home to a small community of around 1,000 people descended from early Portuguese settlers. A boulevard of Portuguese seafood stalls can be found on Danjaro Street, where you can pick the freshest catch of the day and have it cooked your way. The cooks here take their seafood soups seriously, with flavors that are sweet, spicy, and fragrant. In this soup, the Portuguese cooks use halibut steak, as the bones provide a good amount of flavor and gelatin to add depth to the soup. A foundation of turmeric, garlic, sweet shallots, and a spike of sambal, plus a good-quality seafood stock, ripe tomatoes, and Great Northern beans all add to the complexity of this very tasty soup. SERVES 4 TO 6

1 pound fresh halibut steak, cut into 4 pieces

2 tablespoons lemon juice

1 teaspoon salt, or to taste

3 shallots, peeled and cut in half

3 cloves garlic, peeled and left whole

1 piece (1 inch) fresh ginger, peeled and chopped

2 tablespoons Sambal Ulek (page 44 or store-bought)

½ teaspoon ground turmeric

½ teaspoon ground white pepper

¼ cup peanut oil

1 large tomato, diced

1 tablespoon tomato paste

1 can (15 ounces) Great Northern beans, rinsed and drained

3 cups seafood stock

2 green onions (white and green parts), chopped

1. Sprinkle the fish with the lemon juice and salt. Set aside to marinate.

2. Prepare a spice paste by combining the shallots, garlic, ginger, sambal, turmeric, and white pepper in a small food processor. Blend into a smooth paste the consistency of applesauce.

3. Heat the oil in a 3-quart saucepan or soup pot over medium heat. Test if the oil is hot by adding a pinch of the spice paste; it should sizzle immediately. When the oil is ready, add all the spice paste and sauté, stirring as needed to prevent burning, until the spices are aromatic and the oil begins to separate, about 5 minutes.

4. Add the tomato and tomato paste and mix to combine with the paste. Cook until the tomato is soft, 10 to 15 minutes.

5. Add the fish, beans, stock, and green onions and give the soup a gentle stir, taking care not to break the fish. Reduce the heat to low, cover the pot, and simmer until the fish is cooked through, about 15 minutes. Serve immediately.

BUTTERNUT SQUASH SOUP
IN LEMONGRASS COCONUT MILK

If you already have the ingredients on hand for this comforting, creamy soup—especially if you use pre-diced squash from the store—it takes less than 30 minutes to cook, the perfect time to warm up some naan in the oven or cook a pot of rice to serve on the side. A delectable and easy-to-prepare supper, perfectly balanced and healthy, this soup just could not be any better on a chilly day. SERVES 4

2 stalks lemongrass, outer layers discarded, finely chopped

3 shallots, sliced

2 fresh red jalapeño chilies, sliced

½ cup coconut cream

3 makrut lime leaves, stemmed

3 cups diced butternut squash

2 cups coconut milk

2½ cups vegetable or chicken broth

1 tablespoon fresh lime juice

Fish sauce to taste

Salt to taste

1. Begin by preparing a paste by combining the lemongrass, shallots, and jalapeños in a blender and blending until smooth with a consistency that resembles applesauce.

2. Heat the paste and coconut cream in a large pot over medium heat until fragrant and the oils from the coconut cream separate onto the surface, about 5 minutes.

3. Add the lime leaves, squash, coconut milk, and broth and bring to a boil. Reduce the heat to medium low and cook until the squash is fork tender, about 20 minutes.

4. Add the lime juice and season with the fish sauce and salt to taste, stirring well to combine the flavors. Taste and adjust the seasoning with more fish sauce if needed.

THE HUMBLE COCONUT TREE AND ITS GIFTS

Towering palm trees line the shores of coasts across Southeast Asia. The green branches of the trees rustle in the ocean breeze, offering a shady retreat from the equatorial heat. One palm tree of great importance to the people is the coconut palm. For people living in the tropical areas of the world, the coconut palm is the tree of life, and has been an important source of food and shelter for thousands of years. The coconut tree is deeply embedded in the culture and culinary landscape across tropical Southeast Asia, including the Pacific Islands, providing nature's greatest gifts—coconut water and coconut oil—a blessing to our health and well-being. Since time immemorial, this tree has supported the livelihood of millions of people.

Nearly one-third of the world's population depends on coconut to some degree for their food and their economy. The fibrous husk is used for making placemats and baskets while the shell is used to make bowls, spoons, and plates. With a life span of 60 to 80 years, the coconut tree provides meat, juice, milk, and oil and can support three generations—a farmer, his children, and grandchildren.

Coconuts can be eaten in different stages of ripeness. When they are young and green, the clear juice inside, naturally fragrant with a subtle hint of flowers, is known as coconut water. On hot days, coconut water will revive you and replenish your energies. When the coconuts mature, the shell becomes brown and the meat inside is white and dense, ready to be grated and sold at local sundry shops and markets, or used to produce coconut oil, milk, or cream. At a shop, you will find a skillful worker cracking the coconut with an axe over a bin to allow the water within to drain. The white flesh is then held against a powered grater that spins and grates the coconut into a wooden box. Fine shreds of a coconut are collected into clear plastic bags and sold. At home, you can toast grated coconut and use it for garnish in salads and meat dishes such as rendang, or as a breading for deep fried foods or for desserts.

Or you can use the oil, cream, or milk, which are all available store-bought. Coconut oil is pressed from mature coconut flesh. Because it is chemically stable and doesn't oxidize easily, coconut oil is less likely to go rancid or oxidize and can be stored longer than other oils. The oil is solid at room temperature but melts quickly when warmed. Virgin coconut oil has a delightful flavor and is pleasant enough to eat straight from the jar.

To extract the cream, hot water is added to grated coconut and allowed to steep for a few minutes. Then, when cool enough to handle, the coconut is pressed by hand to obtain the cream. This precious extract is used to thicken curries, in cakes, as a topping for pancakes and puddings, and to make tropical frozen delights.

When hot water is added to the pulp a second time, the strained liquid is called coconut milk. This thinner liquid is used in soups, curries, desserts, and drinks, and to cut the heat in spicy dishes. (In the countryside, the pulp which no longer can produce milk is fed to the chickens that roam freely in the yard.)

Both coconut cream and coconut milk are sold canned. But the flavor of fresh-pressed coconut milk is just amazing.

THE HEALTH BENEFITS OF COCONUT OIL

Mother Nature's abundant gifts from the coconut palm are most well-known through modern revelations about its oil. Coconut oil is extracted from mature coconut flesh and comes in two forms: virgin and refined. Virgin coconut oil is preferable for cooking. It is abundant in lauric acid, which can strengthen the immune system, and also possesses a higher amount of phenolic antioxidants. Refined coconut oil undergoes heat extraction in its production and is processed to remove the coconut odor, making it more suitable for cosmetic uses.

What makes coconut oil different from most other edible oils? According to my friend Dr. Karen Parker, a naturopathic physician in Seattle and fellow of metabolic and nutritional medicine at the Metabolic Medical Institute (in affiliation with George Washington University), the difference is in the length of the carbon chain that makes up the structure of the fatty acid. Long-chain fatty acids (LCFAs), which come mostly from animal fats, are the most prevalent fat in the Western world. By comparison, medium-chain fatty acids (MCFAs) do not contain cholesterol or trans fats. Coconut oil is composed mostly of MCFAs, so even though it is a saturated fat (which is normally stigmatized as bad for us), it is healthier than fats containing LCFAs because the body metabolizes MCFAs differently.

When we eat food containing LCFAs, they are broken down into individual fatty acids that are then sent into the bloodstream to be distributed throughout the body and packed away into our fat cells. Coconut oil, though, with its MCFAs, is metabolized differently. When consumed, these fatty acids are broken down and used do not collect in artery walls as plaque.

SIMPLE MALAYSIAN CHICKEN SOUP

This is the chicken soup for whatever ails you. Nutritious, light, and tasty, it is a staple in my family and definitely the first item on the menu when anyone is feeling under the weather. The ginger provides an enzyme called *zingibain* that is both an antioxidant and an anti-inflammatory, helping to relieve joint pain and headaches and fight the achiness of a cold.

SERVES 4 TO 6

3 tablespoons peanut oil

1½ yellow onions, roughly chopped

2 Roma tomatoes, quartered

3 tablespoons Ginger, Garlic, and Cilantro Paste (page 53)

1 teaspoon freshly ground black pepper

1 pound bone-in skinless chicken thighs, cut into 2-inch pieces

3 red potatoes, peeled and cut into 1-inch cubes

2 carrots, peeled and cut into 1-inch pieces

6 cups water

2 teaspoons salt, or to taste

2 tablespoons chopped green onions (white and green parts)

1. Heat the oil in a 6-quart stockpot over medium heat. Add the onions, tomatoes, ginger-garlic paste, and pepper and cook until fragrant and the onions and tomatoes are soft, about 7 minutes.

2. Add the chicken, potatoes, and carrots and mix well to combine with the onion mixture. Add the water and salt and bring to a boil. Reduce the heat to low, cover the pot, and cook until the chicken and potatoes are tender, about 1 hour. Taste and add more salt if needed.

3. Remove from the heat, garnish with the green onions, and serve immediately.

MALAYSIAN-STYLE CHICKEN SOUP
WITH POTATOES AND CARROTS SOTO AYAM

This chicken soup is thicker and heartier than the version on the previous page and excellent during the cold winter months. The sweet cinnamon, licorice-tasting star anise, and whole peppercorns are wonderful warming spices that bring depth to the soup. I always use organic chicken quarters, which are basically the thigh and drumstick part attached, for meat that is tender and tasty. Little cafes and bistros throughout Malaysia serve *soto ayam* along with buttered bread or rice vermicelli; it is extremely popular in the evening among hungry customers after work. SERVES 4 TO 6

5 tablespoons peanut oil

1 cinnamon stick

4 whole cloves

2 whole star anise

2 teaspoons whole black peppercorns

2½ tablespoons Ginger, Garlic, and Cilantro Paste (page 53)

1½ yellow onions, sliced

1 beefsteak tomato, quartered

4 pounds bone-in chicken leg quarters

4 red potatoes, peeled and cut in half

2 carrots, peeled and chopped

7½ cups water

2 teaspoons salt, or to taste

½ small cabbage, cored and tough outer leaves discarded

2 tablespoons chopped fresh cilantro, for garnish

1. Heat 3 tablespoons of the oil in a 6-quart stock-pot over medium heat. Add the spices ginger-garlic paste, onions, and tomato. Cook until fragrant and the onions turn golden and tomato soft, about 7 minutes.

2. Heat the remaining 2 tablespoons oil in a skillet over medium heat. Place the chicken skin side down and allow the skin to cook until evenly light golden brown, about 5 minutes. When the chicken is properly browned the meat will not stick to the pan. Turn the meat and cook the underside until light golden brown, about 5 minutes more. The chicken will be still uncooked in the inside.

3. Add the chicken, potatoes, and carrots to the pot and mix well to combine with the spice mixture. Add the water and salt and bring to a boil. Reduce the heat to low and cook until the chicken and potatoes are tender, about 40 minutes.

4. Meanwhile, peel the leaves from the cabbage and cut each in half.

5. Add the cabbage leaves and continue to cook until the leaves are tender, about 10 minutes. The soup will have reduced and thickened. Taste and add more salt if needed. Remove from the heat, garnish with the cilantro, and serve immediately.

SALADS

In the rustic little town of Tapah, a narrow road shoots off towards the hills and, for 50 miles, winds and twists its way to Malaysia's rooftop, the Cameron Highlands. Here, palm trees and banana trees give way to the deep growth of thick ferns that seem to fan the road.

This picturesque plateau's cool mountain weather makes it an excellent location for growing all of Malaysia's herbs, vegetables, tropical fruits, and even fresh flowers and strawberries. Every day, a train of trucks makes its way down these damp, misty roads headed for the markets that are the hubs for redistribution of the produce.

As you stroll through the markets, you will see piles of fresh herbs of every sort: basil, cilantro, and a variety of mints. A wealth of fresh fruits abounds, including pineapples, star fruit, mangosteens, many kinds of mangoes, papayas large and small, and fruits unknown outside the tropics. This bounty is all neatly stacked on wooden tables and sometimes hung by raffia string. Visitors are awed by the display of colors and sizes, and the cascade of aromas. The torch ginger flowers, in particular, are so aromatic that customers crowd around the stalls just to inhale their aroma. The market is the well from which cooks create a typically Malaysian meal.

The beauty of Malaysian cuisine is that we use herbs with as much confidence as we use lettuce. Slicing an aromatic green may make you feel as if you've wandered into a sprawling, secret garden; the act of preparing a bouquet of basil, mint, limes, lemongrass, cilantro, and makrut lime leaves is part of the culinary adventure even before you taste the dish. The herbs used in Malaysian salads are not only aromatic, but also laden with health-giving properties. Today, dozens of studies in the *Journal of Natural Medicine* confirm that simply including whole foods like fruits and vegetables in one's diet cannot alone fight against diseases; instead, a combined diet rich in whole foods and herbs is the key to preventing diseases. Spices, rhizomes, and aromatics herbs all make up the awesome flavors of the Malaysian salad bowl.

Many of the recipes presented in the chapter will show you how to expertly blend sweet mangoes, pineapple, and coconut with savory shrimp paste and fish sauce, adding spicy flavors of sambals and sour notes of lime or tamarind. Fresh mint, cilantro, basil, and other herbs will supply the fresh finale to your salads.

The most beloved salad in Malaysia is *rojak* (page 111), sold by street vendors and made from a mixture of pineapple, mangoes, star fruit, and pomelo that is drizzled with a dark palm sugar–tamarind sauce and topped with ground roasted peanuts. Sometimes vegetables like water spinach (also called morning glory leaves) and cucumber, or seafood, are added to the salad to give it a unique texture and an extraordinary blend.

Malaysians do not think of salads as something that comes before a meal but rather served with other dishes on the table, making them part of the whole meal. But of course many people in the U.S. prefer to enjoy their salad before the main course or even on its own as a light meal.

One of the secrets to the complexity and depth of a delicious Malaysian salad is the balance of sweet, sour, salty, and hot, most notably in the dressing. The basic Malaysian dressing is a mixture of lime juice for tartness, fish sauce for saltiness, and palm sugar for sweetness and to balance flavor. Savory or umami ingredients like

soy sauce, tamarind, ginger, shallots, garlic, hot peppers, or sambals can be used in the dressing to bring a salad together. Malaysians rarely use oil-based vinaigrettes. However, it would be easy to add your favorite oils (maybe olive oil, avocado oil, or coconut oil): Just drizzle it at the very end after compiling your salad. You should add the oil at the end so that the lime dressing can penetrate the vegetables for maximum flavor; adding the oil too early would coat the vegetables, thereby preventing the citrus from breaking through.

Salad dressings are best and most flavorful when freshly made. Always make the dressing in a separate bowl, whisk well so that all the ingredients are well blended, and then taste and adjust the seasonings. For instance, if your dressing is too salty, balance it with palm sugar;

do not add more lime or lemon juice as it will only increase the saltiness. If it is too spicy, tone it down with palm sugar. If too tart, add more fish sauce. If you added too much palm sugar, balance the dressing with more lime juice. I call for palm sugar because it is light, well rounded, and easily blended with the other ingredients. But if you cannot find palm sugar, light brown sugar can be substituted.

Once you pin down a few dressings and know how to balance the sweet, sour, salty, and hot, the world of fruits and salad greens is in your hands to create any flavorful Malaysian salad. You can use any variety of greens like romaine, arugula, green leaf lettuce, and baby spinach, and vegetables like beets, English cucumbers, and jicama—whatever is in season at your local supermarket.

SWEET MANGO AND CASHEW SALAD
WITH CHILI-LIME DRESSING

I have served this sweet mango salad to thousands of people around the country, from ordinary folks to foodies, and it is always a hit. The key to success is to use ripe, golden mangoes. I opt for golden Philippine mangoes rather than the red Mexican variety because they are less fibrous and extremely juicy. Usually sold in cases of twelve or six, they are in season during the summer months only. You will find them at most ethnic groceries and some select supermarkets. With fried shallots and cashews, the mango salad is an explosion of sweet, sour, and savory flavors on your palate all at once. SERVES 4

¼ cup fresh lime juice

3½ teaspoons liquid palm sugar (see pages 315–316) or honey

1 fresh bird's-eye chili, finely chopped

1 teaspoon salt or 2 teaspoons fish sauce

3 ripe mangoes, peeled and cut into ½-inch dice

¼ cup finely chopped fresh cilantro leaves

¼ cup roasted unsalted cashews

2 tablespoons Fried Shallots (page 56)

1. Prepare the dressing by combining the lime juice, palm sugar, chili, and salt or fish sauce in a small bowl, stirring well to blend the flavors.

2. Combine the mango and cilantro in a large bowl. Pour in the dressing and toss to mix well. Toss in the cashews and fried shallots, mix well, and serve.

CUCUMBER-YOGURT RAITA

This common raita, made with cucumber, beautifully complements dishes such as Tandoori Broiled Salmon (page 186), Salmon in Creamy Tikka Masala (page 192), and Grilled Lamb Chops with Rosemary-Garlic Pesto (page 275). The yogurt should be thoroughly whisked until creamy before mixing in the other ingredients. SERVES 4

- 2 cups plain yogurt, preferably Indian or Greek style
- 1 teaspoon ground cumin
- ¼ teaspoon cayenne pepper
- 1 teaspoon salt, or to taste
- ½ teaspoon freshly ground black pepper
- 1 English cucumber, peeled, seeded, and grated
- ½ cup chopped fresh cilantro leaves

Whisk the yogurt in a bowl until creamy. Add the cumin, cayenne, salt, black pepper, and cucumber and mix well. Cover and refrigerate until ready to serve, about 30 minutes or up to a maximum of 1 hour. After an hour the consistency will be watery. Sprinkle with the cilantro just before serving.

CARROT, APPLE, TOMATO, AND RAISIN RAITA

This is a refreshing salad that I make at home all summer as a wonderful way to cool the palate when eating spicy dishes. My favorite moment is when the plump raisins hidden within the salad burst in my mouth. SERVES 4

- 2 cups plain yogurt, preferably Indian or Greek style
- 1 teaspoon honey, or to taste
- 1 teaspoon salt, or to taste
- ¼ teaspoon freshly ground black pepper
- 2 small carrots, peeled and grated
- 1 Roma tomato, seeded and diced
- 1 green apple, cored and diced
- ¼ cup raisins
- 1 fresh green jalapeño chili, seeded and chopped
- ¼ cup chopped fresh mint leaves
- 1 tablespoon fresh lime juice

1. In a medium bowl, combine the yogurt, honey, salt, and pepper and whisk until well combined and creamy.

2. Add the carrots, tomato, apple, raisins, jalapeño, and mint; mix well. Taste and add more salt or honey if needed. Stir in the lime juice. Serve immediately; or refrigerate for about 30 minutes or up to a maximum of 1 hour and serve chilled; after an hour the consistency will be watery.

ASPARAGUS AND COCONUT SALAD WITH CITRUS DRESSING

The wild fern shoots, or *pucuk paku*, that grow along streams, in paddy fields, and in backyard gardens in Malaysia are popular in a variety of salads, often topped with sambal. Asparagus comes close to the taste of these dark green, crunchy shoots. Boiling the asparagus not only helps retain the vitamins, color, and texture, but most importantly allows the tangy citrus dressing to be absorbed at first contact. Peeling the stems instead of trimming the tough ends means you do not waste the lower stalk. Other vegetables such as artichoke hearts and raw endives work equally well with this recipe. SERVES 6

Juice of 2 limes

1 tablespoon fish sauce

1½ teaspoons liquid palm sugar (see pages 315–316) or 2 tablespoons brown sugar

½ teaspoon salt

1 small white onion, thinly sliced

1 fresh red jalapeño chili, thinly sliced

1 pound asparagus

½ pound medium shrimp, peeled and deveined

1 cup fresh cilantro leaves, coarsely chopped

2 tablespoons grated unsweetened coconut

1 teaspoon Sambal Belachan (page 43) or Sambal Ulek (page 44 or store-bought)

1. To prepare the dressing, combine the lime juice, fish sauce, sugar, salt, onion, and chili in a small bowl. Whisk until the sugar dissolves. Allow the dressing to sit for about 5 minutes for the flavors to infuse.

2. Meanwhile, peel the outer layer of the asparagus using a potato peeler. Cut the stalks in half then wash under cold running water.

3. In a pot large enough to hold the asparagus horizontally, bring salted water to a boil. Drop the asparagus into the boiling water and cook, uncovered, until the shoots are tender when cut with a knife, about 5 minutes. Lift the asparagus out of the pot, drain, and transfer to a serving bowl.

4. Add the shrimp to the boiling water and cook until pink-orange, about 4 minutes. Remove with a slotted spoon and add to the bowl with the asparagus.

5. Immediately pour the dressing over the asparagus and shrimp, sprinkle with the cilantro and coconut, and top with a dollop of sambal. Serve warm.

LONG GREEN BEANS AND ROMAINE SALAD WITH CALAMANSI DRESSING

Calamansi is a tiny lime that is native to Southeast Asia. In Malaysia, they grow like lemons on the tree and we pluck them fresh for salad dressings. They have a special tangerine and lemon-like flavor combination without the tartness of regular limes. Fresh calamansi limes are not widely available in the United States, although they are becoming more and more popular and I do hear about people finding them at farmers' markets in California and other citrus-growing states. Another option would be to grow your own tree if you happen to reside in a warm climate. Pure frozen calamansi juice is an acceptable substitute; it comes in small packets found in the freezer section of Asian supermarkets. Alternatively, you could mix the juice of one orange and one lemon, which freezes well and can be added to any dressing. As for the beans, if you cannot find Asian long beans, substitute common string beans. SERVES 4

2 tablespoons calamansi lime juice or a mix of orange and lemon juice

2½ tablespoons kicap manis (sweet soy sauce; see page 16)

1 tablespoon Sambal Belachan (page 43)

Salt

12 ounces yardlong beans or string beans

1 bunch romaine lettuce, torn into small pieces

2 ripe tomatoes, quartered

Leaves from 2 sprigs Thai basil

1. Make the dressing by combining the lime juice, kicap manis, sambal, and ½ teaspoon salt in a small bowl.

2. Meanwhile, bring a pot of salted water to a boil. Drop in the beans and cook, uncovered, until the tough yardlong beans become tender but slightly crunchy, about 10 minutes (7 minutes for string beans). Drain as soon as they are done.

3. To serve, combine the beans, lettuce, tomatoes, and basil in a large salad bowl. Pour in the dressing and toss to mix well. Serve immediately.

TEMPEH AND ARUGULA
WITH SWEET LIME VINAIGRETTE

In many Western restaurants, it is common to see arugula served with mozzarella or burrata cheese, but I thought it would be wonderful to enjoy arugula's earthiness with mellow, nutty-tasting tempeh instead. In this salad, the crispy tempeh acts as a sponge, absorbing the sweet lime vinaigrette. Tempeh, a vegan cake of fermented soy beans, is a popular protein throughout Southeast Asia, eaten in salad or usually with rice as part of a hot summer meal. It is hearty and mild with an excellent nutrient profile: high in fiber and protein and low in fat with no cholesterol. As a fermented food, it is totally digestible, effectively delivering all the essential nutrients; and since it is browned in coconut oil, it is even healthier: Studies have shown that eating coconut oil increases calorie burning and thus can promote weight loss. SERVES 4

1 package (8 ounces) organic tempeh

4 cloves garlic, pressed

½ teaspoon salt

2 tablespoons rice vinegar

1 tablespoon lime juice

1 teaspoons liquid palm sugar (see pages 315–316)

¼ cup coconut oil

2 cups arugula, washed and dried

1 tablespoon Sambal Ulek (page 44 or store-bought)

1. Cut the tempeh into 2- by 1-inch strips. Put them in a bowl with the garlic and salt and mix gently, as the tempeh is very delicate and can break easily with rough handling. Let the tempeh marinate while you prepare the vinaigrette.

2. Stir together the vinegar, lime juice, and palm sugar in a small bowl. Set aside for the flavors to infuse.

3. Heat the oil in a medium skillet over medium heat. Add the marinated tempeh and cook each side until golden brown, about 10 minutes per side. Remove with a slotted spoon and set on paper towels to drain.

4. To finish the salad, pour half the vinaigrette over the arugula in a large bowl and toss well. Transfer the arugula to a serving plate, then arrange the tempeh strips on the top. Pour the remaining vinaigrette over the tempeh. Place a spoonful of the sambal in the center of the salad or scatter it over the tempeh. Serve immediately.

CAMPARI TOMATO AND BASIL SALAD WITH SOY SAMBAL VINAIGRETTE

Juicy tomatoes, beautifully mounted in bushel baskets at roadside farm stands, are the objects of my affection. I particularly love the sweetness of the little plump Campari tomatoes in summer. I thought up this recipe after tasting countless basil and tomato salads made with Italian balsamic vinaigrette. Replacing those flavorings with Thai basil, soy sauce, sambal ulek, and a splash of fresh lime juice gives the salad all the flavors of the tropics in one bowl. I even enjoy drinking the dressing once the tomatoes are eaten! SERVES 2

2 tablespoons soy sauce

1 tablespoon fresh lime juice

1 teaspoon sesame oil

1 tablespoon Sambal Ulek (page 44 or store-bought)

1 teaspoons liquid palm sugar (see pages 315–316) or honey

½ teaspoon salt, or to taste

8 ripe Campari tomatoes or 5 Roma tomatoes, cut into quarters

½ cup Thai basil leaves, roughly chopped or left whole

2 tablespoons Fried Garlic in Oil (page 56)

1. Prepare the dressing by combining the soy sauce, lime juice, sesame oil, sambal, palm sugar, and salt in a small bowl, stirring well to blend in the flavors.

2. Combine the tomatoes and basil in a bowl. Pour in the dressing and toss to mix well. Top with the fried garlic and serve at room temperature.

SPICY AHI TUNA AND HERB SALAD

This delicious salad is from Kelantan, a remote and unspoiled state on the northeast coast of Malaysia, only a few kilometers from the border with Thailand, and visitors will notice that much of its food tastes familiar, rather like Thai food. Kelantan has one of the best-known vegetable and herb markets in Malaysia. In the Kelantanese kitchen, aromatic herbs are used frequently in salads and paired with seafood. I use ahi tuna here since it is healthy and delicate tasting. The salad's familiar Southeast Asian flavor footprint includes the fiery bite of chilies, the bright spark of lime juice, the deep muskiness of fish sauce, and the aromatic top notes of lime leaves, mint, and cilantro. SERVES 4

1 pound ahi tuna steak (about 1 inch thick)

½ teaspoon salt

¼ teaspoon ground black pepper

¼ teaspoon turmeric

4½ tablespoons fresh lime juice

3 tablespoons fish sauce

3 teaspoons liquid palm sugar (see pages 315–316)

1 green jalapeño chili, stem removed, seeded, and chopped

2 small shallots, thinly sliced

4 makrut lime leaves, stems removed, finely sliced

1-inch piece fresh ginger, peeled and julienned

¼ cup peanut oil

1 cup fresh mint leaves (from 1 bunch), chopped

1 cup fresh cilantro leaves (from 1 bunch), chopped

1 cup Thai basil leaves (from 1 bunch), chopped

1 bunch green leaf lettuce, torn into bite-size pieces

1. Coat the tuna on both sides evenly with the salt, pepper, and turmeric. Set aside to marinate.

2. In a small bowl, combine the fish sauce, lime juice, palm sugar, jalapeño, shallots, makrut lime leaves, and ginger and whisk until the sugar is dissolved. Set aside for the flavors to come together.

3. Heat the oil in a small skillet over medium heat. Add the tuna and cook for about 1 minute on each side for medium-rare. Remove the tuna from the pan and set aside.

4. Place the mint, cilantro, basil, and lettuce in a bowl. Pour in half of the dressing and toss well.

5. Slice the tuna into ½-inch-thick slices and arrange on top of the salad. Pour the remaining dressing over the tuna and serve immediately.

MALAYSIAN POTATO SALAD

In Malaysia, during family potluck gatherings, someone always brings a spicy potato salad made with fresh ground spices. I have tried to keep the authenticity of our family recipe but have altered it by using yogurt instead of mayonnaise. I always keep a bottle of Sriracha next to my stove, since a small dash of this zesty hot sauce is everyone's favorite. Although Sriracha can be hot, here it is mellowed by the yogurt and sour cream. I normally serve the salad warm, but depending on your preference you can serve it chilled. Either way, always dress the potatoes while still warm, as this allows the flavors to be more easily absorbed.

SERVES 4

1½ pounds Yukon gold potatoes, washed and left unpeeled

1 cup plain Greek yogurt

½ cup light sour cream

2 tablespoons extra-virgin olive oil

1½ to 2 tablespoons Sriracha sauce

2 shallots, minced

1 teaspoon freshly ground black pepper

½ teaspoon ground turmeric

Pinch of salt, or to taste

Pinch of sugar

2 hard-boiled eggs, quartered

1. Place the potatoes in a large saucepan, add cold water to cover by about 2 inches, and bring to a boil. Reduce the heat to medium and cook until the potatoes are tender when pierced with a fork, about 20 minutes. Drain.

2. For the dressing, in a small bowl combine the yogurt, sour cream, oil, Sriracha, shallots, pepper, turmeric, salt, and sugar and whisk until well combined.

3. Cut the potatoes into quarters while still hot. Transfer to a large bowl, add the eggs, then pour on the dressing and toss well to combine. It is alright if the eggs crumble as it makes for a tastier salad. Let sit for 5 minutes to calm the Sriracha. Taste and add more salt if needed. Serve warm or cold.

SWEET AND TANGY PINEAPPLE SALAD

There are many types of salads that use pineapples in Malaysia. Resembling Mexican pico de gallo, they are called *achar,* a Hindi word that tells us of its Indian origins. However, these salads have become truly Malaysian in their mix of ingredients, especially the use of sambal tumis. As we know from the sambal chapter (page 39), sambal tumis is one of the foundation cooking pastes, widely used in many kinds of dishes.

This particular achar commonly adorns the tables of Baba and Nyonya communities in Malaysia. It is typically made of small chunks of cucumber and pineapple plus fresh basil leaves, all marinated in a sweet and sour dressing of lime juice, fish sauce, and palm sugar. The use of sambal tumis makes the salad unique, but also characteristic of Baba-Nyonya cooking. You could replace the pineapple with tart green mangoes. And, if you are in a hurry, sambal ulek can be used in place of sambal tumis. The salad is most typically paired with steamed rice and fried fish. SERVES 4

1 fresh bird's-eye chili, finely chopped

¼ cup fresh lime juice

3½ teaspoons liquid palm sugar (see pages 315–316) or honey

1 teaspoon salt or 2 teaspoons fish sauce

2 cups diced fresh pineapple

1 large English cucumber, diced to yield 2 cups

½ cup finely chopped fresh basil leaves, plus 5 whole leaves for garnish

4 to 5 tablespoons Pineapple Sambal Tumis (page 47) or Sambal Ulek (page 44 or store-bought)

3 tablespoons ground peanuts

1. Prepare the dressing by combining the chili, lime juice, palm sugar, and salt in a small bowl, stirring well to blend the flavors.

2. Combine the pineapple, cucumber, chopped basil, and pineapple sambal tumis in a large bowl. Pour on the dressing and toss to mix the salad ingredients well. Serve topped with the peanuts and garnished with basil leaves.

PINEAPPLE, MANGO, AND CUCUMBER SALAD WITH TAMARIND SAUCE

ROJAK

There is a fifth-generation vendor outside the Rocky coffee shop in Bangsar, a neighborhood in the suburbs of Kuala Lumpur, who makes the best version of *rojak*. He cuts sweet tropical pineapples, tart green mangoes, and cucumbers into small, uneven chunks and tosses them with a tangy sauce made of palm sugar, tamarind, sambal ulek, and *hea koh*—a glistening black molasses-like shrimp paste—then tops it all with coarsely ground peanuts. The rigorously authentic version of his secret recipe requires hea koh, which is available in most Asian grocery stores or online. You can still make the salad if you cannot find hea koh, but without it the rojak will not taste quite the same. SERVES 4

¼ cup Tamarind Water (page 54)

3 tablespoons liquid palm sugar (see pages 315–316)

2 tablespoons kicap manis (sweet soy sauce; see page 16), or to taste

1 to 2 teaspoons Sambal Ulek (page 44 or store-bought)

1 tablespoon hea koh (sweet black shrimp paste), optional

2 cups cubed fresh pineapple

1 small cucumber, chopped

1 unripe green mango, peeled and sliced

½ small jicama, peeled and sliced into wedges

½ cup ground peanuts

1. To make the dressing, combine the tamarind water, palm sugar, kicap manis, sambal, and hea koh (if using) in a small saucepan over medium heat. Bring just to a boil. Immediately remove from the heat and set aside to cool.

2. Combine the pineapple, cucumber, mango, and jicama in a serving bowl. Add the dressing and peanuts and toss to coat. Serve immediately.

GREEN MANGO IN LEMON-BASIL DRESSING

I first tasted this salad at an outdoor eatery in the rustic town of Terengganu, in northeastern Malaysia, which is considered the cradle of Malay culture thanks to its traditional way of life. Lemon basil comes into season especially in the fall, and the leaves add a lemony fragrance and herbal flavor to the salad. You will see this beautiful herb in many Southeast Asian markets, but if you cannot find it, substitute mint, rather than the more common Italian basil. You can also increase the amount of sambal ulek in the dressing to 2 tablespoons for more spiciness. I never tire of this salad, especially when served with sticky rice. Each bite is sweet, hot, salty, soft, and crunchy, just like Terengganu itself. SERVES 4

5 tablespoons Tamarind Water (page 54)

2 tablespoons fish sauce

2 tablespoons liquid palm sugar (see pages 315–316) or 2½ tablespoons superfine sugar

1 tablespoon Sambal Ulek (page 44 or store bought)

½ cup lemon basil leaves, chopped

1 unripe green mango, peeled

1 very small jicama, peeled

2 tablespoons peanut oil

2 small shallots, thinly sliced

3 tablespoons roasted unsalted cashews

1. Prepare the salad dressing by combining the tamarind water, fish sauce, palm sugar, sambal, and lemon basil in a small bowl, stirring to blend the flavors. Set aside to allow the sambal and lemon basil to infuse their flavors into the dressing. You should end up with balanced sweet, sour, salty, and spicy flavors with an aromatic hint of lemon.

2. Thinly slice or shred the mango and place in a large salad bowl. Next, cut the jicama in half, then thinly slice and add to the bowl. Add the dressing, toss well, and set aside while you fry the shallots.

3. Heat the oil in a small skillet over medium heat. When the oil is hot, add the shallots and gently fry until golden brown, about 5 minutes. With a slotted spoon, immediately transfer the shallots to the salad, along with 1 teaspoon of the shallot oil from the pan. Add the cashews to the salad and toss well. Serve at room temperature.

CHICKPEA SALAD WITH CUMIN-LEMON DRESSING

This is an old family recipe, usually served to accompany roasted chicken or lamb chops. It's pretty to look at and its taste is warm and comforting. Once cooked, dried chickpeas are amazingly nutty, bright, and fragrant compared to the humdrum flavor of canned ones. The recipe also asks for *amchoor*, a powder made from dried green mangoes; it lifts the lemon and brings life to all the other spices in the dressing. If you do not have amchoor, substitute 1 tablespoon Tamarind Water (page 54), or ½ cup pomegranate seeds. SERVES 4

1 cup dried chickpeas, soaked overnight

3 cups water

1 teaspoon cumin seeds

3½ tablespoons fresh lemon juice

2 tablespoons extra-virgin olive oil

2 teaspoons brown or white sugar, or to taste

1 teaspoon amchoor powder (optional)

½ teaspoon ground paprika

1 teaspoon salt, or to taste

4 green onions, thinly sliced (white and green parts)

½ cup tightly packed fresh cilantro leaves, chopped

1 red bell pepper, diced

1 yellow bell pepper, diced

1 fresh green jalapeño chili, seeded and diced

1. Place the chickpeas in a medium saucepan, add the water, and bring to a boil. Cook until the chickpeas are tender, about 15 minutes. While the chickpeas are cooking, prepare the rest of the ingredients for the salad.

2. Start with the dressing. Heat a small skillet over medium heat. Add the cumin seeds and toast until the seeds are fragrant and appear one shade darker, 1 to 2 minutes. Remove the seeds from the pan and grind to a smooth powder using a mortar and pestle. (You could also use a spice grinder, but for such a small quantity a mortar and pestle is easier.) Place the cumin powder in a bowl and add the lemon juice, oil, sugar, amchoor powder, paprika, and salt and whisk until the sugar is completely dissolved. Taste; if the dressing tastes too tart, add a little sugar to cut the tartness.

3. Add the green onions to a large salad bowl. Next add the cilantro, bell peppers, and jalapeño. Drain the cooked chickpeas and, while still warm, add to the salad. Pour on the dressing and toss well to combine. Serve at room temperature.

RICE NOODLE SALAD WITH SHRIMP AND COCONUT
KERABU BEEHOON

Kerabu beehoon is typically served for lunch at Baba and Nyonya restaurants in the states of Penang and Malacca. It reminds me of the rice vermicelli bowls at Vietnamese restaurants. The dressing of calamansi lime juice, sambal, and palm sugar is absorbed into the vermicelli and forms a delightful balance of sweet, sour, salty, and spicy on your palate. You can use a blend of orange and lemon juice in place of the calamansi juice, if you cannot find it. You could also make the salad with grilled seafood, chicken, or tofu in place of the shrimp.

SERVES 4

DRESSING

- ½ cup plus 2 tablespoons calamansi lime juice
- 4 tablespoons liquid palm sugar
- 2 tablespoons Sambal Ulek (page 44 or store-bought)
- 2 garlic cloves, minced
- 1 teaspoon toasted shrimp paste (see page 116)
- ½ teaspoon salt

SALAD

- ½ pound medium shrimp, peeled and deveined
- 6 ounces dried rice vermicelli
- 8 green onions, thinly sliced (white and green parts)
- 1 cup fresh mint leaves, roughly chopped
- 1 fresh red chili, minced
- 1 small red onion, thinly sliced
- 5 tablespoons toasted grated coconut

1. To prepare the dressing: Combine the calamansi lime juice, palm sugar, sambal, garlic, shrimp paste, and salt in a small bowl and mix well. Set aside.

2. For the salad: Bring 8 cups of water to a boil in a large pot. Add the shrimp and boil until pinkish orange in color, about 2 minutes. Remove with a slotted spoon and set aside.

3. Bring the water back to a boil. Add the vermicelli and boil for about 3 minutes, stirring with a slotted spoon to prevent the noodles from sticking. Drain the noodles and immediately rinse under running water to remove excess starch. Drain the noodles well.

4. Combine the noodles, shrimp, green onions, mint, chili, onion, coconut, and the dressing in a medium bowl and toss well. Serve warm or at room temperature.

SHRIMP PASTE

Throughout the islands and coasts of Southeast Asia, the old tradition of fermenting the bounty of the seas has allowed people to survive year-round on their seasonal catches. Making shrimp paste is one such example, a tradition that is especially robust and still mostly done by fishing families in villages along the coast of the Straits of Malacca and the islands of Pangkor and Penang. There, fishermen are often seen wading in deep water in search of *geragau*, tiny shrimp that are caught at high tide. The larger shrimp or little fishes are thrown back, and the *geragau* that remain are destined to become shrimp paste, a distinctive smoky and salty ingredient that offers complexity and depth to any dish.

They are first rinsed in sea water and placed on stretched mats or large wooden trays to dry under the tropical sun. Once dried, the tiny shrimps are mixed with salt and sun dried again for eight hours. They are then crushed into a paste and fermented in large wooden trays for two weeks. The crushing and drying is repeated from time to time until the shrimp is disintegrated and becomes a dense, dark reddish-brown paste. Finally, the paste is pressed into round or rectangular shapes and left under the sun to dry before it is packed. The shrimp paste, or *belachan* (pronounced buh-LAH-chan and sometimes spelled *blachen* or *blachan*) is package with the family's brand and sold to market vendors for resale to consumers, or to middlemen and distributors.

The complex, savory taste that shrimp paste brings is unparalleled in the world of global cuisine. Don't let the pungent smell deter you, as the smell dissipates during cooking. The flavor of shrimp paste is a little bit of many things: salty, slightly bitter, roasted, and fermented. When it is present in a curry, stir-fry, or condiment, the shrimp paste will act as a hidden ingredient; you taste only a unique complexity and depth unlike anything else you've ever experienced, a *wow* factor that leaves the palate yearning for more. It especially pairs well with chilies.

In Asian groceries, it is easy to find different styles of shrimp paste, each one from a different country; you can also buy it online. There are Malaysian (*belachan*), Indonesian (*trassi*), Thai (*kapi*), Vietnamese (*mam ruoc*), and Filipino (*bagoong*) varieties. Some of them may be dyed a deep pink color, but the reddish-dark brown blocks in white wrappers from Malaysia work best and are most authentic for the recipes in this book. Most of the shrimp paste in the market is raw, so once purchased it's best to store the paste in an airtight bag in the refrigerator.

To toast shrimp paste: If you are going to fry the shrimp paste with other spices or ingredients, then you do not need to cook it first. However, if you are adding it to raw ingredients that will not be cooked, it will be need to be toasted before you use it. The best way to toast shrimp paste is to wrap it in several sheets

of aluminum foil, then bake it in a 350°F oven for about 30 minutes. To test if the paste is fully toasted, press the foil using firm pressure with large wooden spoon. If the paste is completely toasted, the foil will collapse approximately in half as the paste inside crumbles. Allow it to cool before opening the foil. Alternatively, you can cook a larger batch by frying it in hot oil until flaky. Store the cooled toasted belachan in an airtight glass gar in the pantry. Given the high salt content, shrimp paste, whether raw or toasted, has a long shelf life.

There is no substitute for shrimp paste and it should not be confused with fish sauce or anchovy paste, which are very different in characteristics.

VEGETABLES

Anyone, adult or child, who has ever eaten in a Malaysian home will tell you how flavorful, fresh, and exciting vegetables are. "Those delicious morsels of sweet potato in coconut milk; I have never tasted a dish so delicate, well-balanced, and aromatic." "I could eat this for breakfast, lunch, and dinner." And so on. Malaysian home-style vegetables provide diners with and unforgettable experience.

Fortunately, you are able to experience these exquisite flavors in your own home with any vegetables in season using my cooking techniques.

Begin by choosing the freshest vegetables using your eyes, nose, and hands. At the market, choose Asian greens such as baby bok choy with firm stems and light green leaves that are crisp and bunched together in a tight head. Chinese broccoli (*gai lan*) should have large green flat leaves with thick stalks, and tiny yellow flower buds. Cabbage must be firm, have compact heads, and feel heavy. The smaller the cabbage, the sweeter the taste. Asian eggplants are best when they are long and dark purple in color. The skin must be smooth and shiny and when gently pressed the surface should slightly bounce back, which indicates ripeness. Asian long beans, sometimes called yardlong beans, are freshest when they are bright green and have no blemishes. Unlike the common short green beans which are firm, choose long beans that are flexible.

One of the great secrets to creating exciting vegetable dishes quickly is to peel, cut, chop, julienne, blanch, and do all the necessary prep work well ahead of time. Chilies can be chopped and garlic minced using a food processor. Shallots can be sliced, ginger julienned, and green onions chopped, then all these ready-to-use ingredients can be stored in airtight containers and neatly tucked in the refrigerator.

The recipes in this chapter are inspired by Indian, Chinese, and Malay cuisines. Each culinary culture has its own slant and technique. For instance, Okra with Tomato and Onion Masala (page 122), Cabbage Sautéed with Eggs, Turmeric, and Curry Leaves (page 128), Mushroom Masala (page 127), and Malaysian Korma Vegetables (page 144) are all prepared in a typical Indian way—flavored with spice seeds fried in hot oil with curry leaves, onions, and garlic. When the spice seeds come in contact with the hot oil, they come alive and release their flavors, which then unite with the juices of the vegetables to make the dish hearty and exquisite. When cooking with spice seeds, you may want to sprinkle a little water over the vegetables if you find them to be too dry, as this prevents the spices from burning.

Traditional Malay homes, on the other hand, prefer a simmer technique and longer cooking times. Malay cooking calls for a vibrant multi-layered seasoning approach, for instance, by blending shrimp paste, lemongrass, chilies, garlic, and shallots to make a fresh sambal or spice paste. Malaccan-Style Eggplant Sambal (page 125), Stir-Fried Asparagus with Sambal Belachan (page 137), Fried Tofu and Tomatoes in Sweet Soy Sambal (page 139), and Potato Sambal Casserole (page 142) are examples of such cooking methods. When a cook is looking for a sauce-based dish, coconut milk is added. You might also include

some cream or butter if you'd like to mellow down the chilies. The dish is then allowed to simmer in the enriched sauce and enjoyed with steamed jasmine rice. Sweet Potatoes and Baby Spinach Simmered in Coconut Milk (page 141) and Young Bamboo Shoots in Turmeric-Coconut Curry (page 130) are popular Malay-style provincial dishes.

Chinese home-style cooking involves a hot wok over a high flame, with the ingredients stir-fried very quickly. Cooking most vegetables in this group usually begins by stir-frying garlic in hot oil and then adding the vegetables. You would then choose from a combination of cooking sauces like soy sauce, oyster sauce, kicap manis, or fermented soy bean paste plus pepper to further accentuate the flavor. Sesame oil is used only to seal in the flavor and complete the dish. Chinese-style dishes in this chapter include Stir-Fried Asian Greens with Garlic and Oyster Sauce (page 131), Stir-Fried Bean Sprouts with Anchovies and Cilantro (page 145), and Broccoli, Cauliflower, and Shiitake Combination (page 138). The stir-fry method retains much of the vegetables' vitamins and minerals while delivering a lighter tasting dish that is eaten with steamed rice and some meat or seafood dishes.

The recipes in this chapter are slightly modified for a fresher, lighter taste, tailored to today's health-conscious cooks while keeping the traditional flavors alive. Take a little time to choose vegetables that are fresh and in season. With the endless selection of fresh vegetables available, these recipes will help you to create exciting, healthy, and fresh tropical tasting dishes.

OKRA WITH TOMATO AND ONION MASALA

With its bright colors and mellow flavors, this Indian specialty, called "bhindi masala," where okra is slowly cooked in a smooth tomato mixture, is sort of like an okra primavera. It goes well with pinto or black beans, rice pilaf, pasta, or, if you are not vegetarian, chicken or egg dishes. In all my years as a teaching chef, I have never been able to understand why some people cannot appreciate the beautiful green vegetable that is okra. But I suspect it is because they have not learned how to cook it correctly, and think of it as slimy. The proper technique is to always wash and dry okra thoroughly before cutting it, and then during cooking, to push the okra back and forth instead of stirring in circles. SERVES 4

3 tablespoons virgin coconut oil

1 teaspoon cumin seeds

4 garlic cloves, sliced

½ small red onion, diced

2 to 3 sprigs curry leaves

1 teaspoon turmeric

½ to 1 teaspoon chili powder or cayenne

½ teaspoon salt, or to taste

2 beefsteak tomatoes, chopped

8 ounces fresh okra, washed and halved

1. Heat the oil in a medium sauté pan or skillet over medium heat. Once the oil is hot, add the cumin seeds and let sizzle, stirring gently with a spatula or wooden spoon, until they turn one shade darker and become fragrant, about 40 seconds.

2. Add the garlic, onion, and curry leaves and mix well to incorporate into the oil. Stir occasionally to prevent the spices from burning and cook until the onions are light brown, about 5 minutes.

3. Add the turmeric, chili powder, salt, and tomatoes and mix well to combine with the onions in the pan. Allow the tomatoes to cook and break down naturally, about 15 minutes, stirring only occasionally.

4. Add the okra and gently fold them into the tomatoes. Cover the pan and continue cooking, occasionally gently moving the okra back and forth with the spatula or wooden spoon (do not stir in circular motion, or the okra will become slimy), until the okra is tender, about 10 minutes. Taste; add more salt if needed. Serve hot.

MALACCAN-STYLE EGGPLANT SAMBAL

This dish is my version of *Nyonya sambal terung,* the famous eggplant dish served at little Baba and Nyonya home-style cafes in Malacca. A true Nyonya would spend hours and hours pounding her *rempah* (spices) with a *batu lesong* (mortar and pestle), using the *agak agak* approach—meaning no exact measurements, but cooking purely on taste and understanding of the ingredient. But a blender works fine for me. Like all sambal dishes, my simple version begins with an aromatic spice paste; kicap manis adds sweetness and ground cumin prolonged flavor. Long, thin Asian eggplants, which have a sweet and mellow flavor without bitterness, are better than the large oval varieties. Be sure to cook the spice paste completely, until the oils separate from the paste, before adding the eggplant, or the chili will taste raw. The key to maintaining the texture is to not stir the eggplant while it slowly simmers in the sambal sauce, otherwise the dish will end up mushy. This is an excellent side dish that goes well over brown or white rice, with Potato Sambal Casserole (page 142), lamb chops, or baked chicken, or even as a topping for flatbread. SERVES 4

1 piece (2 inches) fresh ginger, peeled and chopped

3 shallots, chopped

4 cloves garlic, peeled and left whole

3 Roma tomatoes, cut in half

5 fresh red jalapeño chilies, cut in half, or 1½ tablespoons Sambal Ulek (page 44 or store-bought)

1 teaspoon ground cumin

¼ cup water

¼ cup peanut oil or canola oil

6 tablespoons kicap manis (sweet soy sauce; see page 16)

4 Asian eggplants (1 pound), sliced in half and then cut into 3-inch pieces

Salt to taste (optional)

1. Make the spice paste by blending the ginger, shallots, garlic, tomatoes, chilies, cumin, and water in a blender until you have a fragrant and smooth bright reddish-orange paste.

2. Heat the oil in a saucepan or 12-inch skillet over medium heat. Carefully add the spice paste to the side of the pan to prevent splattering, then gently move the paste to the middle and stir to incorporate it into the oil. Allow the paste to cook, stirring occasionally to prevent sticking, until the oils separate and appear on the surface, about 15 minutes.

3. Stir in the kicap manis. Gently place the eggplant slices on top of the sambal and do not stir. Cover the pot, lower the heat, and cook until the eggplant is soft, about 15 minutes. Gently fold the eggplant into the sambal. Taste; add a pinch of salt if needed. Serve warm.

STIR-FRIED CABBAGE WITH SOY SAUCE

In Malaysia, Indian-style vegetable dishes are transformed by adding Chinese sauces like soy sauce. When cooking the cabbage, your goal is to get the soy sauce to penetrate the cabbage while preventing the cabbage from becoming soggy. If there is liquid in the wok, the trick is to raise the heat to high and move the cabbage to the sides, creating space in the center of the wok for the water to evaporate. When the wok appears dry, bring the cabbage back to the center and continue to stir-fry. This will keep the cabbage crisp and maintain its texture. This dish is delicious served with Malaysian Korma Vegetables (page 144), and Turmeric Fried Chicken (page 276), and a plate of hot rice. SERVES 4

¼ cup peanut oil

3 shallots, thinly sliced

3 garlic cloves, minced

Pinch of salt

½ teaspoon ground white pepper

1 green cabbage, cored and sliced

1 tablespoon soy sauce, or to taste

3 tablespoons chopped fresh cilantro

1. Heat a wok or a sauté pan over medium heat for about 30 seconds. Once it's hot, add the oil, pouring it around the perimeter of the wok. Add the shallots and cook until lightly brown, 2 to 3 minutes. Add the garlic, salt, and pepper and cook until fragrant, about 1 minute.

2. Add the cabbage and cook until slightly wilted, about 3 minutes. Add the soy sauce, mix well, and continue to cook, stirring, for about 1 minute more. Taste, and add more soy sauce only if needed. Remove from the heat and garnish with cilantro before serving.

MUSHROOM MASALA

Even my youngest son, who is not too keen on vegetables or spicy food, loves this simple Indian-style dish. *Masala* refers to the spice mixture in which the mushrooms are cooked, in this case onion, garlic, turmeric, and chili powder. If the spice mixture begins to appear too dry, add a little water to moisten it and prevent it from burning. The mushrooms will blend their flavor with the spices, creating a mild savory taste. Of course this dish can be served over rice, but we sometimes enjoy it as a pizza topping, in grilled sandwiches, or in omelets.

SERVES 4

¼ cup peanut oil

1 small red onion, minced

4 cloves garlic, sliced

Pinch of salt, or to taste

1 teaspoon ground chilies

½ teaspoon ground turmeric

½ teaspoon ground white pepper

1½ pounds white mushrooms, thinly sliced

3 tablespoons chopped fresh cilantro

1. Heat a wok or a sauté pan over medium heat for about 30 seconds. Once hot, add the oil, pouring it around the perimeter of the wok. Add the onion, garlic, and salt and cook until the onion is lightly brown, about 5 minutes.

2. Add the chili powder, turmeric, and white pepper and cook, stirring to combine the flavors, until the chili powder no longer tastes raw, about 2 minutes.

3. Add the mushrooms and mix well. Lower the heat to medium-low and cook until the mushrooms have cooked down to half their size, about 10 minutes.

4. Taste and add more salt if needed. Raise the heat to high, stir the mushrooms a few times, then allow then to brown undisturbed in order to caramelize on the bottoms, about 2 minutes more. Remove from the heat, garnish with the cilantro, and serve hot.

CABBAGE SAUTÉED WITH EGGS, TURMERIC, AND CURRY LEAVES

When I was growing up, we had a beautiful curry leaf tree in our backyard, and we would pluck leaves from it every day to use in our cooking. The aroma of curry leaves is so remarkable that, even now, when I hold a bag of curry leaves in my hands it inspires me to cook.

We ate this dish often in our home when I was a child, especially with fish curries, such as Salmon in Creamy Tikka Masala (page 192) and Tamarind Fish Curry (page 207), and steamed jasmine rice. The aromatic, peppery-tasting leaves and a hint of golden turmeric dress up the mild, sweet taste of cabbage. In America, curry leaves are usually sold in clear plastic bags. The summer months are the best time to look for them. If you find a good source, I suggest that you buy extra and freeze the rest. Turmeric powder, from a golden root vegetable, has many health benefits and is popular wherever people from India have settled. Its flavor is very subtle but its usefulness is dramatic; it is believed to prevent flatulence and assist with digestion, which is why it is often paired with cabbage. SERVES 4

1 small cabbage

2 tablespoons peanut oil

1 teaspoon black mustard seeds

½ large onion, very thinly sliced

4 cloves garlic, minced

2 sprigs curry leaves, chopped

½ teaspoon ground turmeric

½ teaspoon salt, or to taste

½ teaspoon ground white pepper

2 large eggs, beaten

1. Cut the cabbage in half. Remove and discard the core, and then slice the cabbage into thin ribbons.

2. Heat a wok or a sauté pan over medium heat for about 30 seconds. Once it's hot, add the oil, pouring it around the perimeter of the wok.

Add the mustard seeds, cover with a splatter screen, or partially cover with a lid, to contain the seeds. Cook until you hear the mustard seeds pop, about 1 minute.

3. Add the onion, garlic, and curry leaves and stir-fry until the onion is tender and lightly brown, about 5 minutes. Add the turmeric, salt, and pepper and sauté until fragrant, about 1 minute more.

4. Add the cabbage and cook until slightly wilted and well blended with the onions, about 3 minutes. Push the cabbage to the sides of the pan to make a well in the center and pour in the beaten eggs. Bring the cabbage back to cover the eggs. Allow the eggs to set, 1 to 2 minutes, then scramble gently and toss with the cabbage until well combined. Taste and add more salt if needed. Serve immediately.

YOUNG BAMBOO SHOOTS IN TURMERIC-COCONUT CURRY

If you enjoy artichoke hearts, then you will love the taste of young bamboo shoots, which have a nutty taste and crunchy texture. Here they are curried with ripe tomatoes and coconut milk for a mild-flavored, unassuming dish with notes of sweet and savory—enjoy it for lunch over steamed jasmine rice with a side of fried chicken. You can find young bamboo shoots at most Asian stores, in cans or vacuum-packed in sealed plastic. If you are lucky, you might find fresh bamboo shoots sold from large five-gallon tins. Always select curved shoots with golden tips if you can, as they are sweeter. If you use canned, be sure to rinse them to remove the metallic flavor, then blanch them in boiling water to enliven them. SERVES 4

3 tablespoons peanut oil

1 small onion, minced

5 garlic cloves, minced

2 stalks lemongrass, outer layers discarded, thinly sliced

2 fresh green chilies, chopped

1½ cups canned bamboo shoots, rinsed and blanched

2 tomatoes, quartered

½ teaspoon ground turmeric

2 cups coconut milk

1 tablespoon liquid palm sugar (pages 315–316), or to taste

1 tablespoon fish sauce, or to taste

¼ cup fresh cilantro, roughly chopped

1. Heat the oil in a medium skillet or wok over medium heat. Add the onion and cook, stirring, until lightly browned, about 10 minutes. Add the garlic, lemongrass, and chilies and cook until completely browned and aromatic, about 5 minutes.

2. Add the bamboo shoots, tomatoes, and turmeric. Mix well to combine and cook for another minute.

3. Stir in the coconut milk. Lower the heat and cook, uncovered, stirring occasionally to prevent the coconut milk from burning, for about 20 minutes.

4. Season with the palm sugar and fish sauce, adjusting to taste. Stir in the cilantro and serve warm.

STIR-FRIED ASIAN GREENS WITH GARLIC AND OYSTER SAUCE

SAWI GORENG

A sure way to eat more vegetables—especially powerfully nutritious greens—is to make them as flavorful as possible. Garlic, pepper, cooking sauces like oyster sauce, and fragrant oils like sesame oil are all traditional in the Malaysian-Chinese way of cooking and transform ordinary leafy greens into a sumptuous dish. Chinese-style cooking also uses rapid cooking in a wok over high heat to seal in all the vegetables' nutrients. I developed this recipe with a number of Asian greens, but you can substitute greens of any kind. I encourage you to visit the produce section of a Chinese or Southeast Asian market to pick up some bok choy, choy sum, pea sprouts, or *gai lan* (Chinese broccoli), but you can also use mustard greens, collard greens, or kale. You could also add some diced ham or salted herring along with the garlic. Stir-fried greens go well with roasts, curries, braised meat dishes, and beans. SERVES 4

8 ounces leafy greens of your choice
5 shiitake mushrooms
¼ cup peanut oil
6 garlic cloves, sliced
½ teaspoon ground white pepper
Pinch of salt
2 tablespoons oyster sauce, or to taste
1 teaspoon sesame oil

1. To prepare the greens, place them in a large bowl and rinse thoroughly under tap water. Drain and cut the leaves from the stems, keeping the leaves whole. Cut the stems into 1-inch lengths.

2. Wash the mushrooms and remove the stems under running water. Gently pat dry, then slice both the stems and caps. It is important that the mushrooms are damp so they don't burn in the hot wok.

3. Heat a wok over medium-high heat until the surface is very hot. Add the oil and swirl to coat. Add the garlic and stir-fry until light golden, about 30 seconds.

4. Raise the heat to high, add the greens and mushrooms, and stir-fry until the vegetables start to wilt and reduce by half, about 2 minutes. Add the pepper and salt and mix well. The stems should be tender but not overcooked.

5. Season with the oyster sauce and mix well to combine. Stir in the sesame oil and serve immediately.

HOW TO COOK SUCCESSFULLY WITH A WOK

In a traditional Malaysian kitchen, the "wet kitchen," where the wood and propane fires burned, was always set outside the house, adjacent to the indoor "dry kitchen." From our living room upstairs, I would hear the sound of stir-frying coming from my neighbor's wet kitchen. I was fascinated by the way my neighbor, Auntie Susan, used her reliable two-handled *kuali* (small wok). She seemed to move to a music I could not hear, adding and removing food, lifting and tossing with her metal spatula, as the various ingredients merged into one dish.

Anyone who has ever used a wok knows that food actually tastes better when cooked in a well-seasoned wok. In Malaysian kitchens, most home cooks use a round-bottom wok made of either cast iron or carbon steel. However, getting a round bottom wok to work on an electric stove can pose a challenge, so if you have an electric stove, use a flat bottom wok; I recommend the carbon steel kind, preferably 14 inches in diameter, which is what I use in my classes. Carbon steel provides quick heat conduction and its light weight makes the wok easier to lift from the stove and to store, making it a better choice than traditional cast iron.

I do not recommend stainless steel, aluminum, or nonstick Teflon. The problem is that these types of woks do not generate the high heat necessary to make vegetables crisp and retain their nutrients, nor to effectively sear meat and provide the depth you desire.

Here are some tips to successfully to cook with your wok:

- If you have an iron wok: Season your wok prior to use to prevent rusting, keep food from sticking, and avoid transferring a metal taste to your food. First, preheat the oven to 450°F. Wash the wok, scrub it with soap, and rinse thoroughly with water. This should be the only time your wok makes contact with soap. Dry the wok with a paper towel. Next, lightly coat the wok, inside and outside, with canola, peanut, or coconut oil to season it. Place the oiled wok upside down on a baking sheet to collect any oil that may drip, and bake in the oven for 45 minutes. This creates a polymer seal that adheres to the metal. Allow the wok to cool completely, then thoroughly rinse with hot water and dry. The wok is now seasoned and ready for cooking. After each use, rinse the wok only with hot water. Do not use soap, which breaks down the oil and removes the polymer seal.

- When you are preparing ingredients for the wok, make sure that everything is the freshest and best quality for flavor and nutrition. All vegetables must be clean and dry, not wet, so you do not end up with excess water in the wok. Use a colander to shake off excess water. When using meat, thinly slice it across the grain to ensure even cooking.

- Do not overcrowd your wok. Too many ingredients will end up like a stew. The maximum amount of meat, for example, would be about 1 pound.

- The wok is a very forgiving cooking tool. If you are new to it, I suggest you begin cooking at medium heat. Place the ingredients in the center and then gradually increase the heat to high. Use your spatula to spread the food around the wok, away from the center to seal in all the flavors, as the sides of the wok are hotter than the center. When it is time to add sauce, I suggest that you reduce the heat to low to prevent burning.

- After many years of teaching cooking classes, I like to associate the wok techniques with ships sailing into a harbor and then sailing off to sea. We bring the food to the center, like a harbor, to protect and gather the ingredients and sauces, oils, and spices. Then, the food is sent off to the sides to pick up flavor and sizzle with its own characteristics, only to return again to the harbor of the center. If you imagine this back and forth movement of the food, it is so much like the beauty of a tide, with its relaxing motion that feeds the soul.

Although woks are commonly associated with stir-frying, your wok is actually the ultimate multi-purpose cooking vessel: you can also use it to steam, braise, boil, and fry.

STIR-FRIED BOK CHOY
WITH BACON AND GARLIC

Here is such a simple recipe that can be cooked in less than 5 minutes, yet will complement anything you bring to the table—it's especially excellent with Tamarind-Glazed Roast Duck (page 290). With bits of salty bacon and garlic pieces hidden within the leaves, the bok choy always disappears quickly even among picky eaters. When buying the bacon, avoid specialty flavors such as hickory smoked or applewood, as they would overwhelm the vegetables.

SERVES 4

1 pound baby bok choy

2 tablespoons peanut oil

4 ounces slab bacon, cut into ½-inch pieces

4 garlic cloves, minced

1 fresh Thai green chili, minced

1. Prepare the bok choy by separating the leaves and rinsing away any dirt on the bottom of the bulb under cold running water. Rinse the greens in a large bowl and drain. Roughly chop and set aside.

2. Heat a wok over medium heat until the surface is very hot. Add the oil and swirl to coat the wok surface. Add the bacon, garlic, and chili and stir-fry until much of the bacon fat is rendered, the bacon is crisp, and the garlic appears golden, about 3 minutes.

3. Raise the heat to high, add the bok choy, and stir-fry until the greens start to wilt and reduce by half the amount, about 2 minutes. The stems should be tender but not overcooked. Remove from the heat and serve immediately.

STIR-FRIED ASPARAGUS WITH SAMBAL BELACHAN

A Malay dish made with water spinach (also known as morning glory leaves, or *kang kung*) is so popular that it's called the unofficial national dish of Malaysia. Here, I substitute asparagus, which is readily available and tastes delicious with the complex umami flavor of the shrimp paste (*belachan*) in the sambal. SERVES 4

3 shallots, sliced

4 cloves garlic, peeled and left whole

2 tablespoons Sambal Ulek (page 44 or store-bought)

2 tablespoons soy sauce

½ teaspoon raw shrimp paste (optional)

¼ cup peanut or coconut oil

Salt

1 pound asparagus

1. In a pot large enough to hold the asparagus horizontally, bring salted water to a boil.

2. Meanwhile, place the shallots, garlic, sambal ulek, soy sauce, and shrimp paste (if using) in a small food processor or blender and blend into a smooth paste to make the sambal.

3. Heat the oil in a medium skillet over medium heat. Add the sambal and cook, stirring occasionally, until fragrant and the oils have separated onto the surface of the mixture, about 5 minutes.

4. Trim the tough ends of the asparagus, peel the outer layer using a potato peeler, and then cut the stalks in half. Wash under cold running water.

5. Once the water has come to a rapid boil, drop the asparagus into the boiling water and cook, uncovered, until the shoots are tender when cut with a knife, about 10 minutes.

6. Transfer the asparagus with a slotted spoon to the skillet and gently mix well to combine with the sambal. Allow the asparagus to cook for about 1 minute, then remove from the heat and serve immediately.

BROCCOLI, CAULIFLOWER, AND SHIITAKE COMBINATION

Since this extremely handy dish can be paired with almost any kind of food, I ate it often growing up; it's great with steak or any curry. The oyster sauce is a key flavoring ingredient here, so I would suggest that you do not skip it or substitute: The combination of oyster sauce, chicken stock, and soy sauce provides a complex, layered salty and sweet base for the vegetables. You might also want to substitute or add carrots, bok choy, green bell peppers, or baby corn. SERVES 4

¼ cup peanut oil

4 garlic cloves, sliced

1 piece (2 inches) fresh ginger, peeled and julienned

8 ounces broccoli, cut into 1-inch florets

½ head cauliflower (6 to 8 ounces), cut into florets

6 ounces shiitake mushrooms, washed, stemmed, stems and caps cut in half

¼ cup chicken stock

2 tablespoons soy sauce

2 tablespoons oyster sauce

1 teaspoon sugar

½ teaspoon ground white pepper

1 teaspoon cornstarch mixed with 3 tablespoons water

¼ cup chopped fresh cilantro

1. Heat a wok over medium-high heat until the surface is very hot. Add the oil and swirl to coat. Add the garlic and ginger and stir-fry until they both appear light golden, about 1 minute.

2. Add the broccoli, cauliflower, and mushrooms and mix well to combine. Add the chicken stock, soy sauce, oyster sauce, sugar, and pepper and mix well. Lower the heat to medium and cook until the vegetables are still crisp but a little tender on the inside, about 1 minute.

3. Add the cornstarch mixture; raise the heat to high, and stir-fry until the sauce thickens, about 1 minute. Add the cilantro and toss well before serving immediately.

FRIED TOFU AND TOMATOES IN SWEET SOY SAMBAL

This sweet sambal is a favorite of cooks of northern Malaysia. I first fell in love with it in Langkawi Island, tucked in the northwest corner of the Malay peninsula and a stone's throw from the Thai-Malaysian border. Because tofu absorbs flavors so well, each piece bursts with a caramel-like sweetness from the sweet soy sauce and a smoky flavor that goes well with hot rice. Fried tofu also brings a crunchy texture. You can purchase tofu already fried at most Asian markets or the deli sections of supermarkets with Chinese dishes on sale, or you can buy fresh tofu and fry it yourself. SERVES 4

¼ cup peanut or canola oil

½ yellow onion, minced

2 large ripe tomatoes, finely chopped

2 to 3 tablespoons Sambal Ulek (page 44 or store-bought)

2 pieces (4 inches each) store-bought fried tofu (or fry it yourself), cut into 1-inch cubes

3 tablespoons kicap manis (sweet soy sauce; see page 16)

Pinch of salt

2 green onions (white and green parts), thinly sliced

1. Heat a wok or a large deep skillet over medium heat for about 40 seconds. Once hot, add the oil and heat until the surface shimmers slightly. Add the onion, tomatoes, and sambal ulek and cook, stirring occasionally, until the oils separate and come to the surface, about 15 minutes.

2. Add the tofu, kicap manis, and salt and cook, stirring occasionally, until the oils separate again and the flavors are well blended, about 10 minutes. Transfer to a serving dish and garnish with the green onions.

LONG GREEN BEANS, TOFU, AND BEAN SPROUTS IN COCONUT MILK

A favorite way of cooking vegetables in the Malay style is to simmer in coconut milk. Cut into bite-size pieces, they cook quickly in the liquid and retain perfect texture and flavor. Yardlong beans, the more traditional option for this recipe, are a different species than American string beans. They are string-less and typically grow to be about 18 inches long. They have a sweeter and nuttier flavor than string beans, and when simmered in liquid become vibrant, tender, and delicious. But if you cannot find long beans, you can substitute regular string beans. You could also incorporate butternut squash or tomatoes into the recipe. SERVES 6

3 tablespoons coconut oil

5 large shallots, sliced

2½ cups (one 14-ounce can) coconut milk

8 ounces yardlong beans, cut into 1-inch lengths (1½ cups)

1 block (14 ounces) store-bought fried tofu (or fry it yourself), cubed

1 cup bean sprouts

½ teaspoon salt, or to taste

¼ cup coconut cream

1. Heat the oil in a medium saucepan over medium heat. Add the shallots and stir-fry until aromatic and golden, about 3 minutes.

2. Add the coconut milk, raise the heat to high, and bring to a boil, watching carefully and stirring occasionally so the coconut milk does not overflow. Add the beans and tofu, reduce the heat to medium-low, and cook until the beans are tender and the tofu puffs up in the coconut milk, about 15 minutes.

3. Stir in the bean sprouts, salt, and coconut cream and cook for about 1 minute more. Serve immediately.

SWEET POTATOES AND BABY SPINACH SIMMERED IN COCONUT MILK

This beautiful and easy to prepare dish sums up a typical Malay home-style meal when served with any fried dish (such as fish or chicken), rice, and a small side of sambal. Because it is so mild, sweet potato requires delicate seasoning. To that end, simmer it in a creamy coconut milk broth that features fenugreek seeds, garlic, and shallots. Fenugreek may look like tiny brown stones before cooking, but when these seeds come in contact with hot oil, they soften and release a delicate hazelnut-like flavor that complements coconut milk very nicely. If you are cooking for anyone with nut allergies, toasted fenugreek is a charming alternative. You could replace the sweet potatoes with yams or taro. SERVES 6

3 tablespoons coconut oil

2 large shallots, minced

2 garlic cloves, minced

½ teaspoon fenugreek seeds

2½ cups (one 14-ounce can) coconut milk

1 pound sweet potatoes, peeled and diced

½ cup baby spinach

½ teaspoon salt, or to taste

¼ cup coconut cream

1. Heat the oil in a medium saucepan over medium heat. Add the shallots, garlic, and fenugreek seeds and stir-fry until the mixture is aromatic and the shallots appear golden, about 2 minutes.

2. Add the coconut milk, raise the heat to high, and bring to a boil, watching carefully and stirring occasionally so the coconut milk does not overflow. Add the sweet potatoes, reduce the heat to medium, and cook until the sweet potatoes are tender when cut with a fork, about 15 minutes. When the sweet potatoes are almost cooked, the coconut milk will have transformed from white to a buttercream-like color.

3. Add the baby spinach, salt, and coconut cream and cook until the spinach is wilted, about 5 minutes. Serve immediately.

POTATO SAMBAL CASSEROLE

This marvelous braised potato sambal, called *sambal kentang*, fills me with nostalgic feelings: I remember peeling potatoes and grinding chili paste with my mother and aunties in our open-air kitchen while we bonded and caught up on gossip, surrounded by emerald green foliage. The joy was not only in cooking together but also in anticipating the finished dish— sweet and spicy potatoes that go with virtually anything, but especially with grilled fish and crusty bread. The potatoes are cooked separately then added to the sweet spicy flavoring paste of onion, tomato, palm sugar, and fish sauce. The cooked sambal coats each morsel of potato for a prolonged flavor. If you'd prefer, you can finish the potatoes on the stovetop instead of baking them in the oven; simply add the cooked and quartered potatoes to the skillet with the sambal at the end of step 3 and continue to cook until the sauce has thickened and the sambal coats the potatoes, about another 10 minutes. SERVES 4

1½ pounds red potatoes, washed and peeled

½ small yellow onion, chopped

1 tomato, chopped

1 cup Sambal Ulek (page 44 or store-bought), or 6 fresh red jalapeño chilies

6 tablespoons peanut or coconut oil

½ cup coconut cream

¼ cup water

1 tablespoon fish sauce, or to taste

¼ cup liquid palm sugar (pages 315–316), or to taste

1. Preheat the oven to 350°F. Cover the potatoes with 8 cups water in a pot and cook over medium-high heat until fork tender, about 20 minutes.

2. While the potatoes are cooking, prepare the spice paste by grinding the onion, tomato, and sambal ulek in a food processor until very smooth, adding a little water if needed to keep the blades moving.

3. Heat the oil in a skillet over medium heat. Add the sambal mixture and cook, stirring frequently, until the oil separates onto the surface, about 10 minutes.

4. Add the coconut cream, water, fish sauce, and palm sugar. Cook until the oil once again separates onto the surface, another 10 minutes; the separation indicates the sambal mixture is cooked. Taste and add more fish sauce for saltiness or palm sugar for sweetness as desired.

5. Check the potatoes, and once they are fork tender, remove from the heat and allow to cool before cutting into quarters. Transfer the potatoes to a casserole dish and pour the sambal over them. Bake until the sambal appears to cling on or coat the potatoes, about 25 minutes. Serve warm.

MALAYSIAN KORMA VEGETABLES

When I was growing up, every Christmas morning I woke up to the fragrance of pandan leaf, ginger, and green cardamom pods sautéing in clarified butter as my mother prepared korma, our family holiday tradition. Korma is a mild and creamy cashew curry made with spices, yogurt, and either vegetables or meat. It comes originally from northern India, but this Malaysian recipe is lighter tasting than the versions served in Indian restaurants in the United States. You may buy korma spice powder in most Indian grocery stores, or you can find Baba's Kurma Curry Powder online, just as many Indian and Malaysian cooks living overseas do. You may be able to find fresh or frozen pandan leaves at Asian markets. If you cannot find them, you can omit the pandan, and the korma will still taste incredible. SERVES 4

¼ cup clarified butter (ghee) or extra-virgin olive oil

1 cinnamon stick (about 4 inches)

2 whole star anise

3 green cardamom pods, crushed

2 fresh or frozen pandan leaves (optional)

1 large red onion, chopped

2 fresh green jalapeño chilies, seeded and sliced lengthwise

¼ cup Ginger, Garlic, and Cilantro Paste (page 53)

3 medium tomatoes, cut in half

1 large Yukon Gold potato, peeled and quartered

1 to 2 carrots, peeled and diced

1 cup white mushrooms, halved

¼ cup roasted unsalted cashews

5 tablespoons korma powder

1 teaspoon ground turmeric

½ teaspoon freshly ground black pepper

3 cups coconut milk

1 cup water

1 teaspoon salt, or to taste

1 cup plain yogurt

1 teaspoon lime juice

½ head cauliflower, cut into small pieces

1. Heat the butter in a large heavy pot over medium heat. Add the cinnamon, star anise, cardamom, pandan leaves (if using), onion, chilies, and ginger-garlic paste. Cook, stirring, until the onion is soft, about 10 minutes.

2. Add the tomatoes, potato, carrots, mushrooms, and cashews and mix well. Stir in the korma powder, turmeric, pepper, coconut milk, and water. Cook until the potatoes are tender when cut in half with a spoon, about 10 minutes.

3. Season with salt to taste. Add the yogurt and lime and mix to blend. Add the cauliflower; cook without stirring for about 1 minute. The cauliflower should be still crisp. Remove from the heat and serve warm.

STIR-FRIED BEAN SPROUTS
WITH ANCHOVIES AND CILANTRO

In Malaysia, bean sprouts with anchovies are as common as potatoes are in American restaurants: People order them at most Chinese open-air restaurants. The crispy fried anchovies, soy sauce, and white pepper add an umami taste and aroma to the sprouts, which are otherwise plain tasting. This dish must be eaten immediately after it is cooked, so make sure all your other dishes are ready before you begin. Dried anchovies can be found in most Southeast Asian or Japanese grocery stores, and sometimes in larger supermarkets. After frying, they keep well for several weeks stored in an airtight glass jar; I love to keep a supply of them on hand to liven up any other plain vegetables. SERVES 4

¼ cup peanut oil

2 large shallots, sliced

3 garlic cloves, sliced

2 fresh red chilies, seeded and chopped

¼ cup loosely packed fried anchovies (see note at right)

12 ounces bean sprouts, rinsed and drained

1 tablespoon soy sauce, or to taste

¼ teaspoon ground white pepper

¼ cup chopped fresh cilantro

1. Heat a wok or large, deep skillet over medium-high heat and add the oil. Add the shallots, garlic, and chilies and cook, stirring constantly, until the shallots are golden brown, about 3 minutes. The moisture from the shallots will prevent the garlic and chilies from burning.

2. Raise the heat to high and add the anchovies to the wok, stirring to combine. Add the bean sprouts and toss for 30 seconds.

3. Add the soy sauce and white pepper and continue to stir-fry for about 1 minute more. Stir in the cilantro and then remove from the heat. Serve immediately.

FRYING ANCHOVIES | Anchovies are a concentrated source of glutamic and inosinic acid—two molecules responsible for triggering our savory sensation and providing that rich umami flavor. They add depth of flavor to pretty much anything. Dried anchovies are found in small clear plastic packets from Japan or Thailand and widely sold at most Asian markets. I rinse them in a colander (to remove their saltiness), pat them dry, and then deep-fry over medium heat until crispy, about 1 minute. Do this ahead of time and keep the fried anchovies in an airtight container in the refrigerator for up to 3 months. Fried anchovies can be added to soups, salads, stir-fries, or coconut rice (page 160) for extra umami flavor.

RICE AND NOODLES

For most people around the world, rice is not just another grain; cooked rice is the heart of their existence. The word *nasi* (steamed rice) is synonymous with "food" in the Malaysian national language, and throughout Southeast Asia it is customary to greet someone with a "Hi! Have you eaten rice yet?"

Rice is cooked every day and absorbs homemade curries and sauce from any braised dish. In a typical Malaysian meal, at least four dishes are served: A nicely balanced meal would include a soup, a curry or stir-fried dish, a vegetable or a salad, and a sambal—and steamed rice taking center stage. The many varieties of rice are traditionally prepared using different methods depending on whether the dish is Indian-, Chinese-, or Malay-inspired. Leftover rice is used for fried rice, *nasi goreng*. (See Rice in Asian Diets, page 165, for more.)

In this chapter, I share some of my adventures with rice beginning with my favorite Malaysian Indian recipes—Spiced Clarified Butter Rice with Almonds and Cranberries (page 161) and Fragrant Tomato Rice with Cashews (page 163). These dishes use long-grain basmati rice as the rice does not clump and beautifully showcases the various fruits and nuts layered with spices. These pilafs embellish our family table at every celebration and continue to make new memories as I share them with friends in the United States.

When I reminisce about comfort food prepared by the Malay cooks across the country and dishes enjoyed by all nationalities, it would certainly include Fragrant Coconut Rice on page 160. I recall enjoying this dish at village-style restaurants where the rice is bundled in little green banana leaves with a dollop of sambal within. Likewise, Pineapple Fried Rice with Chicken and Cashews on page 162 and Village Fried Rice with Chicken and Spinach on page 173 are quick and delightful weeknight favorites. Unlike Malaysian Indian pilafs, these dishes

use the common white jasmine rice; although you may use brown jasmine if you prefer. (The white variety is known for its ability to absorb sauces, provide a softer bite, and hold on to the ingredients.) My other favorite is Fried Rice with Shrimp, Bacon, and Eggs on page 175 which also uses jasmine rice and is an example of the Chinese-Malaysian style of cooking. These sorts of wok-fried dishes are also nourishing, and just about anything belongs in fried rice: leftover roast chicken, veggies, ham, or bacon and eggs with a few dashes of Asian pantry sauces. Rice is so versatile that I encourage you to unleash your creative side and have fun with the delightful variety of rice dishes presented in this chapter.

Just as rice is basic to the Malaysian diet, noodles too are enjoyed with the same gusto. Most Asians who live abroad know that the memory of a good noodle dish can haunt you for years. Fortunately, noodles are easy to obtain and are inexpensive. Many types of Asian noodles can be found at your local supermarket; others might require an excursion to an Asian market. (See Asian Noodles on pages 156–157 for more information.) Each type of noodle has its own special character.

In my pantry I stock a variety of rice noodle sticks of all shapes and sizes—yellow pancit Cantonese-style wheat noodles, wonton egg noodles, clear rice and mung bean vermicelli (also known as glass noodles), flat wheat noodles—as each variety clings to the flavorful sauces, broths, or other ingredients in different ways. The convenience and versatility of dried noodles allows

me to create a variety of tasty dishes anytime.

To help you choose the appropriate noodles for the recipes, here are useful ones available in Asian groceries: Noodles such as *pancit canton* or yakisoba have a yellow hue and provide a soft bite. They absorb sauces well and are also suited for pairing with meats and vegetables. Rice vermicelli, delicate in appearance and texture, are popular in soups and stir-fries. Egg noodles are sold fresh in the refrigerated section or dried and they work well in soups or when combined in sauces.

Most noodle dishes require the use of chopped garlic, minced ginger, sliced onions, and chopped cilantro, all of which can be prepped ahead of time and stored in airtight containers in the refrigerator. Dried noodles can also be soaked in hot water until soft, then drained and stored in an airtight bag or container. This makes the whole

cooking process easier and more convenient.

A noodle is never simply one element. Perhaps it's the marriage of coconut broth and just the right addition of aromatics redolent of galangal, lemongrass, and ginger, plus time simmering with chicken and vegetables to form the deeply satisfying Chicken Laksa on page 159. Other times, it is about experimenting with the combination of sauces and sambals tossed with rice or egg noodles and greens in a wok, each strand of the noodles a journey of taste imbued with three cultures in a bite. Traditional Malaysian Stir-Fried Noodles (page 150), Stir-Fried Rice Vermicelli with Mushrooms and Kicap Manis (page 155), and Black Hokkien Noodles with Shrimp and Cabbage (page 170) are examples of these dishes.

TRADITIONAL MALAYSIAN STIR-FRIED NOODLES

MAMAK MEE GORENG

Few traditional Malaysian dishes represent my home country's culinary fusion better than *mamak mee goreng,* literally translated as "Indian Muslim fried noodles." In Malaysia, the noodles are a specialty of the Indian street food vendors who created their own version of stir-fried noodles. The unique flavors come from borrowing Chinese, Western, and Indian ingredients. For instance, Chinese soy sauce and kicap manis, Western tomato ketchup and potatoes, a touch of Malay sambal, and Indian turmeric all help to build depth and flavor in the noodles, which take on a sweet tangy taste that is rich and enticing. The noodles are finished off with a squeeze of lime juice to make the ingredients pop. *Mamak* (Indian Muslim) street vendors have become such experts at cooking this quickly that they can chop the ingredients and do the frying while having a hearty conversation with their customers. You will find mee goreng enjoyed any time of the day or night and prepared in many ways, each rendition given a twist by the local culture.

In this traditional and authentic recipe, I use the common yellow noodles known as *yakisoba,* which you will find in the refrigerator section of any Asian supermarket and probably in major supermarkets too. I pair the noodles with *gai lan,* also called Chinese broccoli. If you cannot find it, you can substitute collard greens, although they are not as sweet. Like most stir-fries, success hinges on having all the ingredients prepared in advance, because the cooking goes very quickly once you start. This stir-fry is so versatile, you may add any other protein, whether chicken, shrimp, turkey, or beef, for a heartier dish. SERVES 4

1 pound fresh yellow noodles (yakisoba)

¼ cup canola or peanut oil

6 cloves garlic, minced

2 tablespoons Sambal Ulek (page 44 or store-bought)

¼ head cabbage, roughly chopped

8 ounces gai lan (Chinese broccoli), thinly sliced

1 medium potato (any kind), boiled, peeled, and cut into 1-inch cubes

8 ounces store-bought fried tofu, thinly sliced

¼ cup kicap manis (sweet soy sauce; see page 16), or to taste

3 tablespoons soy sauce

2 tablespoons tomato ketchup

½ teaspoon ground turmeric

2 large eggs, beaten

3 green onions (white and green parts), thinly sliced

1 lime, cut into wedges

1. Gently rinse the noodles in a colander under hot running water to remove oil, then set aside to drain thoroughly in the colander.

2. Heat a wok or a large deep skillet over medium heat for about 40 seconds. Add the oil, pouring it around the perimeter of the wok to coat the sides and bottom. When the surface shimmers slightly, add the garlic and cook until golden and fragrant, about 1 minute. Add the sambal and cook for another 30 seconds, until fragrant and the oils separate on the surface.

3. Add the cabbage, gai lan, potato, and tofu and stir-fry until the vegetables are slightly wilted, about 1 minute.

4. Now add the drained noodles and toss well to combine with the vegetables, mixing carefully to prevent the noodles from breaking; stir-fry for about 2 minutes.

5. Add the kicap manis, soy sauce, ketchup, and turmeric. Using tongs or two spatulas, toss gently like a salad until the noodles are well coated with the sauces. If the noodles are sticking, add a splash of water and toss well again.

6. Lower the heat to medium-low, push the noodles to one side of the pan, and add the beaten eggs on the opposite side to create a thin layer. Immediately bring the noodles back over the egg. Do not stir or mix at this point; allow the egg underneath the noodles to cook undisturbed for at least 30 seconds.

7. Raise the heat to medium-high, then gently lift the noodles from underneath and stir-fry continuously until the eggs are fully cooked, about 2 minutes; the noodles should no longer appear wet from the eggs. Continue to stir-fry by gently moving the noodles away from the center to the side and back to the center, repeat this motion for about 2 minutes. Taste and add more kicap manis if needed. Toss in the green onions and mix well. Squeeze lime over each portion and serve immediately.

MALAYSIAN WOK-FRIED SPAGHETTI WITH KALE AND SAMBAL

SPAGHETTI GORENG

This is my modern take on the quintessential Malaysian comfort food *mee goreng* (page 150). This common dish is prepared at makeshift stalls and small coffee shops throughout the country. The locals normally gather around popular mee goreng trucks with a plate in their hands as the vendor stir-fries the noodles in a large cast iron wok attached to the trunk. I love this modern adaptation in its use of spaghetti, soy sauce, and sambal, all tossed in the sizzling-hot wok. I have also replaced Asian greens with kale, cabbage, and tofu, as their textures easily pair with spaghetti. Since the recipe uses spaghetti, the noodles will not be as tender as fresh yakisoba in traditional mee goreng; nevertheless, it is satisfying and keeping with the Malaysian style of seasoning. Before stir-frying make sure you have all your ingredients ready to go. This dish is prepared quickly, and any delay in the process or sequence can either overcook the ingredients or make the noodles stick to the wok. And keep in mind as you stir-fry that you want the noodles to make contact with the side of the wok, where it is the hottest, in order to obtain a charred flavor. SERVES 4

¼ cup extra-virgin olive oil or peanut oil

6 cloves garlic, minced

2 large shallots, thinly sliced

2 tablespoons Sambal Ulek (page 44 or store-bought)

½ head cabbage, finely chopped

2 cups chopped kale

8 ounces store-bought fried tofu, thinly sliced

1 pound spaghetti, cooked al dente

¼ cup kicap manis (sweet soy sauce; see page 16), or to taste

3 tablespoons soy sauce

2 large eggs, beaten

1. Heat a wok or a large deep skillet over medium heat for about 40 seconds. Add the oil, pouring it around the perimeter of the wok to coat the sides and bottom. When the surface shimmers slightly, add the garlic and shallots and cook until golden and fragrant, about 2 minutes. Add the sambal and cook for another for another 30 seconds, until fragrant and the oils separate onto the surface.

2. Add the cabbage, kale, and tofu and stir-fry until the vegetables are slightly wilted, about 1 minute.

3. Now add the cooked spaghetti and toss well to combine with the vegetables, mixing carefully to prevent the noodles from breaking;

stir-fry for about 3 minutes. Add the kicap manis and soy sauce and continue to mix well.

4. Push the noodles to one side of the pan. Add the beaten eggs on the opposite side to create a thin layer and then immediately bring the noodles back over the egg. Do not stir or mix at this point; allow the egg underneath to set and to cook undisturbed for at least 30 seconds.

Raise the heat to medium-high, then gently lift the noodles from underneath and stir-fry continuously until the eggs are fully cooked, about 2 minutes; the noodles should no longer appear wet from the eggs.

5. Continue to stir-fry for 1 to 2 minutes more, then taste and add more kicap manis if needed. Serve immediately.

STIR-FRIED RICE VERMICELLI
WITH MUSHROOMS AND KICAP MANIS

This vegan, gluten-free stir-fry is a typical home-style lunch. Morsels of mushrooms, thinly sliced cabbage, and bean sprouts break down in the wok to combine with rice vermicelli. Not only is the stir-fry healthy and the ingredients economical, it is also a good choice for a party. Prepare the vegetables ahead of time and store them in airtight containers for up to three days. Because the vermicelli can easily stick to the pan since it is so light and delicate, here are a couple tips: Start cooking on medium-low heat and then gradually increase the heat at the very end to sear the noodles. And avoid the common mistake of tossing the noodles from the center, as this will break the strands; instead, use your spatula to gently toss the noodles from underneath. SERVES 4

6 ounces rice vermicelli

Boiling water

¼ cup peanut oil

6 cloves garlic, minced

3 large shallots, sliced

1 to 2 tablespoons Sambal Ulek (page 44 or store-bought)

8 ounces button mushrooms, thinly sliced

3 tablespoons soy sauce, or to taste

2 tablespoons kicap manis (sweet soy sauce; see page 16)

½ head cabbage, sliced

8 ounces bean sprouts

½ cup chopped ½-inch fresh chives

1. Place the vermicelli in a large bowl and cover with boiling water. Set aside to soften, about 7 minutes. Once soft, drain the noodles in a colander and set aside.

2. Heat a wok or a large, deep skillet over medium heat for about 40 seconds. Add the oil, pouring it around the perimeter of the wok to coat the sides and bottom. When the surface shimmers slightly, add the garlic, shallots, and sambal. Cook, stirring, until fragrant and the oils have separated onto the surface, about 5 minutes.

3. Add the mushrooms, lower the heat to medium-low, and cook, stirring, until the mushrooms have broken down in the sambal, about 5 minutes. Add the vermicelli, soy sauce, and kicap manis. Raise the heat to medium-high and cook, stirring to prevent the rice vermicelli from sticking to the bottom of the wok, for 5 to 7 minutes.

4. Add the cabbage, bean sprouts, and chives, distributing them evenly around the wok, and continue to stir-fry until the vegetables are slightly wilted, about 2 minutes. Taste and add more soy sauce if needed. Serve immediately.

ASIAN NOODLES

A ten-minute walk from my father's home in the residential community of Limau Manis in Bangsar Park, following a narrow concrete pathway among tropical trees, sits the long row of shop houses on Jalan Maarof. These brick shops with black-tiled roofs and plantation-style shutters, built by the British, were originally homes, but today, stores are on the ground level and living quarters are upstairs. Each day these humble shop houses receive crowds of hungry lunchtime locals in search of the most flavorful noodles. Long-simmering lemongrass coconut soup spiked with chilies, mint, and coriander, with tender slices of chicken and some steamed morning glory are the high point of the day. Fresh lime wedges, slices of fresh pineapple, and bowls of sambal belachan are placed for all at the table.

These noodles vendors began humbly, building their reputations amongst the customers who sit elbow-to-elbow at small round tables, everyone from street workers in bright blue uniforms to established businessmen. These full-flavored noodle dishes epitomize Malaysian cuisine.

To make these dishes at home, you will want to buy Asian noodles. Some noodles can be found at your local supermarket; for others, you might need to take a trip to an Asian grocery store or shop online. When you walk into an Asian grocery store, amid the exotic spices and myriad sauces, you will easily spot a huge variety of fresh and dried Asian noodles. It is often quite a daunting task to select the right one as there are many brands and varieties from Thailand, China, Vietnam, and Malaysia. But we can put most noodles into four categories based on the ingredients: rice, wheat (all European pastas are wheat-based), egg, or bean threads (made from mung beans).

Rice noodles are gluten-free and primarily made with rice flour and water, sometimes with tapioca or cornstarch added. They are sold either dried, or fresh in the refrigerator section. Dried rice noodles need to be soaked in hot water to make them soft and pliable for cooking. However, fresh rice noodles make a tastier choice, as they have a softer texture. Use these, for example, in Char Kway Teow (page 236).

Similar in width to angel hair pasta, thin and delicate **rice vermicelli** are quickly stir-fried with vegetables, meat, or seafood and eaten for breakfast, for example as in Stir-Fried Rice Vermicelli with Mushrooms and Kicap Manis (page 155) and *Bihun Goreng* (page 169). As with all dried Asian noodles, it is best to soak them in hot water until soft before cooking. Alternatively, rice vermicelli can be deep-fried without soaking and used as a crunchy garnish.

Wheat noodles are made with flour, salt, water, and occasionally egg and/or other flavoring ingredients. You will probably see Asian wheat noodles labeled **yakisoba noodles, pancit canton**, or **chow mein noodles** in major supermarkets. They are composed of the same

ingredients but called by different names. In Asian markets, they are also sold fresh (ready to use) or dried. All fresh wheat noodles need to be rinsed in hot water to loosen the strands and to remove excess oil before use. In this book, wheat noodles are used in Traditional Malaysian Stir-Fried Noodles (page 150) and Black Hokkien Noodles with Shrimp and Cabbage (page 170).

Egg noodles are made from wheat, water, and eggs, which give them a yellow color. They are richer and dense in texture and best used in stir-fried, soup-based dishes or boiled so they are soft enough to accept flavoring sauces. The noodles come fresh or dried. Dry egg noodles

need to be soaked in hot water to reconstitute them. If you are using fresh egg noodles, however, separate and loosen the noodles, prior to cooking. They are used in the Malaysian Wantan Noodles with Barbecue-Roasted Pork (page 224) recipe.

Bean thread noodles, also known as glass noodles, are slippery, angel hair–like noodles made from mung beans or yams, so they are gluten-free. The noodles must be soaked in hot water until soft, then rinsed and drained before use. The noodles become transparent when cooked, and are best in soups, stir-fries, and salads, for example in Rice Noodle Salad with Shrimp and Coconut (page 114).

CHICKEN LAKSA

Laksa is associated with the island of Penang, and something I always seek out from the many vendors when visiting. This is my version of the traditional dish, a kind of chicken noodle soup rich with coconut, macadamia nuts, lime, chilies, and ginger. The Nyonya, who originated this dish, also known as the Baba-Nyonya, are descendants of mainly Hokkien Chinese traders from Fujian Province who settled in Malacca and Penang as early as the 15th century. The men who came on Chinese ships to trade within this archipelago married local women and hence Baba and Nyonya clans started. If you have them, use egg noodles or yakisoba; if not, you can use fettuccine. Make the laksa paste ahead of time and you can begin your dish by simply heating the paste in the pan with coconut milk and stock and then proceed with the recipe below. SERVES 6

1 cup Laksa Spice Paste (page 61)

3 cups coconut milk

3 cups good-quality chicken stock

1½ pounds chicken breast, cut into 2-inch pieces

2 small zucchini, chopped

1 cup chopped peeled butternut squash

1 teaspoon sugar

6 Vietnamese mint leaves (also known as *rau ram*), washed (optional)

Salt to taste, plus more for cooking the noodles

1 pound egg noodles, yakisoba, or fettuccine

1 lime, cut into wedges

Sambal Ulek (page 44 or store-bought), for serving

1. Combine the laksa paste, coconut milk, and stock in a deep pot and bring to a boil. Lower the heat and simmer for about 15 minutes. If the stock appears chunky from the lemongrass and galangal of the spice paste, strain through a sieve, then return the stock to a boil.

2. Add the chicken, zucchini, and squash and simmer over low heat until the chicken is cooked through, 10 to 15 minutes. Add the sugar and mint and simmer to infuse the flavors for 1 to 2 minutes. Taste and add salt if needed.

3. Meanwhile, bring a large pot of water and 1 tablespoon salt to a boil. Add the noodles and cook according to the package instructions until just al dente. Drain the noodles.

4. To serve, divide the noodles among serving bowls. Top with the chicken and vegetables and then pour the sauce over the noodles. Serve with the lime wedges and sambal.

FRAGRANT COCONUT RICE

Many Malaysian dishes couple so well with creamy coconut rice. The difference between a good coconut rice and an exceptional one lies in the use of a pandan leaf (screwpine leaf), which infuses the grains with its delightful aromatic essence. If you are able to find and use pandan, make sure you remove the leaf before serving because it is tough to chew.

The traditional name for this dish is *nasi lemak*. It is served piping hot from wooden steamers, and the rice is spooned onto clean banana leaves. In modern kitchens, the rice is best when cooked in a nonstick pot or a rice cooker. Immediately after cooking, the rice may appear wet with coconut cream on the surface; allow it to set before fluffing with a fork. This rice is delicious as a side dish to Sweet and Spicy Prawn Sambal Tumis (page 209), Stir-Fried Asparagus with Sambal Belachan (page 137), or Beef Rendang (page 261). SERVES 4

3 cups jasmine rice

2 cups coconut milk

1 cup water

1 tablespoon salt

1 pandan leaf, tied into a knot (optional)

1 inch fresh ginger, peeled and sliced

2 tablespoons toasted coconut flakes

1. Wash the rice by gently rubbing it with your fingers in a bowl filled with water. When the water becomes cloudy, drain and repeat the process until the water is clear. Drain.

2. Place the rice in a large nonstick saucepan and add the coconut milk, water, salt, pandan leaf (if using), and ginger. Bring to a boil over medium heat. Let the rice boil, uncovered, until steam holes appear in the rice and the surface looks dry, about 10 minutes. Reduce the heat to low, cover with a tight-fitting lid, and cook without stirring until all the liquid is absorbed and the grains are tender and fluffy, about 20 minutes more. Alternatively, combine all the ingredients in a rice cooker and let the machine cook the rice.

3. Toss in the coconut flakes, then fluff the rice. Serve hot or warm.

SPICED CLARIFIED BUTTER RICE WITH ALMONDS AND CRANBERRIES

NASI MINYAK

This dish has been in my family for generations and every time I prepare it, my son Anton remarks, "The house smells of Christmas." It is the incredible aromas of cardamom, star anise, pandan leaf, fresh ginger, almonds, cranberries, and clarified butter as they meet in the pot! The spices perfume the oil, allowing the grains to absorb the aromatic oils and puff up with outstanding flavor. Quick and easy to prepare, I normally serve this pilaf-like rice dish alongside Grilled Lamb Chops with Rosemary-Garlic Pesto (page 275). This would also be an excellent choice to include in your traditional Thanksgiving dinner. SERVES 6

3½ cups long-grain white basmati rice

⅓ cup clarified butter (ghee)

1 cinnamon stick (3 inches)

2 whole star anise

6 whole cloves

5 whole green cardamom pods, crushed

⅓ cup Ginger, Garlic, and Cilantro Paste (page 53)

2 pandan leaves, tied into a knot (optional)

¼ cup dried cranberries

¼ cup almonds

3 cups good-quality chicken broth

1 cup evaporated milk

1. Wash the rice by gently rubbing it with your fingers in a bowl filled with water. When the water becomes cloudy, drain and repeat the process until the water is clear. Drain and set the rice aside.

2. Heat the clarified butter in a large saucepan over medium heat. Add the cinnamon, star anise, cloves, and cardamom pods and cook, stirring, until fragrant, about 2 minutes.

3. Add the ginger-garlic paste, pandan leaves, cranberries, and almonds and cook until fragrant, about 5 minutes.

4. Add the rice and fold to combine with the spice butter; cook until the grains are well coated and the rice appears dry, about 2 minutes.

5. Add the broth and milk and gently stir for 30 seconds. Reduce the heat to low, cover with a tight-fitting lid, and cook without stirring until all the liquid is absorbed and the grains are tender and fluffy, about 20 minutes.

6. Remove the rice from the heat. Discard the pandan and cinnamon stick, then gently fluff the rice with a fork. Serve warm.

PINEAPPLE FRIED RICE WITH CHICKEN AND CASHEWS

Pineapples, the "sweet" of sweet-and-sour dishes, are used in a lot of Malaysian recipes, since they are so widely grown throughout Southeast Asia. This fried rice, a relatively easy week-night meal that is so much tastier and healthier than takeout! Leftover or one-day-old rice works best, because the grain is not as starchy as freshly cooked rice. The firmer the grain, straight from the refrigerator, the easier it is to stir-fry. But first make sure to break the clumps of rice with your hands. You may use any favorite meat—chicken, ham, or shrimp—or keep it vegetarian by swapping in peas, mushrooms, or tofu for the chicken. Be sure to serve with some Sambal Belachan (page 43) to drizzle over the rice. SERVES 4

¼ cup peanut oil

4 shallots, thinly sliced

3 cloves garlic, minced

1 fresh green jalapeño chili, chopped

1½ cups fresh pineapple chunks, cut into bite-size cubes

1 pound boneless skinless chicken thigh, cut into ½-inch pieces

¼ cup roasted unsalted cashews

4 cups cooked jasmine rice (preferably leftovers)

3 tablespoons soy sauce

2 tablespoons tomato ketchup

2 tablespoons fish sauce, or to taste

2 eggs, beaten

Fresh cilantro leaves, for garnish

1. Heat a wok or a large deep skillet over medium heat for about 40 seconds. Add the oil, pouring it around the perimeter of the wok to coat the sides and bottom. When the surface shimmers slightly, add the shallots and stir-fry until light golden, about 3 minutes. Add the garlic and jalapeño and cook, stirring, until fragrant and the garlic appears golden, about 5 minutes.

2. Add the pineapple and chicken and stir-fry, moving the ingredients back and forth in the wok, until the chicken is thoroughly cooked and no longer pink, about 10 minutes.

3. Mix in the cashews, then add the rice, soy sauce, ketchup, and fish sauce and stir-fry, using the spatula to break up any remaining clumps of rice in the wok, until the ingredients are well combined. Cook, tossing the rice, for about 5 minutes.

4. Move the rice to the side of the wok and add the beaten eggs to the other side. Immediately cover the eggs with the rice and allow the eggs to set and cook, undisturbed, for about 2 minutes. Raise the heat to medium-high and gently mix the rice and eggs.

5. Taste and add more fish sauce if needed, and continue to stir-fry for another 2 minutes. Garnish with cilantro and serve immediately.

FRAGRANT TOMATO RICE WITH CASHEWS

This dish evokes in me warm memories of family gatherings at our long dining table: The light chatter, children's giggles and laughter, and eating food lovingly prepared by my mother. The rice is normally made with milk, but for a healthier version I replace the milk with cashews blended with water to make a creamy liquid. (If you use coconut oil instead of clarified butter, this dish is vegan.) For a successful outcome, do not stir too much, but allow the rice to just simmer so the spices slowly release their fragrance into each grain. SERVES 6

3 cups long-grain white basmati rice

½ cup raw cashews

5½ cups water

1 piece (3 inches) fresh ginger, peeled and roughly chopped

2 heads garlic, peeled

¼ cup clarified butter (ghee) or virgin coconut oil

2 bay leaves

6 green cardamom pods, crushed

1 cinnamon stick (2 inches)

2 tablespoons tomato paste

4 Roma tomatoes, chopped

½ teaspoon salt

2 tablespoons raisins

1. Wash the rice by gently rubbing it with your fingers in a bowl filled with water. When the water becomes cloudy, drain and repeat the process until the water remains clear. Drain and set the rice aside.

2. Blend the cashews and 1 cup of the water into a smooth puree in the blender. Remove and set aside in a small bowl. Next add the ginger and garlic to the blender (there is no need to rinse the blender as the ingredients all become part of the final dish) and blend to a smooth paste. Set aside in a separate bowl.

3. Heat a 12-inch skillet over medium heat. Add the butter or oil, bay leaves, cardamom, and cinnamon and cook until fragrant, about 1 minute. Add the ginger-garlic mixture, tomato paste, and tomatoes and cook this intensely fragrant paste until it appears light golden and is reduced to half the quantity, about 6 minutes. Continue to cook, stirring occasionally, until the tomatoes cook down, about 10 minutes more.

4. Carefully add the rice and salt and gently fold the mixture, as you would fold a cake batter. Add the cashew puree and the remaining 4½ cups water and mix gently to keep the grains from breaking. Bring the rice to a boil without stirring and reduce the heat to medium-low. Cover the pot with a tight-fitting lid and cook until the water has evaporated and the rice is dry, 15 to 20 minutes.

5. Uncover and fluff the rice with a fork. Garnish with the raisins and serve warm.

RICE IN ASIAN DIETS

They are three billion people worldwide, mainly in Asia, who rely on rice daily. With 90 percent of global rice grown and eaten in Asia, it is often said that rice is life. Most people's lives are intertwined with rice; rice does not just stand for sustenance, but in almost every country in the continent this staple food is of great cultural and historical significance.

The old-fashioned American "family style" of eating is very similar to the way people eat in Malaysia. Everyone gathers around a table and takes what they want from the center. In a typical Malaysian meal, at least three or four dishes are served, with steamed rice at the heart of the meal. Diners take a little bit from each dish and eat it with the rice, mingling the flavors in their individual plate or rice bowl. Without rice, most other dishes would not be complete. This style of eating is considered essential to an overall balanced diet in which one is less inclined to crave unhealthy food between meals.

CULTIVATION

Traditional rice cultivation is a labor-intensive, arduous task, and the farmer's relationship with his paddy field remains a close one. Most of Malaysia's rice is grown in the northwestern state of Kedah, dubbed the Rice Bowl of Malaysia. If you travel there, you will be awed by the countless shades of green of the vast stretches of paddy fields. You may also spot isolated countryside homes raised on stilts and shaded by a cluster of fruit trees and coconut palms. Narrow walkways wind their way between the *kampung*, or houses, and the adjoining paddy fields.

In the early morning, it is common to see the rice farmers working the fields with water buffaloes pulling a plow in the soft mud. During the planting process, women shield their faces from the sun with huge rim hats tied with a cloth as they perform the back-breaking task of pushing clumps of sprouted rice seedlings into the water-logged earth. They do this with such precision that the planted rows almost always form a neat geometrical pattern. After about two months, the seedlings begin to show their yield, bending the long stalks heavy with rice grains forward; and slowly, over the days, they change color, turning from dark green to pale yellow and then golden brown. The greatest care needs to be taken to protect the paddy. The famers erect homemade scarecrows by lashing two sticks together and dressing them with a tattered straw hat and plastic bags that flutter furiously in the wind to frighten away the hungry birds.

During the harvest, the rice is threshed in the fields and the stalks are cut and tied in bundles. The grain is collected in sacks and taken to the local rice mill. The mountains of straw left behind in the fields are burned to add calcium and other important nutrients to the soil.

After the harvest it is time for celebrations to offer thanks. The entire village is enveloped in festivities that last for days and include feasts, folk dancing, theatre, and shadow puppet performances, all the while making offerings to the spirits of the fields.

TYPES OF RICE

There are many different types of rice used in Malaysian cuisine for different styles of dishes. For instance, white jasmine rice is used daily as a staple. Malaysian Indians prefer to use basmati or long-grain rice because it complements their curries, while Chinese cooks choose short-grain white rice to eat along with stir-fry dishes or in porridges. All these varieties can now be found in a brown rice form in modern supermarkets, which may be a preferred choice for health-conscious consumers. The rice you choose will depend on which style of recipe you're making.

WHITE VS. BROWN RICE

Grains of rice are walled in a tough husk, which must be removed in order for the rice to be consumed. The husk is removed, leaving the bran, which can be brown, reddish, or even black. At this stage the rice is 100 percent whole grain. However, most rice is processed further to remove the bran and germ, which are high in vitamins, minerals, oil, and various phytonutrients. What then remains is the starchy endosperm, the white rice enjoyed throughout the world. It has a more refined texture that enables it to absorb the flavors of sauces, curries, and gravies. Brown rice has had only the husk removed, and retains its bran

and germ. It is more nutritious with a hardy texture, but also takes longer to cook.

JASMINE RICE | This is a variety of long-grain rice grown widely throughout Southeast Asia. It is called jasmine because of its subtle floral aroma. White rice cooks lighter and faster with a relatively soft and sticky texture. Leftover jasmine rice can be used to make fried rice as the rice is not as starchy, so it will not stick to the wok.

BASMATI RICE | Hailing from the foothills of the Himalayas in northern India and Pakistan, basmati rice is a long-grain variety commonly used in Indian, Middle Eastern, and Persian cooking and is available in both white and brown forms. Basmati is known as a dry cultivar, since it doesn't need the flooding that paddy rice requires.

When cooking with brown basmati, the grains need to be soaked for at least 30 minutes before cooking. This allows the grains to absorb water and cook evenly without breaking.

Basmati rice looks long and narrow, and each grain stays firm and separated, never sticky after cooking, making it perfect for pilaf dishes such as Spiced Clarified Butter Rice with Almonds and Cranberries (page 161) and Fragrant Tomato Rice with Cashews (page 163).

Brown basmati rice is also chewier and delightfully nutty and semi-sweet. It goes well when sautéed with spices such as cinnamon, bay leaf, cardamom, cloves, turmeric, or saffron. The gentle aromas when spices and rice are sautéed together are heavenly and can calm the soul. An aromatic curry, grilled fish, or chicken curry layered with spices complements this type of rice. It contains all eight essential amino acids, folic acid, and is very low in sodium and has no cholesterol.

SHORT-GRAIN RICE | This is the kind most commonly grown in the United States. It cooks very quickly, and is often highly polished. Serve this rice steamed with the Chicken Satay on page 217 or Grilled Marinated Lamb Chops Satay on page 223.

CRACKED OR BROKEN RICE | This can be derived from any type of white rice. It is the broken grains and is used for making the rice porridge called *congee*, which is typically enjoyed for breakfast with a dash of soy, sesame oil, and sweet soy sauce and garnished with thinly cut ginger. This rice is also ideal for young children or people who are ill since it is easy to digest.

GLUTINOUS ("STICKY") RICE | Short-grained glutinous rice can come as either white, the refined variety, or black, with the bran left intact. Glutinous rice is sticky when fully cooked and the black variety, which is packed with antioxidants, takes on a burgundy color. Sticky rice is usually either steamed or made into pudding-like desserts, such as Malaysia's

famous black rice pudding, *pulut hitam*, or the Sweet Sticky Rice with Mango on page 301. The rice needs to be soaked overnight to soften before cooking, otherwise, the grains will take a long time to cook.

RED RICE OR CARGO RICE | A long-grain unpolished rice whose bran is left intact. When cooked, red rice takes on a firm and chewy texture, with a sweet, nutty taste. The rice's red color is derived from anthocyanins, the same group of phenolic compounds that lend unique red and purple colors to radicchio, purple cabbage, red onions, and many other vegetables. In Malaysian cuisine, red rice is often served with seafood curries or roasts, and cooked with ginger, fenugreek, and coconut milk. Spice Island Prawn Curry on page 182, Swordfish in Tamarind, Lemongrass, and Pineapple Curry on page 198, Tamarind Fish Curry on page 207, and Roast Chicken with Fragrant Lemongrass on page 278 are all excellent with this rice.

Whatever rice you choose to cook, remember that all rice must be washed. Washing is essential to rid the rice of the dust gathered while sitting in a box or gunny sack before being packed to the stores. The clearer the water after washing, the longer the rice will keep after it is cooked. I normally wash my rice by rinsing it three times before cooking. Uncooked rice grains should be stored in an airtight container in a cool, dry place. Stored properly, they will keep fresh for about 1 year.

FRIED RICE WITH ANCHOVIES, SHRIMP, AND CABBAGE
NASI GORENG

Back in my home country, *nasi goreng* (fried rice) is a typical dish enjoyed for breakfast or as a light lunch. Leftover rice from the previous night's dinner is stir-fried with sambal, garlic, anchovies, shrimp, and any cabbage-family vegetable that might be in the refrigerator, such as cabbage, broccoli, or other greens. Fried dried anchovies add savory flavor. I do not recommend using the canned ones since they are oily, the texture is soft, and the taste is very salty. SERVES 3 TO 4

¼ cup peanut oil

3 cloves garlic, minced

½ small red onion, thinly sliced

3 tablespoons Sambal Belachan or Sambal Ulek (page 43 and 44, or store-bought)

⅓ cup fried anchovies (see note, page 145)

8 ounces shrimp, peeled and deveined

3 eggs

2½ cups cooked jasmine or basmati rice (preferably leftovers)

1 teaspoon salt, or to taste

1 teaspoon sugar

½ small head cabbage, shredded

1. Heat a wok or a large deep skillet over medium heat for about 40 seconds. Add the oil, pouring it around the perimeter of the wok to coat the sides and bottom. When the surface shimmers slightly, add the garlic, onion, and sambal and cook, stirring constantly, until the oils separate onto the surface and the paste is aromatic, about 5 minutes.

2. Add the anchovies and shrimp and stir-fry until the shrimp is pink, about 4 minutes.

3. Break the eggs into the wok and mix well to combine with the shrimp mixture. Now add the rice, salt, and sugar and stir-fry, using the spatula to break up any clumps of rice in the wok and mixing until the ingredients are well combined, about 5 minutes.

4. Add the cabbage and continue to stir-fry until the rice is soft, the eggs are well incorporated, and the cabbage is wilted. Taste and add more salt if needed. Stir-fry for another 1 to 2 minutes, then serve immediately.

STIR-FRIED VERMICELLI WITH CHICKEN

BIHUN GORENG

Whenever I am invited to a potluck, this is one of my favorite contributions. The simple recipe has been in my family for 40 years, a dish my mother often prepared for birthday parties, Sunday brunches, and the short road trips we took to breezy seaside destinations. *Bihun goreng*, or wok-fried rice vermicelli, uses very thin rice noodles similar in texture to capellini or angel hair pasta. It is perfect for lunch too, and is gluten free. The wonderful part about creating this dish is that you may use any vegetable sitting in your refrigerator. Be sure that all of your ingredients are washed, cut, and lined up in the order in which they will be used in the wok, since this recipe is done very quickly. SERVES 4

1 package (8 ounces) dried rice vermicelli

¼ cup canola or peanut oil

2 shallots, thinly sliced

3 cloves garlic, minced

3 boneless skinless chicken thighs, cut into 1-inch pieces

½ teaspoon ground turmeric

5 tablespoons soy sauce

1 tablespoon kicap manis (sweet soy sauce; see page 16)

¼ teaspoon freshly ground black pepper

¼ head cabbage, finely chopped

1 cup bean sprouts

1. Place the noodles in a large bowl and cover with room temperature water; soak for about 30 minutes or until soft and pliable. Once the noodles feel soft, drain in a colander and set aside.

2. Heat a wok or a large deep skillet over medium heat for about 40 seconds. Add the oil, pouring it around the perimeter of the wok to coat the sides and bottom. When the surface shimmers slightly, add the shallots and stir-fry until golden and soft, about 5 minutes. Next add the garlic and continue to stir-fry until fragrant and light brown, about 1 minute.

3. Add the chicken and turmeric and stir-fry until the meat is no longer pink and thoroughly cooked, about 10 minutes.

4. Add the noodles and mix well. Add the soy sauce, kicap manis, and pepper and stir-fry, gently moving the noodles away from the center to the side and back to the center and repeating this motion until the noodles are no longer wet, about 5 minutes.

5. Add the cabbage and bean sprouts and stir-fry, pushing the noodles to the side of the wok and then back to the center, until the vegetables are slightly wilted, about 2 minutes. Dish out the noodles and serve immediately.

BLACK HOKKIEN NOODLES WITH SHRIMP AND CABBAGE

After World War II, Chinese Fujian (Hokkien) sailors created a dish in Malaysia using surplus egg noodles from the factories where they worked. These round Asian noodles were braised in dark, sweet and fragrant soy sauce and traditionally tossed with prawns, cabbage, and fish paste shaped into spheres. Rich in protein and low in fat, fish balls made of pulverized white fish were added for their sweet and chewy texture, which enhanced the taste of the noodles.

This simple dish reminds me of my late father. Whenever he came home late after work, he would bring back a packet of these hot noodles from the Chinese restaurant in our residential neighborhood of Lucky Gardens in Bangsar. The noodles were neatly wrapped in a plastic-lined old newspaper tied with bright pink raffia string. All of us children would be excited, anticipating slurping up the thick black noodles. You might be surprised to learn that after 32 years, that noodle vendor's son is now running the same stall and dishing out the same famous noodles.

When I make this dish, I use udon, fresh yellow yakisoba noodles, or sometimes dried *pancit canton* (chow mein noodles); all are readily available in most Asian supermarkets, and pancit canton is also sold in most major supermarkets (you could use spaghetti). It's authentic to use fish balls or seafood balls (found in the frozen section of Asian supermarkets and many major supermarkets), which have a chewy texture that goes well with the noodles. But it's the sauces that make this dish divine: Make sure to taste a few strands of noodles after adding the sauces to make sure the flavors are blended properly; you should have a balance of sweet and salty. If the noodles seem too dry, add more of each of the sauces in equal amounts. SERVES 4

8 ounces (1 package) dried pancit canton noodles or yakisoba, or udon

4 ounces pork belly, skin discarded, cut into small lardons

1 tablespoons canola or peanut oil

4 cloves garlic, minced

1 piece (2 inches) fresh ginger, peeled and julienned

12 ounces shrimp, peeled and deveined

8 ounces fish balls, sliced (optional)

5 tablespoons kicap manis (sweet soy sauce; see page 16)

2 tablespoons soy sauce

2 tablespoons oyster sauce

¼ cup plus 2 tablespoons chicken stock

¼ teaspoon white pepper

¼ head cabbage, finely chopped

¼ cup chopped fresh chives

1. Remove the noodles from the package. If using dried pancit canton noodles, place them in a large bowl, cover with room temperature water, and let soak for 10 minutes, or until the noodles are slightly soft. Once the noodles feel soft, drain and set aside. If using fresh yakisoba noodles, place them in a bowl and add hot tap water to cover. Use tongs to loosen and separate them. Drain in a colander and repeat rinsing the noodles in hot water until no longer oily. Set aside.

2. Heat a wok or a large deep skillet over medium heat for about 40 seconds. Add the pork belly and oil, pouring the oil around the perimeter of the wok to coat the sides and bottom. The fat will melt and you will be left with small crispy lardons. Add the garlic and ginger and stir-fry until fragrant and golden, about 2 minutes.

3. Add the shrimp and fish balls (if using) and stir-fry until the shrimp is no longer pink, about 3 minutes.

4. Add the noodles and mix well to combine with the seafood. Add the kicap manis, soy sauce, oyster sauce, ¼ cup chicken stock, and the white pepper and stir-fry by gently moving the noodles away from the center to the side and back to the center, repeating this motion for about 3 minutes.

5. Add the cabbage and chives and cook, tossing the noodles, until the vegetables are slightly wilted. Continue to stir-fry, pushing the noodles to the side of the wok and then back to the center several times, until the noodles have charred a little, about 2 minutes. Add the remaining 2 tablespoons chicken stock and mix well. Serve immediately.

VILLAGE FRIED RICE WITH CHICKEN AND SPINACH

During my travels back to Malaysia, I always look forward to visiting Perak, a provincial town located in the northwest coast, which served as a backdrop for the 1999 movie *Anna and the King.* Here, the busiest eateries by far are the humble mom-and-pop shops. Come midday, the air is laden with aromas of *nasi goreng* (fried rice). Nasi goreng is also enjoyed for breakfast, lunch, and dinner and definitely the dish for grab-and-go eating for most Malaysians. At home, I cook fried rice when there's leftover rice in the refrigerator and I feel pressed for time. It is a great way to use up whatever fresh vegetables are still in the bin, such as bok choy, carrots, mushrooms, green peppers, or any leafy greens. SERVES 4

¼ cup peanut oil

4 shallots, thinly sliced

3 cloves garlic, minced

3 fresh green bird's-eye chilies, chopped

1 pound boneless skinless chicken thighs, cut into ½-inch pieces

4 cups cooked jasmine rice (preferably leftover)

¼ cup soy sauce, or to taste

¼ cup kicap manis (sweet soy sauce; see page 16)

2 tablespoons oyster sauce

2 eggs, beaten

2 cups fresh baby spinach leaves

Fresh cilantro leaves, for garnish

1. Heat a wok or a large deep skillet over medium heat for about 40 seconds. Add the oil, pouring it around the perimeter of the wok to coat the sides and bottom. When the surface shimmers slightly, add the shallots and stir-fry until light golden, about 3 minutes. Add the garlic and chilies and continue to stir-fry, moving the ingredients away from the center to the side and back to the center, until the mixture is fragrant and the garlic is golden, about 5 minutes.

2. Add the chicken and stir-fry until the chicken is cooked thorough and no longer pink, about 10 minutes.

3. Add the rice, soy sauce, kicap manis, and oyster sauce and stir, using the spatula to break up any clumps of rice, until the ingredients are well combined. Cook, tossing the rice, for about 5 minutes more.

4. Move the rice to the side of the wok and add the beaten eggs to the other side. Immediately cover the eggs with the rice and allow the eggs to set and cook, undisturbed, for about 2 minutes. Raise the heat to medium-high and gently mix the rice and eggs. Add more soy sauce if needed, then continue to stir-fry, moving the rice back and forth, for another 2 minutes.

5. Toss in the spinach and stir-fry until the leaves are wilted and thoroughly mixed in with the rice, about 4 minutes. Garnish with the cilantro and serve immediately.

FRIED RICE WITH SHRIMP, BACON, AND EGGS

This dish is my saving grace on a busy and cold rainy winter day because it can be made quickly and is a wonderful way to use leftover rice. It is also the first dish I taught my sons to cook on their own as they are always hungry. Bacon goes beautifully with the more traditional ingredients of shrimp, ground pork, broccoli, and eggs; and the combination of salty, crispy bacon and rice makes it the ultimate comfort food. At home I use a wok to stir-fry as its concave structure provides a perfect heat consistency, and a well-used wok lends that smoky flavor necessary for fried rice. Start your cooking on medium heat until all the ingredients are cooked, then increase the heat to high just to finish off the dish with a smoky flavor. Sometimes, after the rice is cooked, I let it sit in the wok for 5 minutes on low heat to give it a crispy layer underneath, which is my children's favorite part. SERVES 4

6 ounces slab bacon, cut into ½-inch-thick pieces

1 small red onion, thinly sliced

3 cloves garlic, minced

6 ounces ground pork

1 teaspoon ground turmeric

½ teaspoon ground white pepper

½ teaspoon crushed red chili flakes

8 ounces medium shrimp, peeled and deveined

½ head broccoli, cut into small florets (about 2 cups)

½ cup frozen green peas, thawed

3 cups cooked jasmine rice

3 eggs, beaten

¼ cup fish sauce, or to taste

1. Heat a wok over medium heat until the surface is very hot. Add the bacon and fry until much of the bacon fat is rendered and the bacon is crisp, 7 to 10 minutes.

2. Add the onion and garlic and stir-fry until the onion is wilted and the garlic is golden, about 5 minutes.

3. Add the pork, turmeric, white pepper, and chili flakes and stir-fry until the pork is no longer pink, about 5 minutes.

4. Add the shrimp, broccoli, and peas and continue to stir-fry until the shrimp are pink and cooked through, about 5 minutes.

5. Add the cooked rice, eggs, and fish sauce. Reduce the heat to medium-low while you mix the ingredients; continue to stir-fry, breaking the clumps of rice in the wok, until the ingredients are well combined, about 5 minutes.

6. Increase the heat to high and stir-fry constantly for about 3 minutes. Taste and add more fish sauce if needed. Stir-fry for about 1 minute more, then serve immediately.

SEAFOOD

When I was growing up, seafood was so significant. My mother would make simple, delicious fish dishes. Sometimes, she would dust wild tilapia with delicate ground turmeric, salt, and pepper and pan-fry the fish in coconut oil until crispy and golden. Other times, she simmered wild pompano in fresh coconut milk with ripe tomatoes and aromatics, or wok-fried large prawns with bits of coconut flakes.

In the summer, calamari straight from the fishmonger was cleaned and then tossed into a hot wok with shallots, garlic, lemongrass, and a dollop of sambal, and eaten with a plate of piping hot rice and a side of green mango salad. These simple home-style dishes would take me to food paradise.

Malaysian cooks are brilliant with cooking fish and shellfish because seafood is so abundant year-round. With the South China Sea to the east and the Indian Ocean on the west, fish and shellfish are crucial sources of protein in our diet. Malaysia's long eastern coast is dotted with rustic fishing villages and tall palm trees. Fisherman in colorful prahu boats leave in the early evenings, carrying with them grilled squid stuffed with coconut rice to take to sea, and return at sunrise with their ocean bounties. From their jetties, this fresh seafood finds its way to markets nearby.

Some of the favorite fish and shellfish from this region are golden pompano, mackerel, tilapia, red snapper, grouper, tuna, shrimp, squid, scallop, clams, and crabs. Often fish, prawns, and squid are also ground into a paste to form fish balls, which are used in soups and stir-fry dishes.

In this chapter, I use the term prawns and shrimp interchangeably, and in the recipes, when "prawns or shrimp" are called for, I suggest you use the medium size ones unless otherwise noted. While Americans tend to prefer boneless fish fillets, cooks in many parts of the world prefer to cook a whole fish, or cut it cross-wise into thick bone-in steaks. They use the fish bones too, since bones contain collagen and gelatin to lend flavor and richness to the dish. Malaysian cuisine, influenced as it is by India, China, and Portugal, has developed many ways to cook fish, including simmering, braising, stir-frying, pan-frying, and grilling.

The local fish found in American markets, e.g., sole, flounder, halibut, cod, and salmon, can easily be substituted, since it is the cooking techniques and fresh sauces, aromatic herbs, and spices that create the vibrant and exceptional flavors.

Fish served with spiced sauce or sambal, such as Crispy Cod in Sweet-and-Sour Sauce (page 196) and Pineapple Sambal Prawns (page 204), is common among the Chinese and Nyonya cultures. Adding coconut milk results in a creamier sauce, mellows out the spices, and binds the sharpness of chilies, as in the classic Malay Tilapia Baked in Coconut Sambal (page 189) and Tilapia Simmered in Creamy Tomato Sauce (page 193). On the other hand, a sambal with greater proportions of vinegar or coconut oil can be used as a flavorful marinade for seafood, as in Broiled Black Cod Laksa (page 197) and Sweet and Spicy Prawn Sambal Tumis (page 209) which put a modern twist on traditional Malay cooking. When oil and vinegar take a back seat to spices

you have a wet spice rub, excellent for grilling, broiling, or baking for a smoky Indian style of flavoring—as in Tandoori Broiled Salmon (page 186) and Baked Fish with Fennel, Turmeric, and Olive Oil (page 195). Spice Island Prawn Curry (page 182) uses a variety of spices as well, but in a more complex manner, along with island nuts and citrus which gives it an Indian Muslim character.

Tamarind, the sour fruit from a local tree, is often used by local cooks to bring sourness to a dish instead of lemon. The traditional Malaysian aromatics of lemongrass, makrut lime leaves, ginger, shallots, curry leaves, and fresh mint enhance the natural sweetness of fish and shellfish; while turmeric, coriander, fenugreek, and cumin contribute their savory or fragrant flavors.

What makes Malaysian food so characteristic is not only the ingredients but also the way that you cook, developing and layering flavors as you cook. By applying these layers of flavor to your own local seafood, you may enjoy an endless variety of authentic dishes presented in a creative and delicious way.

MALAYSIAN CHILI PRAWNS

Just after sunset in Kuala Lumpur, the locals and tourists sit at curbside tables indulging in a large platter of chili prawns served right from the blazing wok. The scene is pleasantly noisy with shouted food orders, but no one seems to mind because this is one of Malaysia's most popular dishes. It is filled with layers of flavor using ingredients from the cupboards of Chinese, Indian, and Malay cultures. It's best to use a wok for this recipe since the hot wok will create a marvelous caramelized crust on the surface of the prawns. Chili prawns are traditionally served with Chinese-style steamed buns, but a French baguette is a fantastic substitute. In my home, we cannot resist dipping bread into the sauce, making a delicious mess. Instead of prawns, you could also use crabs in their shell, as they do in Singapore; whichever you choose, the key is the delightfully luscious creamy chili sauce. SERVES 4

3 tablespoons store-bought bottled chili sauce

¼ cup ketchup

1½ tablespoons soy sauce

1½ teaspoons sesame oil

5 tablespoons peanut or canola oil

4 garlic cloves, minced

1 piece (2 inches) fresh ginger, peeled and julienned

3 to 4 fresh red chilies, finely chopped

½ cup (from 3 sprigs) curry leaf

1 pound tiger prawns or large shrimp, peeled and deveined

½ cup low-sodium chicken broth

1 egg, lightly beaten

1 teaspoon sesame seeds

1. Combine the chili sauce, ketchup, soy sauce, and sesame oil in a bowl.

2. Heat a wok or a large deep skillet over medium heat for about 40 seconds. Add the oil, pouring it around the perimeter of the wok to coat the sides and bottom. When the surface shimmers slightly, add the garlic, ginger, chilies, and curry leaves and stir-fry until fragrant and the garlic is golden in color, about 5 minutes.

3. Add the sauce mixture to the wok and mix well. Allow the sauce to simmer for about 2 minutes.

4. Add the prawns and stir-fry over high heat, pressing the prawns against the hot wok until they are seared, about 1 minute. Pour in the broth, mix well, and allow the prawns to cook in the broth for about 2 minutes.

5. Add the egg. Mix and cook until the sauce thickens, about 1 minute more. Remove from the heat. Garnish with the sesame seeds and serve immediately.

SPICE ISLAND PRAWN CURRY

This recipe is a celebration of the street vendors of Penang, known as the Spice Island and Malaysia's legendary food capital. Penang's unique culinary journey threads through more than one hundred years of British colonial rule, during which it hosted spice traders from all over the world. This curry originated with the Nasi Kandar peddlers, the early Tamil Muslim settlers who sold their curries and rice from bamboo containers balanced on a pole slung across their shoulders.

The prawns are seared in a hot wok with curry leaves to provide an exceptional aroma of fresh herbs, then they are left to slowly simmer in a delicious curry sauce of coconut milk mixed with a spice paste of macadamia nuts, ginger, jalapeño, and a combination of spice seeds. If you wish to do some cooking in advance, you can cook the spice paste and then store it in the refrigerator until you are ready to cook the prawns. This sauce pairs well with other seafood; replace the prawns with lobster, crab, clams, or mussels if you wish. Making a trip to an Indian grocery store for the curry leaves is worth the effort. SERVES 6

SPICE PASTE

- ½ small red onion, chopped
- 4 cloves garlic, peeled and left whole
- 1 piece (2 inches) fresh ginger, peeled and chopped
- 4 fresh red jalapeño chilies, chopped
- 4 candlenuts or macadamia nuts, smashed
- 1 teaspoon chili powder
- ½ teaspoon fennel seeds
- ½ teaspoon cumin seeds
- ½ teaspoon mustard seeds
- ½ teaspoon coriander seeds
- ½ teaspoon ground turmeric

PRAWNS

- 1 pound tiger prawns or large shrimp, shelled and deveined
- Juice of 1 lime

Pinch of salt
- 6 tablespoons peanut oil
- Leaves from 3 sprigs curry leaf
- 2 Roma tomatoes, quartered
- 1¾ cups coconut milk
- 1 cup water
- 2 to 3 tablespoons liquid palm sugar (see pages 315–316)
- 1 to 2 teaspoons salt, or to taste

1. Make the spice paste: Combine all the ingredients in a food processor and blend to a smooth paste, adding just a little water (about ¼ cup) to facilitate the blending. Set the spice paste aside.

2. Meanwhile, sprinkle the prawns with the lime juice and salt and set aside to marinate for 15 minutes.

3. Heat 2 tablespoons of the oil in a wok or saucepan over high heat. Add the curry leaves and prawns and sear for about 30 seconds, until the prawns are coated with the fragrant curry leaf oil but not cooked. Remove the prawns and curry leaves, and set them aside.

4. Wipe the wok clean (it's not necessary to wash it) and heat over medium heat. Add the remaining 4 tablespoons oil and then the spice paste. Cook, stirring, until the spice paste is fragrant and the oils have separated onto the top, about 15 minutes.

5. Add the tomatoes, coconut milk, water, palm sugar, and salt and mix well. Reduce the heat to medium-low and let the curry simmer, stirring occasionally to prevent the coconut milk from burning, until fragrant and the oils have separated again, about 15 minutes.

6. Add the prawns and curry leaves and cook for another 2 to 3 minutes, until the prawns are pink and cooked through. Serve warm.

MALAYSIAN COCONUT-BUTTER PRAWNS

This dish, popular at Kuala Lumpur's al fresco restaurants, is a recent invention that blends the Chinese method of cooking rapidly in a wok with the Indian pantry ingredients of coconut, curry leaves, and chilies. You will find unsweetened grated coconut in the frozen section of any Asian market, or dried coconut flakes in the baking section of most grocery and health-food stores. Once the coconut is fried until golden, you can store it in an airtight container in the refrigerator for up to 3 months, or freeze it for up to a year. It is wonderful to have at hand and can be used in place of panko or bread crumbs to lend a tropical coconut flavor to breaded and fried foods. SERVES 4

6 tablespoons unsweetened grated coconut

2 tablespoons peanut oil

2 tablespoons butter

1 egg yolk, beaten

6 fresh green bird's-eye chilies, chopped

4 cloves garlic, minced

Leaves from 3 sprigs curry leaf

1 pound large or jumbo tiger prawns or shrimp, peeled and deveined

2 tablespoons Chinese rice cooking wine

1 tablespoon soy sauce

1 teaspoon sugar

Pinch of salt

1. Heat a dry wok over medium-high heat. Add the grated coconut and cook, stirring constantly to prevent burning, until golden, 2 to 3 minutes. Transfer to a small bowl and set aside.

2. Wipe the wok clean and return to medium heat. Add the oil and butter. When the butter sizzles, immediately add the beaten egg and, using a metal spatula, swirl the eggs until they turn light golden brown, about 45 seconds. Add the chilies, garlic, and curry leaves. Stir-fry until the leaves turn dark green and fragrant, the garlic is golden, and the chilies have softened, about 3 minutes. The egg will continue to cook and become crispy.

3. Add the prawns, rice wine, soy sauce, sugar, and salt and continue to stir-fry until well combined. Raise the heat to high, add the coconut, and continue to stir-fry until the prawns are fully cooked, about 2 minutes. Serve immediately.

PRAWN MASALA IN BASIL CREAM SAUCE

One evening, having run out of curry leaves, I rushed to an Asian store desperate to get my hands on some. To my dismay, the last pack of leaves looked hopelessly shriveled and lacked that peppery aroma. But the fresh basil next to it brimmed with aroma and I could not resist the temptation to bring some home. I had planned for a quick dinner with sautéed shrimp and tomatoes. The licorice-like aroma of the basil turned out to be a great addition to the sweetness of the browned onions and the complexity of the spices. This makes a wonderful meal served with brown basmati rice. SERVES 4

¼ cup peanut oil

½ teaspoon cumin seeds

1 small red onion, minced

2 Roma tomatoes, quartered

2 garlic cloves, minced

1 teaspoon chili powder or Sambal Ulek (page 44 or store-bought)

½ teaspoon ground turmeric

1 pound large prawns or shrimp, peeled and deveined

1 cup fresh basil leaves

1 to 2 teaspoons salt, to taste

¼ cup cream

1. Heat a large sauté pan over medium heat for about 40 seconds, then add the oil. When the surface shimmers slightly, add the cumin seeds and cook for about 10 seconds, until the seeds sizzle in the hot oil. Add the onion and cook until browned, about 10 minutes.

2. Stir in the tomatoes, garlic, chili powder, and turmeric and cook until the tomatoes are soft and the pot is fragrant, about 12 minutes.

3. Add the prawns and basil, massaging the basil leaves between your hands to release their aroma as you add them to the pan. Cook until the oils separate onto the surface and the prawns are pink, about 3 minutes. Season with salt.

4. Mix in the cream and then remove from the heat and serve warm.

TANDOORI BROILED SALMON

While I love tandoori—a style of cooking that uses the intense heat of a clay oven (*tandoor*) to cook marinated meat—I have a few problems with many restaurant versions. First, the dishes are often tinted with red food coloring as a substitute for paprika, and second, they often include low-quality spice blends that lack flavor and aroma. With my family's spice combination, a freshly made masala featuring turmeric, cumin, paprika, and a fresh paste of ginger, garlic, and cilantro, you will be rewarded as if you had a large tandoor oven in your backyard. The ginger-garlic-cilantro paste helps tenderize the fish. The result is a broiled salmon that is succulent, perfectly charred on the outside, and moist and flaky on the inside with an enticing citrus aroma. This delicious tandoori is best enjoyed with a yogurt raita (page 98) and warm buttered naan. SERVES 4

1 large fillet of salmon (about 20 ounces), or 2 salmon steaks (10 ounces each)

2 tablespoons Ginger, Garlic, and Cilantro Paste (page 53)

2 teaspoons paprika

1 teaspoon ground cumin

1 teaspoon ground turmeric

½ to 1 teaspoon pure chili powder or cayenne, to taste

Juice of 1 lime, plus lime wedges for serving

5 tablespoons extra-virgin olive oil

2 teaspoons salt, or to taste

1. Place the salmon on a baking sheet. In a small bowl, mix together the ginger-garlic paste, paprika, cumin, turmeric, chili powder, lime juice, oil, and salt, and then rub the combined ingredients all over the salmon. Cover and allow the fish to marinate in the refrigerator for 4 hours, or preferably overnight.

2. Preheat the oven to 400°F. Bake the fish for about 10 minutes. Heat the broiler and broil the fish directly under the broiler until golden brown, about 2 minutes. Serve immediately with lime wedges.

TILAPIA BAKED IN COCONUT SAMBAL

Baking fish in banana leaves (or parchment paper) keeps the fish moist and seals in the flavors. This cooking technique is popular among the Nyonya community of Malacca, an inter-marriage between Chinese and Malay cultures. You can substitute tilapia with black ling cod if you'd like. The recipe is best as part of a full Malaysian meal, served with Fragrant Coconut Rice (page 160) or Green Mango in Lemon-Basil Dressing (page 112). SERVES 4

8 cloves garlic, peeled and left whole

¼ cup Sambal Ulek (page 44 or store-bought)

2 candlenuts or macadamia nuts

6 tablespoons peanut oil

1¼ cups coconut milk

2 tablespoons fish sauce, or to taste

¼ cup liquid palm sugar (see pages 315–316), or to taste

4 makrut lime leaves, thinly sliced

4 tilapia (or any white fish) steaks (about 8 ounces each), skinned and boned

Banana leaves (or parchment paper)

1. Preheat the oven to 400°F. Prepare the spice paste by grinding the garlic, sambal, and candlenuts in a mini food processor until very smooth, adding a little water if needed to keep the blades moving.

2. Heat the oil in a skillet over medium heat. Add the spice paste and cook, stirring frequently, until the oil separates onto the surface, about 10 minutes.

3. Add 1 cup of the coconut milk, the fish sauce, palm sugar, and lime leaves, and continue to cook, stirring, until the oils separate onto the surface again, about 10 minutes more.

Taste and add more palm sugar if you like your sambal sweet, or more fish sauce if you prefer it salty. Turn off the heat and set aside.

4. Cut each banana leaf large enough to enclose the fish steaks. Gently heat each leaf by holding it over the flame of your burner for a few seconds just to warm it up; this will prevent the leaf from tearing when you use it as a wrapper. (Or you can use parchment paper instead.)

5. Place each piece of fish in the center of a banana leaf. First drizzle the coconut mixture generously over the fish, and then the drizzle the remaining coconut milk on top, using about 1 tablespoon per portion. To create a pouch to enclose the fish, first fold the sides of the leaf to the center of the fish so that they overlap, then bring the top and bottom to the center; lift and tuck one end of a top flap into the pocket of the other to seal. Be careful not to wrap it too tightly or the filling will squeeze out. If needed, secure the leaf with a toothpick. Repeat until all the fish are wrapped.

6. Place the fish parcels on a baking sheet and bake for about 25 minutes. Serve immediately, but be cautious: Hot steam will release when you open the leaves.

MAKRUT LIME LEAVES

The makrut lime, also called *limau purut* ("stomach lime") in Malaysia, is unique among the citrus family in that the fruit and juice are rarely eaten; instead, the leaves are used throughout Southeast Asia due to their beautiful bouquet of floral lime-lemon aroma. The British originally called them *kaffir* limes, but because today that word is widely seen as offensive, I prefer the Thai name, *makrut*. However, you still might find them labeled any number of ways in Asian markets where they are sold.

Although the trees are indigenous to Southeast Asia, they are now being cultivated widely, including in Hawaii. The leaves are forest green in color, have a unique double shape that looks like two leaves joined end to end with a mid-rib through the middle. In Malaysia, the trees are planted abundantly in most home gardens and the leaves are used almost daily in cooking.

The leaves may be used whole, torn into smaller pieces, or thinly slivered to impart their lemony aroma to broth, stews, stir-fry dishes, curries, and unique and refreshing salads. To slice them into slivers, remove the thick mid-rib, stack the leaves together, roll them up tightly, and then slice crosswise with a sharp knife.

Makrut lime leaves complement dishes that contain coconut cream, fresh basil, chilies, cilantro, cumin, lemongrass, galangal, ginger, garlic, shallots, mint, tamarind, or turmeric. Dark green, knobby, and wrinkled, the makrut lime fruit itself is rarely used in cooking since it does not contain much juice; but the zest, containing strong aromatic oils, is often used to flavor desserts. It is also used as an effective cleanser and added as a natural deodorizer to shampoos.

SALMON IN CREAMY TIKKA MASALA

Tikka masala is a gorgeous curry blend of black mustard seeds and nutty fenugreek seeds with a tomato sauce enriched with cream. Most tikka dishes you find in restaurants use leftover tandoori chicken, but I like to use fish. You can use almost any fish, such as swordfish, halibut, cod, or snapper, as long as it is a good-sized steak. The key to tikka is the sauce. There are no hard and fast rules; if you love a creamier dish, finish it off with additional butter. You can greatly speed things up by making the tikka masala mixture, without the cream, ahead of time and keeping it in your freezer. You can also use this mixture as a rub on seafood or other meats prior to grilling. SERVES 4

3 tablespoons coconut oil

1 teaspoon black mustard seeds

1 teaspoon cumin seeds

1 teaspoon fenugreek seeds

1 onion, minced

6 cloves garlic, thinly sliced

1 piece (1 inch) fresh ginger, peeled and thinly sliced

3 Roma tomatoes, chopped

1 tablespoon tomato paste

1 tablespoon chili powder or cayenne

½ teaspoon ground turmeric

1 teaspoon salt, or to taste

½ cup cream

1½ pounds bone-in salmon steaks, cut in half at the bone

1. Heat the oil in a medium saucepan over medium heat. Add the mustard seeds and cover with a splatter screen, or partially cover with a lid, to keep the mustard seeds from popping out of the pan. Cook until you hear the seeds pop, about 30 seconds. Add the cumin seeds and fenugreek seeds and stir and cook, uncovered, until the cumin seeds are fragrant, about 30 seconds more. Next add the onion, garlic, and ginger and cook, stirring, until the onions are soft and lightly browned, about 10 minutes.

2. Add the tomatoes, tomato paste, chili powder, turmeric, and salt. Cook, stirring, until the tomatoes break down, about 4 minutes. Add a little water to the pan if necessary to prevent the spices from sticking. Taste and add more salt if needed. Remove from the heat and allow the mixture to cool for about 2 minutes before blending.

3. Transfer the mixture to a blender, add the cream, and blend to a smooth puree.

4. Return the mixture to the same pan, and bring to a soft boil, adding a little water if the mixture is too thick. Lower the heat, gently add the fish, cover, and cook until the fish is cooked through, about 10 minutes. The fish should easily flake when ready. Serve warm.

TILAPIA SIMMERED IN CREAMY TOMATO SAUCE

TILAPIA MASAK MERAH

Masak merah means "red sauce," but for me, it also means the kind of soul-warming dish that I hunger for after trudging home from work on a frigid winter day. To make this classic Malay dish, you might like to embrace the Malaysian approach to preparation in the kitchen. Keep some peeled garlic and shallots ready in an airtight container in the refrigerator, coconut milk in the pantry, dry spices like turmeric and coriander in the cabinet, a few fresh tomatoes on hand, and fillets of tilapia in the freezer. With all ingredients at the ready, it is a simple a matter to pull it all together into something flavorsome. The secret to a good masak merah is in the spice paste made of dried chilies, which lend a deep reddish hue and depth of flavor you would not obtain from using fresh red chilies. However, it is important that the chilies are completely softened in boiling hot water before blending, otherwise the dish will have a raw aftertaste. I also use good-quality fish stock and coconut milk, which mellow out the tartness in the tomatoes. SERVES 4

8 shallots, minced

4 cloves garlic, minced

4 candlenuts or macadamia nuts

4 dried red chilies de arbol, soaked in boiling water until soft and drained

1 cup water

¼ cup peanut or coconut oil

1 teaspoon ground turmeric

1 to 2 teaspoons ground coriander

1½ cups fish stock

2 tomatoes, quartered

1½ cups coconut milk

Pinch of salt, or to taste

Pinch of freshly ground black pepper

1 pound tilapia fillets, cut into 4-inch pieces

1. Prepare a spice paste by blending the shallots, garlic, candlenuts, chilies, and water in a blender until very smooth.

2. Heat the oil in a saucepan over medium heat. Add the spice paste and cook until fragrant and the oil has separated onto the surface, about 10 minutes.

3. Add the turmeric and coriander and mix until the dry spices are well incorporated into the mixture. Add the stock and tomatoes. Simmer until the tomatoes are soft, about 5 minutes.

4. Add the coconut milk and bring it to a boil. Season with salt and pepper. Add the fish, give it a gentle stir, and reduce the heat to low. Simmer until the oils have separated onto the surface and the fish is cooked through, about 4 minutes. Serve warm.

BAKED FISH WITH FENNEL, TURMERIC, AND OLIVE OIL

This simple baked fish is my standby weeknight dish that quickly goes from the oven to the table. I created it to teach my sons Malaysian home cooking, as it is a recipe that could be easily remembered when they were studying away from home.

Pompano fish tastes pleasantly sweet, and when marinated with ground fennel, turmeric, salt, and olive oil becomes magically caramelized. The olive oil is the key to sealing in the spices, making the fish moist and tender to the bones. While the fish is baking, I cook a pot of brown rice and stir-fry some bok choy with bacon (page 135) or Asian greens (page 131). Everything is finished at the same time and a complete home-cooked dinner is set on the table to enjoy. SERVES 4

2 pounds pompano fish, cut into 2-inch pieces

Juice of 1 lime

1 teaspoon ground turmeric

1 teaspoon chili powder

1 teaspoon ground fennel

1 teaspoon ground coriander

1 teaspoon garlic powder

2½ teaspoons salt, or to taste

¼ cup extra-virgin olive oil

1. Preheat the oven to 400°F.

2. Place the fish in a large bowl. Add the lime juice and rub it all over the fish. Allow to sit for 5 minutes to give the fish a lovely citrus aroma. Rinse the fish and pat dry with a paper towel so that the lime won't overpower the fish.

3. Place the fish on a foil-lined baking sheet. Sprinkle the turmeric over the fish followed by, one at a time, the chili powder, fennel, coriander, garlic powder, and salt. Rub each fish steak thoroughly with the ground spice on both sides. Pour the oil over the fish, making sure each steak is well coated.

4. Bake the fish for about 20 minutes. It should flake easily when pulled with a fork and look evenly brown. Transfer the fish to a serving plate and serve hot.

Baked Fish with Fennel, Turmeric, and Olive Oil served with Sweet Potatoes and Baby Spinach Simmered in Coconut Milk (page 141), rice, and Sambal Ulek (page 44)

CRISPY COD IN SWEET-AND-SOUR SAUCE

Although the recipe includes a sweet-and-sour sauce, this Malaysian dish is different than sweet-and-sour fish served at Chinese-American restaurants. First, the fish is coated with turmeric and salt to provide a savory base. Then a lovely tropical combination of Sriracha, rice vinegar, palm sugar, fish sauce, ginger, and tomatoes yields a more Southeast Asian style of sweet, sour, salty, and spicy (without the use of MSG or cherry-red food coloring). I like using rice flour or potato starch instead of cornstarch for frying: The fish turns out crisper and the sauce does not end up as gooey as when using cornstarch. And you will also notice that your leftovers will not congeal when taken out of the refrigerator the next day. Enjoy this dish with some stir-fried greens and a plate of brown rice. SERVES 4

SWEET-AND-SOUR SAUCE

- ½ cup unsalted fish stock
- 3 tablespoons ketchup
- 2 tablespoons rice vinegar
- 3 tablespoons liquid palm sugar (see pages 315–316) or brown sugar
- 1 tablespoon Sriracha sauce
- 2 to 3 tablespoons fish sauce, to taste

- 8 pieces fresh cod fish fillet (5 to 6 ounces each)
- 1 teaspoon salt
- ½ teaspoon ground turmeric
- ½ cup rice flour or potato starch
  Vegetable or peanut oil, for frying
- 4 cloves garlic, minced
- 1 piece (1 inch) fresh ginger, peeled and finely sliced
- 1 small white onion, thinly sliced
- 2 Roma tomatoes, quartered
- 1 red bell pepper, diced
- 1 tablespoon potato starch or cornstarch mixed with 3 tablespoons water

- 3 green onions (white and green parts), thinly sliced

1. Prepare the sauce: Combine the stock, ketchup, rice vinegar, palm sugar, Sriracha, and 2 tablespoons fish sauce in a bowl; mix well to combine. Set aside.

2. Rinse the fish and pat dry with a paper towel. Season with the salt and turmeric, then coat the fish evenly with the rice flour or potato starch.

3. Heat about 2 inches of oil in a medium skillet over medium-high heat. To check if the oil is hot enough, drop in a 1-inch cube of white bread. The bread should brown in about 40 seconds.

4. Gently place the coated fish into the hot oil and fry, turning once, until medium golden brown in color on both sides and crispy, about 10 minutes total. Remove and set aside on a serving plate.

5. Carefully discard most of the hot oil, leaving about ¼ cup in the skillet. Reduce the heat to medium and add the garlic, ginger, and onion and stir-fry until golden and fragrant, about 5 minutes.

6. Add the tomato and bell pepper and stir well to combine. Add the sweet-and-sour sauce, reduce the heat to low, and simmer until the tomatoes are soft, about 5 minutes. Taste and add more fish sauce if needed. Stir in the potato starch mixture and cook until the sauce thickens, about 1 minute. Pour the sauce over the fish on the serving plate. Garnish with the green onions and serve hot.

BROILED BLACK COD LAKSA

If you have laksa spice paste in the refrigerator, this recipe is incredibly easy, yet so good that nobody will believe it took less than 10 minutes to prepare! The delicateness of black cod is enhanced by the superb blend of laksa spice paste, which adds a nuance of citrusy lemongrass, galangal, and shallots along with a hint of savory turmeric. Brushing olive oil over the spice paste will prevent it from burning and will allow the flavors to go right through to the bone. SERVES 4

½ cup Laksa Spice Paste (page 61)

3 tablespoons coconut oil or extra-virgin olive oil

1 teaspoon fish sauce, or to taste

2 to 3 black cod steaks (8 to 10 ounces each)

1 to 2 tablespoons extra-virgin olive oil

Leaves from 3 sprigs fresh basil, chopped

1. Preheat the broiler. Mix the spice paste, oil, and fish sauce in a small bowl. Taste and add more fish sauce if the paste is not salty enough.

2. Place the fish steaks on a foil-lined baking sheet. Spread the laksa mixture on both sides of the steaks to allow it to penetrate the fish. Lightly coat the spice paste with oil.

3. Broil the fish (do not turn), until opaque in center, about 6 minutes. Transfer to serving plates and sprinkle with the basil.

SWORDFISH IN TAMARIND, LEMONGRASS, AND PINEAPPLE CURRY

ASAM PEDAS

Whenever the tamarind trees in our yard in Malaysia began to fruit, those few days were called *asam pedas* days. *Asam* ("sour") *pedas* ("hot") is a delightful piquant fish stew flavored with fresh lemongrass, juicy pineapples, and tamarind. We mostly used black pomfret or golden pompano, purchased fresh from the fish seller who went from street to street in the mornings, and we would cook the fish within an hour or two. In this version, I use swordfish, which is both tasty and easy to find. However, if you can visit an Asian seafood market, do yourself a favor and purchase a golden pompano instead as it makes a perfect match.

There are geographical variations in the way asam pedas is prepared. Nyonya cooks rely heavily on makrut lime leaves, galangal, ginger, and chilies for the aromatic foundation paste. My family loved to use spices like turmeric paired with candlenuts, lemongrass, tamarind, pineapples, and chilies. All the flavors work in harmony to bring forth a delicious tangy hot and sweet stew. To experience an authentic taste of asam pedas, I recommend you use tamarind water made from fresh tamarind pulp, commonly sold in block form or as concentrated liquid paste at Asian and Mexican supermarkets. SERVES 4

¼ cup Sambal Ulek (page 44 or store-bought)

5 whole candlenuts or macadamia nuts

1 piece (1 inch) unpeeled fresh turmeric, or ½ teaspoon ground turmeric

2 teaspoons shrimp paste

5 shallots, peeled and left whole

3 cloves garlic, peeled and left whole

1 stalk lemongrass, outer layers discarded, thinly sliced

½ cup water

6 tablespoons peanut oil

1 cup Tamarind Water (page 54) mixed with 1½ cups water

2 Roma tomatoes, cut into wedges

1 cup fresh pineapple chunks

5 makrut lime leaves, stemmed (optional)

2 to 3 teaspoons liquid palm sugar (see pages 315–316), to taste

1 teaspoon salt, or to taste

2 swordfish steaks (10 to 12 ounces each), trimmed and cleaned

6 sprigs Vietnamese mint (rau ram), whole sprigs tied into a knot (optional)

1. To make the spice paste: Combine the sambal, candlenuts, turmeric, shrimp paste, shallots, garlic, lemongrass, and water in a blender and blend to a smooth paste. Make

sure the paste is very smooth, otherwise the sauce will be filled with stringy lemongrass threads. The paste should be creamy and orange in color.

2. Heat the oil in a medium saucepan over medium heat. Add the spice paste and cook, stirring occasionally, until most of the moisture has evaporated, the paste is fragrant, and the oils have separated onto the surface, about 10 minutes.

3. Add the tamarind water, tomatoes, pineapple, lime leaves, 2 teaspoons palm sugar, and salt and mix well. Bring to a boil and then reduce the heat and simmer gently for about 10 minutes.

4. Add the fish and Vietnamese mint leaves (if using), and cook until the fish is opaque and cooked through, about 10 minutes. Taste and add more salt or palm sugar if necessary. Serve immediately.

PENANG OYSTER OMELET

OR CHIEN

Oyster omelet, locally known as *or chien*, is a favorite hawker food in Penang. Delicious oysters are hidden within the eggs, which are seasoned with soy sauce, kicap manis, and sesame oil, so each bite of the omelet is complex with layers of flavors. A light cornstarch mixture is poured into the skillet before the oysters, which creates a slight gooey layer that complements the eggs. For this recipe you can use fresh shucked oysters or plump oysters from a jar. SERVES 4

2 cups shucked fresh oysters or jarred or canned oysters, drained

¼ cup flour, for cleaning the jarred or canned oysters

4 eggs, beaten

1½ tablespoons soy sauce

½ teaspoon kicap manis (sweet soy sauce; see page 16)

1 teaspoon sesame oil

¼ teaspoon ground white pepper

2 tablespoons peanut oil

3 cloves garlic, minced

2 tablespoons cornstarch mixed with 1 cup water

3 green onions (white and green parts), chopped

1. Put the oysters in a large bowl, then add the flour and 2 cups water. Using your hands, gently mix the oysters in the flour mixture. The flour mixture will help get rid of any soil and sand in the oysters. Transfer the oysters to a colander and rinse thoroughly under cold running water until all the flour is washed off. Set the oysters aside.

2. In a medium bowl, combine the eggs, soy sauce, kicap manis, sesame oil, and pepper. Mix well.

3. Heat the oil in a large skillet over medium heat. When the oil is hot, add the garlic and cook, stirring, until golden brown and fragrant, about 30 seconds. Pour the cornstarch mixture into the pan. Allow the mixture to set until it appears translucent and bubbly, about 1 minute.

4. Place the oysters and green onions evenly over the mixture. Pour half the beaten egg mixture over the oysters. Cook until the eggs are set on the bottom and appear light brown when lifted with a spoon, about 5 minutes.

5. Pour in the remaining egg mixture and swirl the pan. Using a flat spatula, divide the omelet into four portions. Carefully flip each section and cook until the underside is light golden brown and no longer appears wet. Serve immediately.

PORTUGUESE DEBAL PRAWNS

When the Portuguese ruled Malacca from 1511 to 1641, many local Malaccan Portuguese integrated into the Malaysian way of life while retaining their culinary culture, an influence that endures even after all this time. I travel each year with a group of foodies to a small district called Portuguese Settlement just 30 minutes' walk east from central Malacca town. One of the highlights is enjoying the variety of seafood grilled under the open sky at the waterfront jetty restaurants, which are mostly family run. The cooks wrap the prawns in aluminum foil with a hot sauce (*debal* comes from the Portuguese word for devil, *diabo,* to describe its devilishly hot flavor) and grill them over hot charcoal. I have toned the level of heat way down in this recipe; however, if you enjoy it spicy simply double the amount of jalapeño and sambal. The result is a simply addictive dish of buttery-tasting prawns infused with the tangy chili sauce that might become your favorite prawn dish. SERVES 4

¼ cup peanut oil

1 teaspoon salt

1 fresh green jalapeño chili, sliced

4 cloves garlic, minced

1 to 2 tablespoon Sambal Ulek (page 44 or store-bought)

1 pound large prawns or shrimp, peeled and deveined

2 tablespoons butter

1. Heat a large sauté pan over medium heat for about 40 seconds and then add the oil. When the surface shimmers slightly, add the salt and jalapeño and stir-fry for about 30 seconds.

2. Add the garlic and stir-fry until the garlic is golden, about 1 minute. Add the sambal and prawns and stir-fry until the oils separate onto the surface and the prawns are pink, which means it is fully cooked, about 4 minutes.

3. Add the butter and mix well. Taste and add more salt if needed. Transfer to a serving platter and serve hot.

PINEAPPLE SAMBAL PRAWNS

I will never forget a particular culinary experience, when I dined in a Nyonya home imbued with the old world atmosphere of Malacca. The food the family served brought back memories of my late grandmother's cooking. Everything had the right balance of richness, acidity, sweetness, and spice. With the first bite of fresh tropical pineapple and wild ocean-caught prawns braised in a sweet, tangy curry sauce, I immediately started thinking of reproducing it in my own home to capture that feeling. The only challenge is that typical Nyonya cuisine often requires the painstaking effort of pounding and grinding ingredients with a stone mortar and pestle. This is my simplified version, which is easier to make at home with a blender when there is little time to spend preparing complex dishes. When served with steamed white rice, the pineapple prawn sambal will take you to that old home in Malacca, too.

It is best to use fresh pineapple rather than canned because the texture is better. The dried chilies de arbol provide a rich red hue and add complexity. You can purchase dried red chilies in any Mexican grocery store and many supermarkets. SERVES 4

6 dried red chilies de arbol, soaked in boiling water until soft, drained and water reserved

1 large yellow onion, chopped

3 Roma tomatoes, chopped

½ teaspoon toasted shrimp paste (see page 116), optional

5 tablespoons coconut oil

1 cup fresh pineapple chunks

1 pound medium tiger prawns or shrimp, peeled and deveined

2 to 3 tablespoons liquid palm sugar (see pages 315–316), to taste

1 to 2 tablespoons fish sauce, to taste

1. Prepare the spice paste by combining the chilies, onion, tomatoes, and shrimp paste (if using) in a blender and blending to a smooth paste. Add some of the chili soaking water to help with the blending if needed. You should have about 3 cups bright orange spice paste.

2. Heat the oil in a medium sauté pan or wok over medium heat. Carefully add the spice paste and bring to a boil. Add the pineapple and simmer, uncovered, until the spice paste thickens, the pineapple cubes are tender, and the oils have separated onto the surface, about 15 minutes.

3. Add the prawns, 2 tablespoons sugar, and 1 tablespoon fish sauce and cook, stirring, until the prawns are pink, about 3 minutes. Taste and add more sugar or fish sauce if needed. Serve warm.

KAM HEONG CLAMS

Kam heong literally means "fragrant and golden." This dish is a recent invention by Cantonese cooks and became popular at seafood restaurants throughout Malaysia, where the cook relies heavily on curry leaves to elevate the flavors and impart their delightful peppery aroma to the clams. I make the clams the authentic way by using tiny dried shrimp, stir-fried until crispy, to provide a complex saltiness. Most Malaysians would agree that without these dried shrimp the taste would not be the same. You can find the little dried shrimp (which are somewhat like anchovies) in packages in most Asian grocery stores and in many large supermarkets. However, if you are unable to find them, you can omit them. You can also make the recipe with calamari, prawns, or crab. Whichever way, serve with a bowl of piping hot rice—quintessentially Malaysian. SERVES 4

1½ pounds Manila clams

Salt

3 tablespoons oyster sauce

3 tablespoons dark soy sauce

1 teaspoon sugar

¼ cup peanut oil

1 tablespoon dried shrimp, soaked in water until soft, drained, and minced

1 piece (1 inch) ginger, peeled and julienned

4 cloves garlic, minced

3 shallots, sliced

4 fresh green bird's-eye chilies, chopped

Leaves from 3 sprigs curry leaf

1 tablespoon curry powder

1. Clean and scrub the clams thoroughly. Soak the clams in water with 1 tablespoon salt for 30 minutes, then rinse in cold water and drain.

2. Meanwhile, combine the oyster sauce, dark soy sauce, and sugar in a bowl and stir well.

3. Heat a dry wok over medium-high heat. When the surface shimmers slightly, add the oil around the perimeter of the wok to coat, and then add the dried shrimp and fry until crispy, about 2 minutes.

4. Add the ginger, garlic, shallots, chilies, and curry leaves and cook, stirring, until fragrant and the mixture is golden in color, about 10 minutes. Add the curry powder and stir for about 30 seconds to cook off the raw taste.

5. Toss in the clams and the oyster sauce mixture, and give everything a good stir. Cover the wok and let the clams cook until they open up, about 15 minutes. If some of the clams do not open, raise the heat to high, give the mixture a good stir, cover, and cook for another few minutes. Discard any clams that still don't open. Transfer to a serving platter and serve immediately.

MY MOTHER'S FISH CUTLETS

These *cutlets,* as we call them in Malaysia, are similar to the crab cakes served in American restaurants. In Malaysian Indian homes, they are served as a main course, rather than an appetizer, usually along with rice, a vegetable dish, and lentil soup. I use rice flour as a binder in order to give the cakes a nice crunch that all-purpose flour would not. The rice flour also creates a lighter texture and does not absorb too much oil. Rice flour is available at most Asian grocery stores or you may also purchase it online. If you like, you could also dip the fish cakes in egg white and then roll them in breadcrumbs until well coated before frying. I leave the choice entirely to you. At my home, leftovers are turned into mini salmon burgers or sliders to make a filling dinner the next day. SERVES 4

1 pound salmon or snapper fillets

½ teaspoon ground turmeric

1 tablespoon salt, or to taste

½ cup water

½ small white onion, finely diced

1 piece (1 inch) fresh ginger, peeled and minced

Leaves from 2 sprigs curry leaf, minced

1 fresh green jalapeño chili, seeded and chopped

½ teaspoon ground cumin

½ teaspoon ground fennel

2 egg yolks, beaten

2½ tablespoons rice flour

Canola oil, for frying

1. Place the fish in a shallow pan and add the turmeric, salt, and water and bring to a boil. Simmer until the fish is done (it should flake easily when pulled with a fork), 5 to 7 minutes.

2. Transfer the fish to a medium bowl and discard the water. Use a fork to flake the fish, discarding the skin. To the same bowl, add the onion, ginger, curry leaves, jalapeño, cumin, and fennel and mix well. Taste and add more salt if needed. Stir in the egg yolks and rice flour.

3. To make the fish cutlets, take about 3 tablespoons of the fish mixture, about the size of a lime, and roll into a ball with the palms of your hands. Then gently flatten to a disk. Oiling your hands may be helpful. You should end up with 8 to 10 cakes.

4. Heat about 2 inches oil in a medium skillet over medium-high heat. To check if the oil is hot enough, drop in a 1-inch cube of white bread. The bread should brown in about 40 seconds.

5. Working in batches to avoid overcrowding the pan, gently place the fish cakes in the hot oil and fry until slightly golden on the bottoms, about 3 minutes, then carefully flip and continue cooking for an additional 3 to 5 minutes. Remove the fish cakes to a plate lined with paper towels. Serve hot.

TAMARIND FISH CURRY

My mother prepared this curry most Sundays to be savored with our weekend crepes. I now do the same in my Seattle kitchen. She always used golden pompano fish, but I believe that wild king salmon, when in season, is an excellent substitute due to its fat content. The high-point of the curry is the tamarind, which gives it a sour taste that is balanced by coconut milk and spices. The tamarind pulp used to make the tamarind water is widely sold in a cylindrical bottle at most Asian and Mexican stores. If you can find fresh tamarind pods, you may also enjoy squeezing the pods for their pulp, which is such a pleasurable thing to do, and your curry will end up much tastier. For a more substantial dish, add some okra or potatoes.

SERVES 6

¼ cup coconut oil

½ teaspoon cumin seeds

½ teaspoon mustard seeds

½ teaspoon fenugreek seeds

1 white onion, chopped

3 cloves garlic, minced

Leaves from 3 sprigs curry leaf

1 to 2 fresh green jalapeño chilies, cut into half lengthwise and seeded

2 tomatoes, cut in half

½ small eggplant, cut into 1-inch cubes; or 3 small Indian eggplants, halved

2 to 3 tablespoons curry powder, preferably Baba's fish curry powder

½ teaspoon ground turmeric

1¼ teaspoons salt, or to taste

1 cup Tamarind Water (page 54)

3 king salmon steaks (6 to 8 ounces each), cut in half at the bone

1½ cups coconut milk

1. Heat the oil in a medium saucepan over medium-high heat. Add the cumin seeds, mustard seeds, and fenugreek seeds and cook, stirring, until fragrant, about 40 seconds.

2. Add the onion, garlic, curry leaves, jalapeños, tomatoes, and eggplant and cook, stirring, until fragrant of peppery curry leaf and the eggplant becomes soft, about 15 minutes.

3. Add the curry powder, turmeric, and salt and mix well. Add the tamarind water and bring to a boil. Add the fish and give it a stir—gently, to prevent the fish from breaking into pieces. Reduce the heat to low and simmer until the fish is done, 7 to 10 minutes. The fish should easily flake when done.

4. Gently stir in the coconut milk and bring to a soft boil. Taste and add more salt if needed. Serve warm.

GRILLED BLACK COD WITH SWEET SOY SAMBAL

At open-air markets and fairs in Malaysia, you can smell the distinct aroma of grilled fish even before you approach the colorfully tented stalls. People often stand in long lines to select a fish from an assortment laid out on crushed ice and then wait patiently while the fish is cleaned and grilled. Among the more popular fish used are stingray, skirt wing, and wild sardines, although at home I like to cook wild black cod. The fish is seldom eaten by itself, but is accompanied by a slightly spicy sambal for dipping on the side, which perfectly complements the mild, sweet, and slightly flaky flesh of the fish. SERVES 4

2 pieces wild black cod fillet (8 to 10 ounces each)

3 tablespoons kicap manis (sweet soy sauce; see page 16)

1 tablespoon freshly ground black pepper

½ teaspoon ground turmeric

½ teaspoon garlic powder

1 teaspoon salt, or to taste

1 tablespoon coconut oil

½ lime, cut into wedges

3 tablespoons Sambal Ulek or Sambal Belachan (page 44 or 43, or store-bought)

1. Prepare the fish by gently rubbing each piece with the kicap manis, pepper, turmeric, garlic powder, and salt. Marinate in the refrigerator for 1 hour.

2. Heat the oil in a cast iron grill pan over medium heat. Grill the fish, turning once, until cooked through, about 4 minutes per side. The kicap manis will caramelize on the surface when the fish is cooked. Squeeze a little lime over the fish and enjoy with the sambal on the side.

SWEET AND SPICY PRAWN SAMBAL TUMIS

In Malaysia, this prawn sambal is popular everywhere, from school canteens to work cafeterias, from hawker stalls to restaurants, and especially in home kitchens. Malaysians love to eat prawn sambal tumis for breakfast with rice, as the sambal is naturally sweet from tomatoes and shallots. When cooked, the sambal relish is ready to accept any main ingredient such as fish, clams, mussels, crab, and scallops. When making the sambal, it is very important that the onions are browned and the tomatoes are soft before adding in the spice paste, as to build the correct foundation of flavors. This allows each ingredient time to release its own juices into the dish. Make sure the sambal tastes perfectly balanced (sweet, sour, salty, spicy). You can customize the sambal by adding more palm sugar to obtain a sweeter finish, or add more sambal ulek for a spicier dish. SERVES 4

SPICE PASTE

¼ cup Sambal Ulek (page 44 or store-bought)

5 shallots, peeled and cut in half

4 cloves garlic, peeled and left whole

3 Roma tomatoes, chopped

½ cup water

PRAWNS

5 tablespoons coconut oil

1 Roma tomato, quartered

½ small white onion, sliced

1 pound medium tiger prawns or shrimp, peeled and deveined

3 tablespoons liquid palm sugar (see pages 315–316), or to taste

2 tablespoons fish sauce, or to taste

Pinch of salt, or to taste

1. Prepare the spice paste: Combine the sambal, shallots, garlic, tomatoes, and water in a blender and blend into a smooth paste. You should have about 2 cups.

2. Heat the oil in a medium skillet or wok over medium heat. Add the tomato and onion and cook until the onions are browned and the tomatoes soften, about 15 minutes.

3. Carefully add the spice paste and cook, stirring occasionally, until the paste thickens and the oils have separated onto the surface, about 15 minutes.

4. Add the prawns, sugar, fish sauce, and salt and cook, stirring, until the prawns are pink in color and the oils separate again onto the surface, about 5 minutes. Taste and add more palm sugar, fish sauce, or salt if needed. Serve warm.

STREET FOOD

It is all about socializing and eating al fresco. The streets themselves are transformed into makeshift restaurant corridors, where the "restaurants" are humble booths, with each vendor specializing in only one signature dish. Even as a little girl, I always loved going to hawker stalls and would sometimes stand mesmerized, watching the vendors put together a meal in a few minutes.

Just like my professional education, these hawkers too have stoked the fires in me to keep sharpening my culinary abilities, to be passionate about acquiring knowledge, and to impart these specialties to home cooks.

One of the great joys of street food eating is starting the morning with white coffee and a plate of the famous Char Kway Teow (page 236). Just watching the street cook practice her craft is in itself amazing: Surrounded by locally produced ingredients, she stands over a large wok fired by a noisy gas stove. With a long ladle, she instinctively and quickly spoons just the right amount of oil, minced garlic, fresh rice noodles, bean sprouts, cooking sauces, wild prawns, and sausage into the wok to create an irresistible dish. During cooking, tiny droplets of oil in the wok may catch fire, rendering an unmistakable smoky flavor to the noodles.

Come midday, most locals hunt down the finest bowl of *asam laksa,* in which mackerel caught off the coast and the freshest aromatics are used to make a seafood broth painstakingly prepared before dawn. The broth, poured over a bowl of fresh rice noodles, exudes aromas of lemongrass, *bunga kantan* (or torch ginger), and tangy tamarind. Colorful accoutrements such as julienned cucumber, fresh red chilies, minced onions, lettuce, fresh pineapple, and mint leaves finish the dish.

Other popular dishes include Nasi Lemak, or coconut rice with anchovies, a dollop of sambal, and peanuts bundled in a banana leaf (page 233), Beef Rendang (page 261), and Hainanese Chicken Rice (page 215), which is roast chicken plated with rice cooked in chicken broth and garlic.

Despite the emergence of modern restaurants throughout Malaysia, at dusk the locals still consider the finest food to be from the humblest operations, like the veteran satay seller. Surrounded by bamboo containers in which he totes all his food and a few stools for customers, he prepares only one dish, chicken or beef satay, grilled, drenched in peanut sauce, and served with cucumber and rice cakes. He has no refrigerator or even storage. His sticks of satay are grilled on a charcoal fire and served immediately to hungry customers waiting in line to order. The cooking is non-stop, with smoke from the charcoal grill lingering in the still night air until the last stick is delivered. Among the customers are the many women, referred to throughout Asia as "plastic-bag wives," who are too busy to prepare food after work. Instead, they return home laden with plastic bags filled with street food from nearby stalls and push carts.

The dishes in this chapter are carefully selected for their popularity and as part of the tapestry of Malay, Chinese, Indian, Malay,

and Nyonya cuisines. Just like authentic street food, nothing is made ahead of time and no refrigeration is needed in between steps; everything is made fresh from start to finish. Some of the recipes—curry puffs (page 242), Roti John (page 220), Ginger-Sesame Chicken Wings (page 241), and Five-Spice Savory Potatoes (page 239)—also make irresistible finger foods. Remember, though, that pushcart vendors specialize in only one signature dish and make it over and over again, so although the idea of "street food" might seem simple, some of these recipes are quite complex. It would be best to attempt one recipe at a time. Attempting any of these recipes will help you become a better cook, since street food is all about developing a multitude of flavors using only the ingredients available to you.

HAINANESE CHICKEN RICE

This recipe originated in China, in the southernmost island of Hainan, and made its way to Malaysia with early Chinese immigrants. It has since become a favorite among the locals and was adopted as a part of Malaysia's culinary culture. The town of Ipoh, a center for Hainanese immigration, is worth exploring for some of the best places for Chicken Rice. Poached chicken, fragrant rice, chili sauce, and garnishes for serving are all part of this wonderful dish. The flavorful chicken broth used to poach the chicken seasons the rice as well. Everything comes together on the table. SERVES 6

CHICKEN

- 1 small whole chicken (3½ pounds), cleaned
- 6 cloves garlic, smashed
- 1 piece (2 inches) fresh ginger, peeled and smashed
- 6 green onions, folded in half
- 3 tablespoons shaoxing rice wine
- 2 tablespoons light soy sauce
- 2 tablespoons rice vinegar
- 1 teaspoon fish sauce
- 8 cups water

RICE

- 3 tablespoons reserved chicken fat, or peanut oil
- 3 cups jasmine rice
- 2 cloves garlic, finely chopped
- 1 piece (1 inch) fresh ginger, peeled and sliced
- 1 pandan leaf, fresh or frozen (optional)

SEASONING SAUCE

- 3 tablespoons light soy sauce
- 1 tablespoon sesame oil

CHILI SAUCE

- 3 tablespoons Sambal Ulek (page 44 or store-bought)
- 3 cloves garlic, peeled and left whole
- ⅓ cup rice vinegar
- ⅓ cup granulated sugar
- ½ teaspoon salt
- Juice of 1 lime

FOR SERVING

- 1 cucumber, sliced
- 2 green onions (white and green parts, sliced

1. Poach the chicken: Begin by trimming the fat surrounding the inner part of the chicken cavity and set it aside for the rice. Place the chicken into a stockpot that is tall enough to allow the chicken to be covered with water. Insert the garlic, ginger, and green onions into the cavity of the chicken. Next pour the rice wine, soy sauce, vinegar, and fish sauce into the cavity, then secure the opening with a short bamboo skewer.

2. Add the water to cover the chicken and bring to a boil, then reduce the heat to medium-low and simmer until the meat is tender, about 1 hour or so. The chicken thigh joint will easily pull away from the body when the meat is done. While the chicken cooks, skim any froth from the surface of the broth.

3. Make the rice: Cook the reserved chicken fat in a 3-quart heavy saucepan over medium heat, stirring occasionally, until the fat is rendered and the solids have shrunk considerably. Discard the solids.

4. While waiting for the fat to break down in the pan, wash the rice by gently rubbing it with your fingers in a bowl filled with water. When the water becomes cloudy, drain the water and repeat the process until the water is clear. Drain well.

5. Add the garlic, ginger, and pandan leaf (if using) to the chicken fat and cook over medium heat, stirring, until the garlic is golden and fragrant, about 1 minute. Add the rice and carefully mix until the grains are well coated with the fat.

6. Add 4½ cups of the broth from the chicken pot to the rice and bring to a boil (keep the remaining broth to serve with the chicken). Boil until the liquid on the surface is evaporated and small bubbles appear from holes in the rice, 3 to 4 minutes. Cover, reduce the heat to low, and cook until the rice is tender and the rest of the liquid is absorbed, about 20 minutes. Remove from the heat and let stand, covered and undisturbed, for about 5 minutes. Fluff the rice with a fork and cover. Alternatively, you can cook the rice and broth in a rice cooker.

7. While the rice is cooking, make the seasoning sauce and chili sauce: Mix the soy sauce and sesame oil in a small bowl; set the seasoning sauce aside. Blend the chili sauce ingredients in a mini food processor until smooth. Transfer to a small bowl for serving and set aside.

8. To serve: Once the chicken is cooked, carefully lift the chicken and allow the broth to drain from the cavity into the pot. Strain the broth into a clean pot and reserve to serve with the chicken. Allow the chicken to cool slightly on a plate before cutting. De-bone the chicken (the bones will easily come off since the chicken will be very tender) and slice into 3-inch pieces, then arrange on a serving platter. Place the cucumber on the platter.

9. Drizzle the seasoning sauce over the sliced chicken and cucumber. Set the bowl of chili sauce on the table. Pour the broth into individual bowls and sprinkle with the green onions. Serve the rice on individual plates. Enjoy while still warm.

CHICKEN SATAY KAJANG

Small pieces of meat grilled over an open flame are found the world over. The Turks have their kebab, the Greeks have their souvlaki, and the Japanese have their yakitori. In Southeast Asia, we call this treat *satay:* thin, marinated strips of meat on bamboo skewers, cooked over a flaming grill. Watching a satay chef at work is truly entertaining. Standing over the hot grill, he holds a palm leaf fan in one hand to fan the fire and with the other he skillfully turns over several skewers at a time to ensure that each morsel is evenly cooked. Chicken and beef are both traditional, but it is the marinade that makes satay distinct. For an authentic flavor, grilling over charcoal flames is best, but these also taste good when broiled (about 3 minutes per side). Whether under the broiler or on the grill, make sure to presoak the bamboo skewers in water for 30 minutes so they do not burn. MAKES 20 SKEWERS

1 piece (1½ inches) unpeeled fresh galangal, chopped

2 stalks fresh lemongrass, outer layers discarded, thinly sliced

6 shallots, sliced

3 fresh red bird's-eye chilies, chopped

1½ teaspoons ground turmeric

1½ teaspoons ground coriander

3 tablespoons sugar

1 teaspoon salt

1 pound boneless, skinless chicken thigh or breast meat, sliced into thin 1-inch strips

2 tablespoons canola or peanut oil mixed with 2 tablespoons water, for basting

Perfect Peanut Sauce (page 62)

1 cucumber, sliced

1 small red onion, roughly chopped

1. To make the spice paste, combine the galangal, lemongrass, shallots, chilies, turmeric, coriander, sugar, and salt in a food processor and blend to a smooth paste. Add a little water to facilitate the blending if needed.

2. Combine the spice paste with the chicken in a bowl and knead well in order for the spices to penetrate the meat. Cover the bowl, refrigerate, and marinate for about 12 hours, or preferably overnight.

3. Soak 20 bamboo skewers in water for 30 minutes. Thread the chicken pieces onto each skewer, making sure the tip of each skewer is not exposed. For convenience, satay can be made up to this stage several hours ahead of cooking, the meat well covered with foil and refrigerated.

4. Heat the grill to high. Grill the skewered chicken, basting once or twice lightly with the oil and water mixture to keep the meat moist. Turn frequently to prevent the meat from burning. Grill until the meat is slightly charred on the outside and cooked inside, about 7 minutes. Serve hot with peanut sauce, cucumbers, and onion.

MALAY-STYLE ROASTED CHICKEN RICE
NASI AYAM

On those days when it's crisp, clear, and the sky looks like Malaysia in January instead of a typical grey canvas day in Seattle, I feel especially homesick for the bright tropical sun warming up my cheeks and yearn for a plate of *nasi ayam*, from the rustic stalls of the Malay cooks in the little town of Johor, which borders Singapore. There is nothing more comforting and nothing that captures the essence of Malay home-style food than nasi ayam, tender roasted chicken browned from sweet soy sauce with rice plumped with chicken broth and the savory aroma of star anise. Delicious, uplifting, and definitely a reminder of home for me. Don't hold back on the chili and sweet soy sauce, since the chicken is subtly flavored; drizzling the sauce over every spoonful adds to the flavor of this dish. SERVES 4

CHICKEN AND BROTH

- 6 pounds bone-in chicken leg quarters (about 4 leg quarters), rinsed and trimmed of fat
- 1½ white onions, cut into halves
- 8 cloves garlic, smashed
- 1 piece (2 inches) fresh ginger, peeled and sliced
- 2 whole star anise
- 1 cinnamon stick
- 8 cups water

RICE

- 3 cups basmati rice
- 3 to 4 tablespoons clarified butter (ghee)
- 1 whole star anise
- ½ cup Ginger, Garlic, and Cilantro Paste (page 53)

ROAST CHICKEN

- 3 tablespoons kicap manis (sweet soy sauce; see page 16)
- 3 tablespoons light soy sauce
- 2 tablespoons sesame oil

CHILI SAUCE

- 4 fresh red jalapeño chilies, seeded and chopped
- 3 cloves garlic, peeled and left whole
- ⅓ cup rice vinegar
- Juice of 1 lime
- ⅓ cup granulated sugar
- ½ teaspoon salt

FOR SERVING

- 1 English cucumber, sliced
- 2 green onions (white and green parts), sliced
- 1 tablespoon Fried Shallots (page 56)
- ¼ cup kicap manis (sweet soy sauce; see page 16)

1. Make the chicken and broth: Add the chicken, onions, garlic, ginger, star anise, and cinnamon to a large stockpot. Add the water and bring to a boil over high heat. Reduce the heat to medium-low and allow the chicken to simmer, undisturbed, until cooked through, about 1 hour or so. Skim any frothy impurities from the surface of the broth as it cooks.

2. Meanwhile, make the rice: Wash the rice by gently rubbing it with your fingers in a bowl filled with water. When the water becomes cloudy, drain the water and repeat the process until the water is clear. Drain and set the rice aside.

3. Preheat the oven to 350°F.

4. Heat the clarified butter in a large saucepan over medium heat. Add the star anise and ginger-garlic paste and stir-fry until fragrant, about 2 minutes. Add the rice and fold to combine with the spiced butter; cook until the grains are well coated and rice appears dry, about 2 minutes. Ladle 6 cups of the broth from the chicken pot into the rice. Bring the rice and broth to a boil and boil until the liquid on the surface is evaporated and small bubbles appear from holes in rice, 3 to 4 minutes. Cover, reduce the heat to low, and cook until the rice is tender and the liquid is absorbed, about 15 minutes more. Remove from the heat and let sit, covered and undisturbed, for about 5 minutes. Fluff rice with a fork and cover.

5. Roast the chicken: When the chicken is thoroughly cooked, carefully remove it from the stockpot using tongs and place on a large baking sheet. Keep the remaining broth on a slow simmer over low heat.

6. Combine the kicap manis, light soy sauce, and sesame oil in a bowl and mix well. Drizzle the sauce evenly over each piece of chicken. Roast the chicken until it is perfectly browned; this will only take 5 to 10 minutes since the chicken is already cooked.

7. While the chicken is roasting, prepare the chili sauce: Combine the chilies, garlic, rice vinegar, lime juice, sugar, and salt in a mini food processor and pulse into a coarse paste.

8. To serve: Divide the chicken and cucumber between 4 dinner plates. Strain the broth into a clean pot or bowl. Pour about 1 cup broth into each of 4 individual bowls and garnish with the sliced green onions and fried shallots. Press about 1 cup of rice into a small bowl, then invert onto one of the individual dinner plates. Repeat with the remaining rice and dinner plates. Divide all the chili sauce and kicap manis into small dishes so everyone has their own. Enjoy while hot or warm.

ROTI JOHN

MALAY-STYLE CHICKEN OMELET SANDWICH

This sandwich first appeared in the '60s when an Englishman asked a Malaysian hawker for a hamburger. Having no hamburger to offer, the hawker had the ingenious idea to fry up a patty of minced lamb, onions, and eggs. Thus, Roti John was born—but how did it get the name? The story goes that as the street vendor handed the sandwich to the Englishman he said, "*Silakan makan roti, John*": "Please eat this bread, John"—John being the generic name given to Westerners in the region. Our legendary John loved the panini-like sandwich and thus it became part of the Malaysian street food scene.

I prefer fresh minced chicken, but you could also use leftover roast chicken, ground beef, lamb, or even canned tuna in the egg mixture. For a vegetarian version, substitute a mixture of peas, red peppers, and potatoes for the meat.

When making Roti John, you add the wet egg mixture to the pan as if you are making an omelet, but then you add the bread over this mixture and finish cooking the sandwich in the pan. Don't forget a slather of mayonnaise on the bread for that melt-in-your-mouth experience. SERVES 2

6 tablespoons extra-virgin olive oil

1 small onion, minced

3 cloves garlic, minced

1 teaspoon salt, or to taste

¼ teaspoon freshly ground black pepper

8 ounces ground chicken or ground pork

1½ teaspoons curry powder

4 slices (1-inch-thick) white bread or Japanese shokupan bread

4 eggs, beaten in a large bowl

1½ tablespoons mayonnaise

1. Heat 5 tablespoons of the oil over medium heat in a large deep skillet wide enough to hold 2 slices of bread side by side. Add the onion, garlic, salt, and pepper and stir-fry until the onion is golden and translucent, about 5 minutes.

2. Add the ground chicken and mix well. Stir-fry, using your spatula to break up any clumps of meat, until the meat is no longer pink and much of the moisture has evaporated, about 15 minutes. Add the curry powder and continue to cook, stirring, to cook off the raw taste of the curry, about 3 minutes. Taste and add more salt if needed.

3. While the meat is cooking, lightly toast 2 pieces of the bread either using a toaster or on a cast iron pan. Set aside.

4. Add the cooked meat mixture to the bowl of beaten eggs and immediately mix well to combine. The mixture will look like a wet omelet.

5. Wipe out the pan, set it back over medium heat, and coat with the remaining 1 tablespoon oil. Pour the beaten egg and meat mixture into the pan. Now place the 2 toasted bread slices directly on top of the wet egg and meat mixture and gently press the bread down so the filling sticks to the bread. Using your spatula, constantly tuck the wet filling from the side under the bread. There should be no filling

spilling out from the sides. Cook until set, about 5 minutes.

6. Toast the remaining 2 slices of bread and spread them with the mayonnaise.

7. Once the egg mixture is set, carefully flip the egg mixture and bread using a flat spatula. Place the remaining bread, mayonnaise-side down, on top to form an omelet panini. Press the bread with a spatula so it all sticks together. Transfer the sandwiches to a cutting board and slice in half while hot. Serve immediately.

SATAY-STYLE GRILLED MARINATED LAMB CHOPS

If I had to pick my favorite region for barbecue, it would have to be Southeast Asia. In my homeland of Malaysia, pushcart satay vendors at night markets and along main streets grill marinated chicken and beef cubes on bamboo skewers over red hot charcoal grills. It gives off an inviting aroma mixed with the smoke, enticing hungry patrons to flock to their stalls. This lamb chop satay is prepared differently than the Chicken Satay Kajang on page 217. Instead of lacing the meat on skewers, the entire chops are marinated in a classic mix of coriander and sweet soy, flavors that are enhanced by the charred amber-colored fat from the meat. Serve the chops with a squeeze of fresh lime juice for a vibrant flavor. SERVES 4

1 teaspoon coriander seeds, crushed

1 teaspoon black peppercorns, crushed

¼ teaspoon white peppercorns, crushed

½ teaspoon cumin seeds, crushed

1 teaspoon salt

½ cup kicap manis (sweet soy sauce; see page 16)

¼ cup extra-virgin olive oil

3 tablespoons fresh lime juice

12 lamb loin chops (about 4 pounds)

4 limes, quartered

1. Combine the coriander seeds, black and white pepper, cumin, salt, kicap manis, oil, and lime juice in a food processor and process into a rough, aromatic paste for the marinade.

2. Place the lamb chops in a bowl. Pour the marinade over the chops and rub all over to infuse the flavors into the meat. Allow the lamb chops to marinate for at least 1 hour, or preferably overnight, covered and refrigerated, for the fullest flavor.

3. Heat the grill to a medium-hot fire. Grill the lamb chops on one side for about 5 minutes, then turn and continue grilling for an additional 5 minutes, until just cooked through. Transfer the lamb chops to a platter, garnish with the lime wedges, and serve.

Satay-Style Grilled Marinated Lamb Chops served with Spiced Clarified Butter Rice with Almonds and Cranberries (page 161)

MALAYSIAN WANTAN NOODLES WITH BARBECUE-ROASTED PORK

Every time I visit Malaysia, a stop at the famous wantan noodles stall on Burma Road in Penang is on my must-do list. This wantan noodle recipe is different from similar "wonton" noodles served in Hong Kong–style eateries. While those are typically served in a chicken broth, in Malaysia wantan noodles are usually thin Asian-style egg noodles tossed in a sweet molasses-like soy sauce and sesame oil, served on a plate alongside succulent pieces of char siu pork, pork-filled dumplings, and bok choy. SERVES 4

WONTONS

- 6 ounces ground pork
- 1 egg yolk
- 1 teaspoon grated fresh ginger
- 2 teaspoons soy sauce
- 1 teaspoon oyster sauce
- 1 teaspoon sesame oil
- ⅛ teaspoon ground white pepper
- 1 package square wonton wrappers (you will need 25 wrappers)

SEASONING SAUCE

- 6 tablespoons kicap manis (sweet soy sauce; see page 16)
- 4 tablespoons oyster sauce
- 4 tablespoons light soy sauce
- 4 tablespoons sesame oil
  Ground white pepper

WANTAN NOODLES

- 4 pickled green chilies, thinly sliced
  Five-Spiced Barbecue-Roasted Pork (page 235), cut into bite-sized pieces
- 15 ounces fresh egg noodles (wonton noodles)
- ½ bunch (8 ounces) bok choy, cut into 2-inch lengths

1. Begin by preparing the wontons: Combine the pork, egg yolk, ginger, soy sauce, oyster sauce, sesame oil, and pepper in a bowl and mix well using a fork until you obtain a smooth, thick paste.

2. Place a wonton wrappers on a cutting board or clean surface. Make sure your hands are clean and dry before filling the wrappers. Place a teaspoon of the pork mixture in the center of the wonton wrapper. Using a small pastry brush, lightly moisten the edges of the wrapper with a little water. Fold the wrapper to form a triangle shape and seal the edges together, then press on the edges to thin out the dough.

Bring the corners together and squeeze to form a bundle. If the corners do not stick, try sealing them with a pat of water. Repeat to fill 25 wrappers. (Alternatively, you may double the filling recipe, fill 50 wontons and freeze half of them for later use.) Set the wonton, aside on a plate until ready to cook.

3. Prepare the seasoning sauce: For each serving, combine 1½ tablespoons kicap manis, 1 tablespoon oyster sauce, 1 tablespoon light soy sauce, 1 tablespoon sesame oil, and a pinch of white pepper in a small bowl.

4. Prepare the wantan noodles and condiments: Put the pickled chilies in a small bowl and arrange the roasted pork on a platter.

5. Bring two large pots of water to a rapid boil over high heat so that you can cook the noodles in one pot and wontons in the other at the same time. While waiting for the water to come to a boil, separate and loosen the noodles into 4 individual portions on a cutting board. Separating the noodles and cooking the portions individually will prevent the noodles from sticking together. Set aside until ready to cook.

6. Add the bok choy to one pot of boiling water and cook until tender but still crisp, about 30 seconds. Remove with a slotted spoon, drain well, and set aside. Return the water to a rolling boil.

7. Drop one portion of the noodles into the same pot in which you cooked the bok choy and cook until tender, about 5 minutes. Carefully taste the noodles; they should be tender. Using a large sieve or slotted spoon, remove the noodles and run them under tap water for 5 seconds. Drain and transfer the noodles to a bowl.

8. Add one portion of the seasoning sauce to the noodles, and give them a good toss to combine the flavors. Transfer to a plate and set aside. Repeat, cooking and saucing the remaining noodles.

9. Meanwhile, add the wontons in batches to the other pot and cook until they rise to the top, about 2 minutes per batch, stirring occasionally to keep them from sticking to the bottom of the pot. Drain the wontons.

10. To serve, garnish each plate with pickled green chilies. Add the bok choy, 5 wontons each, and the roasted pork. Serve immediately.

PENANG VEGETABLE SALAD WITH SWEET POTATO SAUCE

PASEMBUR

The tourists who throng Georgetown's popular beachfront called Gurney Drive often order *pasembur* from food trucks fronting the esplanade. Here under a big shady tree, the vendors sell this piled-high salad consisting of crispy coconut fritters, fresh shredded jicama, hard-boiled eggs, julienned cucumber, and crispy tofu pieces drenched in a creamy sweet potato–peanut sauce, a combination of sweet, tangy, and nutty with a hint of spice that is hard to resist. SERVES 4

SWEET POTATO SAUCE

- 3 medium sweet potatoes
- 1½ cups water
- 1 cup tamarind water (page 54) or ¼ cup tamarind concentrate dissolved in 1 cup hot water
- 1 cup roasted unsalted peanuts
- 2 to 3 tablespoons liquid palm sugar (see pages 315–316)
- ½ teaspoon salt, or to taste

SPICE PASTE

- 5 shallots, peeled and left whole
- 3 cloves garlic, peeled and left whole
- 1 teaspoon Sambal Ulek (page 44 or store-bought)
- ½ cup water
- 3 tablespoons peanut oil

SALAD

- 2 tablespoons peanut oil
- 6 to 8 ounces store-bought fried tofu, cut into ½-inch strips
- 1 small cucumber, peeled and cut into matchsticks
- 1 small jicama, peeled and cut into matchsticks
- 2 hard-boiled eggs, halved

1. Start the sweet potato sauce: Wash and scrub the sweet potatoes to remove any dirt. Steam the sweet potatoes in a steamer basket set in a pot of water over high heat until they are soft when pierced with a knife, about 15 minutes. While the sweet potatoes are cooking, prepare the spice paste.

2. Make the spice paste: Place the shallots, garlic, sambal, and water in a blender and blend until pureed. Heat the oil in a wok over medium heat. Add the blended spice paste and stir well. Cook, stirring occasionally, until the oils separate and come to the surface, about 15 minutes.

3. Finish the sauce: Carefully remove the skin from the hot sweet potatoes and add the sweet potatoes and water to the blender, along with the tamarind water and peanuts. Process until pureed.

4. Add the blended sweet potato sauce to the wok with the spice paste and mix well. Reduce the heat to low and simmer for 10 to 15 minutes, until the oils rise to the surface. Add the palm sugar and salt to taste and cook for another 1 minute. Remove from the heat.

5. Heat the oil in a skillet over medium heat, add the tofu and fry, stirring occasionally until crispy, about 10 minutes. Drain on a paper towel.

6. To serve the salad: Fill each plate with the tofu, cucumber, jicama, and eggs. Serve the sweet potato sauce in a bowl alongside or ladle it over the salad. The salad is best served warm.

PENANG, THE PEARL OF THE ORIENT

Across Southeast Asia street food abounds, but nowhere else is street food eaten with more gusto than in legendary Penang. A little island situated off the northwestern coast of the Malay Peninsula fronting the Indian Ocean, Penang is Malaysia's culinary capital, a small island with big flavors. The street food, or hawker food, as it's locally known, is part of the fabric of the city. The hawkers, from their tiny pushcarts or booths, prepare amazing creations that attract food hunters and tourists alike. Each day, customers make beelines for the one stall that prepares one dish better than anyone else.

How did Penang come to be so world famous? Captain Francis Light, an English trader, acquired Penang from the Sultan of Kedah in 1786 on behalf of the East India Company. The British East India Company declared Penang a free port to attract trade away from the Dutch, who were then the colonial rulers of the Dutch East Indies. This strategy drew many immigrant traders to Penang. Settlers were allowed to claim whatever land they could clear. In 1826, Penang grew from a busy transit port to become a major trading post for lucrative trade in tea, spices, porcelain, and cloth, as well as a staging post for the opium trade between India and China. The island beckoned settlers and traders from around the world—Europeans, Eurasians, Jews, Thais, Burmese, Chinese, Indians, Sikhs, and Armenians as well as Arabs and Acehnese. They brought with them their cultures and traditions as well as their culinary skills, making Penang a multicultural melting pot of distinctive traditions living side by side.

This peace was shattered by the bombs of World War II and the Japanese Occupation from 1941 to 1945. Although the British briefly reclaimed Penang following the war, Malaysia (then known as the Federation of Malaya) became independent soon after. As with all newly independent states in the post-war era, Malaysia has seen its fortunes rise and fall, but has come into its own since the 1960s, with the creation of the Association of Southeast Asian Nations in 1967.

Today, Georgetown, the capitol of Penang, is a popular tourist destination, not least for its symphony of sounds along the Street of Harmony, as it is called. While bells of St. George's Church, the oldest Anglican church in Southeast Asia, toll, one can also hear the call to prayer from its many mosques (*masjid*), the Buddhist chants in Sanskrit from Goddess of Mercy Temple, and the cacophony of the faithful in the Sri Maha Mariamman Hindu temple.

There is also an amazing rhapsody of aromas, coming from both the flowers that the faithful donate and the burning candles and incense that drift out onto the streets from these many houses of worship.

But the true glory of the street life in Georgetown comes from the thousands of restored shop homes, with their historical sweep of architectural styles and world-renowned street food carts parked in front. Off the streets are mazes of alleyways, sometimes called *five-foot ways* for their narrow passages, in which many homeowners will set up stalls for selling home cooked specialties. Stop at one such "café" for a short break of shave ice with mung beans and tapioca, or sit down on humble plastic stools to enjoy a plate of mee goreng with a cup of coffee, then go for a Chinese vendor's peanut pancake filled with coconut and sweetened corn. You will surely enjoy your taste of the theater of daily life.

The streets of Penang are a constant reminder of its multicultural society and celebrated by several generations of vendors who infuse a sense of pride into their specialized dishes. Craftsmanship remains valued here and everything is created by hand using only the freshest ingredients sourced locally within the island.

NASI LEMAK

It's hard not to love *nasi* (rice) *lemak* (rich and creamy), so popular that its greatest advocates insist on calling it the country's national dish. Throughout my school years, I would savor nasi lemak, wrapped in green banana leaves, at least three times a week. Inside the bundle was warm coconut rice infused with the vanilla-like aroma of pandan leaves and citrusy ginger accompanied by a hardboiled egg, crispy fried anchovies and peanuts, a few slices of cucumber, and a dollop of sambal; flavors that are still etched in my mind.

Since all the side condiments can be served at room temperature, they can be made well in advance. I always prepare more than I need at one time so I can enjoy this dish again whenever I want. For instance, the fried peanuts and anchovies, which bring complexity and crunch to the dish, can be fried and then stored in an airtight container at room temperature. The sambal can be stored in the refrigerator or freezer and then microwaved when you need it. When all of the main preparations are done ahead of time, you are only left with cooking the coconut rice, which should be served piping hot along with warm hard-boiled eggs and fresh slices of cucumber. SERVES 6

COCONUT RICE

- 3 cups basmati rice
- 1 tablespoon salt
- 4 cloves garlic, smashed
- 1 piece (1 inch) fresh ginger, peeled and sliced
- 2 pandan leaves, tied into a knot
- 3 cups coconut milk
- 1½ cups water

FRIED PEANUTS AND ANCHOVIES

- ⅔ cup peanut or canola oil
- 1 cup raw peanuts with skin on
- 1½ cups dried anchovies, washed and drained

ANCHOVY SAMBAL (*SAMBAL IKAN BILIS*)

- 6 tablespoons Sambal Ulek (page 44 or store-bought)
- 4 cloves garlic, peeled and left whole
- 1 piece (1 inch) fresh ginger, peeled and sliced
- 4 shallots, peeled and cut in half
- ¾ cup water
- 6 tablespoons peanut oil
- 1 teaspoon salt, or to taste
- 1 tablespoon sugar, or to taste
- ½ medium onion, thinly sliced
- 3 tablespoons Tamarind Water (page 54), or 2 tablespoons tamarind liquid concentrate

ACCOMPANIMENTS

- 6 banana leaves (12 by 9 inches each), cleaned
- ½ small cucumber, sliced
- 3 hard-boiled eggs, cut in half

1. Prepare the coconut rice: Wash the rice by gently rubbing it with your fingers in a bowl filled with water. When the water becomes cloudy, drain the water and repeat the process until the water is clear. Place the rice in a large saucepan and add the salt, garlic, ginger, pandan leaves, coconut milk, and water. Bring to a boil over medium heat, then simmer, uncovered, until steam holes appear in the rice and the surface looks dry, about 10 minutes. Reduce the heat to low, cover with a tight fitting lid, and cook, without stirring, until all the coconut milk is absorbed and the grains are tender and fluffy, about 20 minutes more. (Alternatively you can cook all the ingredients in a rice cooker.) When the rice is done, discard the garlic, ginger, and pandan leaves and stir the rice.

2. Meanwhile, fry the peanuts and anchovies: Heat the oil in a wok or skillet over medium-low heat. When the oil shimmers, add the peanuts and cook until they turn brown, about 5 minutes. Transfer the peanuts with a slotted spoon to a paper towel to drain.

3. Next, carefully add the dried anchovies and stir-fry, moving the anchovies back and forth, until golden brown and crispy, about 7 minutes. Transfer the anchovies to a paper towel. Discard the oil. Set aside half of the anchovies to serve with rice and use the other half for the sambal.

4. Prepare the anchovy sambal: Blend the sambal ulek, garlic, ginger, shallots, and ¼ cup water in a blender to a smooth paste with the consistency of applesauce. Heat the oil in a wok or skillet over medium heat. When the oil is hot, add the sambal paste, salt, and sugar and stir-fry until fragrant and the oils separate onto the surface, about 10 minutes. Add the onion and cook until the onion is soft, another 5 minutes. Add the tamarind water and remaining ½ cup water and mix well to combine with the paste. Now add half the crispy anchovies and allow to cook for 5 minutes. Taste the sambal and add more sugar or salt if needed; you want a balanced sweet-salty taste. Turn off the heat.

5. To serve, line each diner's plate with a banana leaf. Place about 1 cup of the cooked coconut rice in the middle of the leaf. (If you like, press the rice into a bowl first and then invert it onto the plate for a neat domed shape.) Put about 3 tablespoons of the anchovy sambal on top of the rice. Place a few sliced cucumbers, half of a hard-boiled egg, and finally 1 tablespoon each of the peanuts and fried anchovies around the rice. Serve warm.

FIVE-SPICED BARBECUE-ROASTED PORK

CHAR SIU PORK

In the days of my childhood, the traveling barbecue vendor would announce his arrival by hitting a bowl with a pair of wooden chopsticks, making a sound like "tok tok tok tok." Our young hearts were cheered by this sound and by the prospect of his specialty, char siu roasted pork, which we called *babi tok*. I created this recipe remembering my childhood days and now my children love the barbecued pork too. It is tender with the perfect amount of sweetness and a deep reddish-brown hue derived from the combination of the sauces and Chinese five-spice powder. The sweet barbecue pork also makes an excellent appetizer, served on top of sliced cucumber with a touch of Sriracha. An important point: You want to only use pork shoulder with enough marbling so the meat will not be dry once cooked. Once the meat is popped into the oven, do not attempt to baste it at all; leave it undisturbed in order to obtain its reddish-brown hue. SERVES 4

¼ to ⅓ cup sugar

6 tablespoons soy sauce

3 tablespoons kicap manis (sweet soy sauce; see page 16)

1 tablespoon rice wine

1 teaspoon sesame oil

1 teaspoon five-spice powder

12 ounces pork shoulder, cut lengthwise into 8- by 2½-inch strips

2 cucumbers, peeled and sliced, for serving

1. In a large, shallow bowl, combine the sugar, soy sauce, kicap manis, rice wine, sesame oil, and five-spice powder and whisk until the sugar is completely dissolved. Add the pork and mix well to coat each piece. Cover, refrigerate, and marinate for at least 24 hours, or preferably 48 hours. The longer the meat marinates, the better it tastes.

2. When ready to cook the pork, preheat the oven to 350°F. Place the pork pieces on a wire rack set over a baking sheet to collect any drips. Discard the marinade. Roast the pork until thoroughly cooked, about 1 hour; the meat will take on a reddish-brown hue when done. Set the meat aside to rest for about 5 minutes. Then slice the meat again about ½ inch thick across the grain and serve with the cucumbers.

PENANG'S FAMOUS CHAR KWAY TEOW

The island of Penang, besides its many old world charms, has over time become a legendary food heaven. In every corner, you will find an eatery, either in the form of a colorfully decorated stall or an ingeniously crafted pushcart under a huge shady raintree. Walking past, you will be mesmerized by the dazzling array and the mouthwatering aromas bellowing from bright charcoal fires, and with the clanging of large ladles on metal woks as busy hawkers create their delicious masterpieces. Eating out has become a way of life for most Penang folks, and many tourists too. Synonymous with Penang's street food is the dish known as *char kway teow,* a rather simple stir-fried dish of flat rice noodles, bean sprouts, sometimes Chinese sausage, wild prawns, plenty of chopped garlic, egg, and soy sauce.

To make it in the most typically Penang way, I suggest using fresh rice noodles. Most Asian markets sell them, perfectly cut into strands and labeled *sha ho fun* in clear Styrofoam trays. At home it's fun to get your hands into these sticky noodles, but first you need to run the noodles under boiling water to remove the oil coating, and then separate them into ribbons. The key is to cook the noodles as soon as you can after you buy them. If you refrigerate the noodles, they will harden and be difficult to separate, which defeats the point of getting them fresh. To achieve the delicious smoky flavor known as *wok hei,* a Cantonese term, I suggest you use a well-seasoned carbon steel wok, not a nonstick skillet. SERVES 4

1 pound fresh rice noodles

3 tablespoons canola or peanut oil

4 cloves garlic, minced

2 large shallots, sliced

1 fresh red jalapeño chili, sliced

8 ounces large shrimp, peeled and deveined

¼ cup soy sauce, or to taste

2 tablespoons kicap manis (sweet soy sauce; see page 16)

½ teaspoon pure ground chilies or chili powder

2 large eggs, beaten

1 cup bean sprouts

½ cup chopped (½-inch) fresh chives

1. Run the noodles under boiling water to remove the oil coating. Separate the noodles into ribbons (as shown in the photograph on page 238,), working gently as they are quite sticky and delicate. Set aside.

2. Heat a wok or a large deep skillet over medium heat for about 40 seconds. Add the oil, pouring it around the perimeter of the wok to coat the sides and bottom. When the surface shimmers slightly, add the garlic, shallots, and chilies and cook, stirring, until fragrant, about 4 minutes. Add the shrimp and cook, stirring, for about 2 minutes more.

3. Add the noodles, soy sauce, kicap manis, and chili powder. Raise the heat to medium-high and cook for about 2 minutes, lifting carefully and gently tossing as the noodles will break into pieces with rough handling. Add the eggs and cook, lifting and gently tossing again, until the eggs are fully cooked, about 2 minutes; the noodles should no longer appear wet from the eggs.

4. Add the bean sprouts and chives and cook, stirring, until the vegetables are slightly wilted. Taste and add more soy sauce if needed for desired saltiness. Serve immediately.

FIVE-SPICE SAVORY POTATOES

I often serve these potatoes at home get-togethers as a healthier and more flavorful alternative to French fries or store-bought chips. I wanted to spice up potatoes without heat, so that both kids and adults can enjoy each morsel. To achieve this, I use *panch phoran* (literally "five spices"), not to be confused with Chinese five-spice, a ground spice mixture that is more robust. The Indian version is a beautiful and aromatic medley of whole seeds—nigella (black onion seeds), black mustard, fenugreek, fennel, and cumin seeds—that is milder, with a subtle peppery flavor that is good for vegetable dishes. You can find this ready-made mix at any Indian grocery, or you can make your own by combining 1 tablespoon of each of the five seeds listed above (all of which can be purchased online). SERVES 4

¼ cup virgin coconut oil or extra-virgin olive oil

1 teaspoon panch phoran

1 red onion, minced

Leaves from 2 sprigs curry leaf

4 cloves garlic, sliced

1 teaspoon garam masala

½ teaspoon ground turmeric

½ to 1 tablespoon chili powder or cayenne

½ teaspoon amchoor (mango) powder

6 medium red potatoes, peeled, cut in half, and sliced

¼ cup water

1 teaspoon salt, or to taste

1. Heat the oil in a medium saucepan over medium heat. Add the panch phoran and allow the spices to sizzle. Using a wooden spatula, move the spices back and forth in the pan (do not stir them in a circular motion, as this prevents aromatic oils from releasing) until fragrant and the spices appear one shade darker, about 1 minute.

2. Add the onion, curry leaves, and garlic and sauté until the onion is well softened, about 5 minutes.

3. Add the garam masala, turmeric, chili powder, and amchoor powder and stir well. Add the potatoes and mix to combine so that the spices coat the potatoes. Add the water to prevent the spices from burning and fold the potatoes gently. Lower the heat, cover the pan, and cook, moving the potatoes back and forth occasionally, until the potatoes are soft and the oils have separated to the top, about 20 minutes. Add the salt, gently stir, and taste; add more salt if needed.

COOK'S NOTE | Keep the spices moving as you add them, as ground spices burn easily, making the dish bitter. The volatile oils in panch phoran all help in digestion, while black mustard is a good source of omega-3 fatty acids. Panch phoran goes very well with lentils, beans, vegetable stir-fries, and even with fish.

GINGER-SESAME CHICKEN WINGS

These sweet, sticky wings are a great finger food that is healthy but still flavorful, with a combination of sweet hoisin and salty soy. This is a resourceful way to use many of the bottles of Asian sauces you might have in your pantry! If you are feeding a crowd, I recommend making a double batch, as the wings disappear quickly. SERVES 6

½ cup sweet Thai chili sauce

3 tablespoons peanut oil

3 tablespoons rice vinegar

3 tablespoons hoisin sauce

3 tablespoons soy sauce

1½ tablespoons ground ginger

1 tablespoon sesame seeds

2 pounds chicken wings

1. Combine the chili sauce, oil, vinegar, hoisin sauce, soy sauce, ginger, and sesame seeds in a bowl and whisk well to make a marinade.

2. Place the chicken wings in a large glass bowl, pour the marinade over, and mix well to coat each piece. Cover, refrigerate, and marinate for at least 24 hours, or preferably 48 hours. The longer the wings marinate, the better they taste.

3. When ready to cook the chicken wings, preheat the oven to 350°F. Line a baking sheet with foil and arrange the chicken wings on the sheet. Discard the marinade. Bake the wings until thoroughly cooked, about 45 minutes. Serve warm.

CHICKEN AND SWEET POTATO CURRY PUFFS

As far back as I can remember, I always craved this savory snack during afternoon teatime. I would eagerly volunteer to take a short walk to the roadside stall two blocks from our home. The vendor, an industrious elderly woman who knew my mother well, had two large woks, with hot oil bubbling, from which she would pull out the puffs and serve them to the long line of customers. For your convenience, I have adapted this recipe to use store-bought puff pastry and to bake the puffs instead of frying them. Alternatively, you can use store-bought or homemade pie dough, and deep-fry them as our local *amah* did. MAKES 22 CURRY PUFFS

1 carrot, peeled and diced

1 medium sweet potato, peeled and diced

1 small Yukon Gold potato, peeled and diced

1 cup frozen petite peas, thawed

2 tablespoons vegetable oil

Leaves from 2 sprigs curry leaf, finely chopped

1 piece (2 inches) fresh ginger, peeled and minced

2 garlic cloves, chopped

8 ounces boneless skinless chicken breasts, diced

2 tablespoons curry powder

1 tablespoon sugar

2 teaspoons salt, or to taste

1 pound frozen puff pastry, thawed

1 large egg, lightly beaten with 1 teaspoon water

1. Set up a steamer by bringing a couple of inches of water to a boil in a large pot. Steam the carrot, sweet potato, potato, and peas in a steamer insert until the vegetables are tender, about 10 minutes.

2. Heat the oil in a medium skillet over medium heat. When hot, add the curry leaves, ginger, and garlic and cook until the garlic is golden and the spices release a fragrant scent, 1 to 2 minutes. Add the chicken and curry powder and cook, stirring as needed, until the meat is no longer pink, about 7 minutes.

3. Add the steamed vegetables, season with the sugar and salt, and cook until the ingredients are well combined, 3 to 4 minutes. Remove from the heat and let cool completely.

4. Preheat the oven to 400°F. Lay one pastry sheet on a lightly floured surface. Roll out the dough to thin it slightly and increase the size by about 1 inch all around. Cut out 3-inch circles. Repeat with the remaining pastry. You will need about 22 circles.

5. Lightly brush the edges of the dough rounds with the beaten egg. Place 1 tablespoon of the cooled filling in the center of each and then fold over the dough to form a semicircle. Gently seal the edges with a fork and place the curry puffs on a baking sheet. Brush each pastry with egg and bake until golden brown, about 25 minutes. Serve warm.

MINIATURE FRIED ROLLS

Crispy on the outside and mouthwateringly savory inside, these rolls are a popular roadside snack usually picked up by people in a hurry, to be eaten in the car or on the long journey home on the bus after work. Sometimes, customers get the stall operator to cut the rolls into bite-size pieces and pour the spicy chili-garlic sauce over the whole thing in a takeaway container. These rolls are often sold together with curry puffs (page 242) and other deep-fried snacks. A note about the name: These rolls are called *spring rolls* throughout Malaysia. However, in Vietnam, Thailand, and Hong Kong, the name *spring rolls* refers to steamed rolls made with rice paper shells and filled with lettuce and other mild cooked fillings. The deep-fried rolls here are also often called *egg rolls,* especially in Chinese restaurants.

MAKES 25 MINIATURE FRIED ROLLS

DIPPING SAUCE

- ¼ cup water
- ½ cup sugar
- ½ cup rice vinegar
- 1 teaspoon minced garlic
- 5 fresh red jalapeño chilies, minced
- ¼ cup fish sauce
- Juice of ½ orange

SPRING ROLLS

- 8 ounces shrimp, shelled and deveined
- 8 ounces ground pork
- 1 (5-ounce) can whole peeled water chestnuts, chopped
- 6 shiitake mushrooms, thinly sliced
- 3 green onions, (white and green parts), chopped
- 3 cloves garlic, peeled and left whole
- 2 tablespoons kicap manis (sweet soy sauce; see page 16)
- 2 tablespoons fish sauce
- 1 teaspoon sugar

- 1 (16-ounce) package 5-inch square spring roll wrappers (sometimes called egg roll wrappers)
- 1 large egg, lightly beaten with 1 teaspoon water
- Vegetable or peanut oil, for deep frying

1. Make the dipping sauce: Bring the water to a boil in a saucepan. Add the sugar and vinegar and stir well to dissolve. Add the garlic and chilies and bring to a boil. Add the fish sauce and orange juice and simmer over low heat until the sauce thickens, about 15 minutes. Remove from the heat and set aside to cool. The sauce can be refrigerated for up 6 hours.

2. Make the filling: Combine the shrimp, pork, water chestnuts, mushrooms, green onions, and garlic in the bowl of a food processor. Pulse a few times until the ingredients are well combined but not mashed. Transfer to a bowl. Stir in the kicap manis, fish sauce, and sugar and mix well.

3. Lay 1 spring roll wrapper on a cutting board or clean surface. Put about 1 teaspoon of the filling in the center, about 1 inch from the edge closest to you. With a pastry brush, lightly brush the sides of the wrapper with the beaten egg to keep the spring rolls sealed during cooking. Fold the end closest to you once over the filling. Bring both the sides of the wrapper to the center. Gently squeeze the wrapper with your fingers to make sure no air is trapped within and start to roll firmly into a cigar-like shape. Place the spring roll on a plate. Repeat with the remaining wrappers and filling.

4. In a wok or large heavy pot, heat 2 to 3 inches of oil over medium heat. Test if the oil is hot enough by placing a chopstick into the pot; if the oil starts to bubble around the chopstick, then the oil is ready for frying. Add a few spring rolls, one at a time. Do not overcrowd the pot or the spring rolls will become soggy. Fry, turning occasionally, until the rolls are golden and crisp, 5 to 7 minutes. Remove and drain on a paper towel. Repeat until all the rolls are fried. Serve hot with the dipping sauce.

MEATS

My mother, a spice merchant, would say, "Some spices are just made for meat dishes." I believe the big difference between cooking in Asia and cooking in Europe and North America lies not in the varieties of spices—cinnamon, cloves, star anise, cardamom, black pepper, coriander, cumin, and nutmeg—that are used all over the world, but rather by how the spices are used in everyday dishes.

In Malaysian cooking, spices flavor the oil and bring complexity and depth to all kinds of dishes—but particularly to meats and poultry. They are partnered in this approach with aromatics (galangal, lemongrass, makrut lime leaves, ginger, garlic, shallots, onions), while sauces and vinegars (oyster sauce, hoisin sauce, soy sauce, fish sauce, rice vinegar) provide layers of salinity that salt alone cannot.

In my kitchen, I enjoy the traditional approach to cooking meat but I also enjoy giving Western-style dishes a Malaysian twist: Grilled Skirt Steak Rendang (page 257) served fajita style with tortillas; Pork Spareribs in Malaysian BBQ Sauce (page 272), which is closely related to American-style barbecue; and Grilled Lamb Chops with Rosemary-Garlic Pesto (page 275).

Curries and stews, such as Butter Chicken Masala (page 269), Malaysian Chicken Curry (page 283), Spicy Beef with Corn and Potatoes (page 253), Chicken and Lentil Dalcha (page 250), and Chicken Korma in Almond Cream (page 260) are commonly slow-cooked. Curries always begin by flavoring the oil with whole dry spices such as cloves, cinnamon, cardamom, and star anise, which draws out the unique essence of each spice and infuses the dish with those flavors. Then fresh spices such as curry leaves, pastes with ginger and garlic, and shallots or onions are added as a second layer to create depth. As the spices cook with the meat, they help tenderize

it, making the meat supple and moist. Adding ground spices somewhat in the middle of the cooking process keeps them from burning and adds even more robust flavor, while also sometimes helping to thicken the sauce or gravy.

Alternatively, ground spices on their own also work wonderfully as rubs when combined with coconut or olive oil and applied to the meat's surface before grilling or frying. I use these spice rubs for Oven-Baked Chicken Tandoori (page 255), Turmeric Fried Chicken (page 276), and Pan-Roasted Chicken with Spiced Rosemary (page 286).

Although many people have health concerns about eating meat, many cuisines around the world have been able to mitigate the potentially harmful effects of meat with the use of health-promoting herbs, spices, and vegetables. Cumin, coriander, ginger, star anise, turmeric, fenugreek, cinnamon, cloves, and cardamom, some of which are native to Southeast Asia, are used regularly in Malaysian meat dishes. Although many studies have shown the healthful properties of these spices, sadly none of the spices are listed in the U.S.D.A.'s food pyramid.

When it comes to marinating, braising, or stir-frying, sauces that are generally used in the Southeast Asian region are indispensable in Malaysian cooking, including soy sauce, oyster sauce, chili sauce, hoisin sauce, fish sauce, and kicap manis (sweet soy sauce). These can be used individually or combined as one would use stock or wine in French cooking. For instance, a few tablespoons each of oyster sauce, soy sauce, kicap manis, and rice vinegar, sealed with a few drops of sesame oil along with some minced garlic and freshly grated ginger, is an excellent marinade for any meat. The meat can then be grilled, baked, or stir-fried in a hot wok to give those flavors a big hit. Even if you are in the midst of stir-frying and your dish seems to lack something, a dash of fish sauce will surely wake it up. Grilled Coconut-Lemongrass Chicken (page 287), Tamarind-Glazed Roast Duck (page 290), and Braised Pork Belly with Soy Garlic Sauce (page 258) are recipes that use these sauces to bring dimension to meat. Because these condiments taste salty, they can often replace salt but are actually lower in sodium.

Last, a method common to all kinds of Malaysian dishes is creating a *rempah,* or spice paste, by blending fresh aromatics, tropical fruits, and Asian herbs. These seasonings (lemongrass, ginger, galangal, makrut lime leaves, hot fresh chilies) differentiate Malaysian cuisine from its Indian and Chinese neighbors. Frying the spice paste in coconut or olive oil sets the foundation, after which you can add any meat or poultry of your liking. Then follow with some liquid—perhaps coconut milk for a creamy finish, tamarind water for a tangy dish, or your own homemade broth. The end result is a flavorful one-pot dish. Once your meat is tender and cooked, simply season with salt, fish sauce, and freshly ground pepper, and maybe add some cilantro, basil, mint, or dill.

Cooking on a day-to-day basis becomes a cinch, because you can store these flavoring pastes in the freezer and use them when you need them. You will notice even leftovers will taste as though they are fresh when cooked with these aromatics.

Among the dishes in this book where aromatics make the biggest difference are Curry Kapitan (page 289), Chicken Opor in Spiced Coconut Milk (page 281), and Grilled Coconut-Lemongrass Chicken (page 287). These signature dishes of Malaysia show how much can be done with aromatics. You could also stuff a whole chicken with fresh aromatics instead of lemons, as I do for Roast Chicken with Fragrant Lemongrass (page 278). These aromatics-based dishes will go well with so many other foods, from Western-style meals to other Southeast Asian ones.

I encourage all of you to be creative. Use other meats (like goat instead of lamb), stock up on a variety of Asian sauces, delve into the Southeast Asian world of aromatics, and grind spices that are readily available in stores into fragrant spice powders to add a new dimension to your everyday dishes.

CHICKEN AND LENTIL DALCHA

When I was growing up, *dalcha* was a popular home-style stew in which any of a variety of meats (usually mutton) would be cooked with lentils and spices until tender, and then enjoyed with roti or bread. My favorite version of dalcha is made with chicken and yellow split lentils. I make this one-pot dish as often as I can because it takes such little effort and cooking it over low heat allows time for the spices and flavors to come together, mellow, and create a full-flavored dish. For me, the enjoyable part of making dalcha is browning the onions and cinnamon, as the scent is divine and makes the stew more interesting. You could vary it by using any kind of beans, lentils, or split peas, or substituting parsnips or potatoes for the carrots. SERVES 4

½ cup split yellow lentils (*toor dal*) or yellow split peas

6 tablespoons clarified butter (ghee) or coconut oil

1 medium yellow onion, minced

3 cloves garlic, minced

1 cinnamon stick

3 Roma tomatoes, halved

1 teaspoon freshly ground black pepper

2 pounds chicken drumsticks (5 or 6 pieces)

4 cups chicken broth

1 to 2 teaspoons salt

½ teaspoon ground cumin

¼ teaspoon ground turmeric

½ cup baby carrots, whole

1. Wash the lentils by gently rubbing them with your fingers in a bowl under cold running until the water runs clear. (The running water allows debris, such as tiny stones or outer skin, to float to the top instead of sinking to the bottom with the lentils.) Drain the lentils and set aside.

2. Heat 4 tablespoons of the clarified butter or oil in a Dutch oven or other heavy pot over medium heat. When the oil is hot, add the onion, garlic, and cinnamon and stir once, then cook until the onions are soft and brown, about 5 minutes.

3. Add the tomatoes and cook until they are a little soft but not broken down, about 5 minutes.

4. Meanwhile, heat the remaining 2 tablespoons clarified butter or oil in a medium cast iron pan. Sprinkle pepper all over the chicken. When the oil is hot, carefully place the chicken in the pan and cook until browned on both sides, about 10 minutes.

5. While the chicken is browning, add the lentils and broth to the Dutch oven with the onion mixture, stir, and bring to a boil.

6. Add the browned chicken pieces to the lentils, then season with the salt, cumin, and turmeric. Cover, reduce the heat to medium-low, and simmer, stirring intermittently, until the lentils are soft and the chicken is cooked through, about 40 minutes. Skim off any foam that may appear on the surface during cooking. Add the carrots and continue to cook, covered, until the carrots are tender, 5 to 6 minutes more. Taste and add more salt if needed. Serve immediately.

CURRIED BEEF WITH OKRA

While many people make hamburgers or meatloaf with ground beef, my family loves this quick recipe featuring sautéed ground beef and okra. My aunties from Ipoh, a rustic town in the Kinta Valley, made it for family get-togethers, and even among the many other dishes, it always appealed to everyone's appetite. Okra lends a sweet and crunchy texture that complements the beef. I add the tomatoes near the end so they are half cooked. Their plump juicy sweetness, together with the perfectly spiced beef, makes a deeply satisfying dish, best served with some baked potatoes. SERVES 6

¼ cup peanut oil

1 small white onion, thinly sliced

1 tablespoon Ginger, Garlic, and Cilantro Paste (page 53)

1 pound lean ground beef

1 to 2 tablespoons curry powder, to taste

½ teaspoon ground turmeric

½ teaspoon ground black pepper

8 ounces okra, rinsed

1 teaspoon salt, or to taste

2 Roma tomatoes, quartered

1. Heat the oil in a large sauté pan over medium heat. When the oil is hot, add the onion and cook until soft and evenly brown, about 5 minutes. Add the ginger-garlic paste, stir, and cook for about 1 minute.

2. Add the ground beef, curry powder, turmeric, and pepper, mix well, and cook until the meat is no longer pink, about 7 minutes.

3. Add the okra and salt and fold once to combine with the meat. Lower the heat to medium-low, cover, and continue to cook until the okra is soft but still slightly crisp, stirring back and forth occasionally, about 10 minutes.

4. Toss in the tomatoes and cook until they are heated through, half cooked, and the oil appears on the surface, about 3 minutes. Give the mixture a stir once to combine the flavors and then serve warm.

SPICY BEEF WITH CORN AND POTATOES

When I tasted this Southwestern-inspired dish in a cozy restaurant in Los Angeles, I thought it was good but needed a kick of spice and a Malaysian twist. So I added ginger, cinnamon, and cloves to enhance the sweetness of the corn, and used that old Malaysian trick of adding a squeeze of lemon juice and some ground chilies to make all the flavors pop. Serve over sliced avocado for a creamy texture, and enjoy with either tortillas or Indian flatbreads such as roti. SERVES 6

¼ cup peanut oil

1 yellow onion, chopped

1 piece (1-inch) fresh ginger, peeled and minced

3 cloves garlic, sliced

1 cinnamon stick

2 whole cloves

1 pound lean ground beef

3 to 4 red potatoes, washed and grated

1½ teaspoons salt, or to taste

1 teaspoon ground chilies

½ teaspoon ground turmeric

1 cup corn kernels

2 tablespoons lemon juice

1 avocado, pitted and sliced, for serving

6 warm tortillas or rotis, for serving

1. Heat the oil in a large sauté pan over medium heat. When the oil is hot, add the onion, ginger, garlic, cinnamon, and cloves and cook until onions are soft and evenly brown, about 5 minutes. Remove and discard the cloves.

2. Add the ground beef and salt and mix well. Add the potatoes and give the mixture a good stir. Cook until the beef is soft and no longer pink, about 15 minutes.

3. Stir in the ground chilies, turmeric, and corn and continue to cook until the corn is soft, about 15 minutes. Taste and add more salt if needed. Add the lemon juice and stir to combine. Serve warm with the avocado and tortillas or roti.

OVEN-BAKED CHICKEN TANDOORI

Although there are numerous upscale Indian Tandoori restaurants in urban areas in Malaysia, makeshift stalls that sit alongside these restaurants seem to have grown in popularity. These cooks construct clay ovens in large empty oil drums and showcase pieces of chicken on skewers in glass cases. The chicken is most often enjoyed with Malaysian *roti canai* (flaky bread) and a hot cup of *teh tarik* ("pulled tea"). You'll notice that the Malaysian style of tandoori is not red like the tandooris found in most Indian restaurants. The spices are also lighter; cumin, coriander, paprika, and turmeric flavor the chicken while yogurt and ginger tenderize it, for meat that is crispy on the outside and succulent inside. SERVES 6

3 pounds skinless bone-in chicken thigh meat
  Juice of 1 lemon
1 cup plain yogurt, whisked until smooth
¼ cup Ginger, Garlic, and Cilantro Paste (page 53)
2 teaspoons paprika
1 teaspoon garam masala (see Note)
1 teaspoon ground cumin
1 teaspoon ground coriander
1 teaspoon ground turmeric
1 teaspoon salt, or to taste
2 limes, cut into wedges

1. Make a deep cut on each side of the chicken pieces, deep enough to touch the bone. Place the chicken in a glass bowl and rub each piece thoroughly with the lemon juice. Set aside for about 15 minutes.

2. Meanwhile, in a bowl, combine the yogurt, ginger-garlic paste, paprika, garam masala, cumin, coriander, turmeric, and salt. Whisk until you have a smooth marinade. Taste and add more salt if needed. Pour the marinade all over the chicken and mix thoroughly, making sure the marinade goes into the slits in the chicken. Cover and refrigerate for at least 24 hours or preferably 48 hours.

3. Preheat the oven to 400°F. Grease a baking sheet.

4. Take the chicken out of the bowl, removing as much marinade as possible, and place on the baking sheet. Roast for about 30 minutes. Set the oven to broil and broil the chicken, flipping once, until golden brown on both sides, about 2 minutes total. Transfer to a platter and garnish with lime wedges. Serve hot.

COOK'S NOTE | To make homemade garam masala, combine 1 tablespoon cardamom seeds, a 2-inch cinnamon stick, 1 teaspoon cumin seeds, 1 teaspoon whole cloves, 1 teaspoon black peppercorns, and ¼ teaspoon ground nutmeg in a coffee grinder or spice grinder and grind to a smooth powder. You should have a little over ¼ cup. Store in an airtight container.

PORTUGUESE DEBAL PORK

The word *debal* here is a Malaccan creole word for "devil," referring to the fiery spiciness of the dish. Red in color from the abundant use of chilies and spiked with tart vinegar and black pepper, debal pork had its beginnings in Goa, the former Portuguese province in India. When the Portuguese colonists came to Malacca, they took local wives and assimilated into the local culture; their descendants still reside at the famous Portuguese Settlement in Malacca. Debal curry is popular here and it is traditional to prepare on the day after Christmas using leftover meat. My family, although we are not Malaccan, also made this dish on Boxing Day. Meat and potatoes are the usual, but sometimes cabbage and long beans are added. The pork curry is slow-cooked for an hour in a fresh-flavored chili paste until the meat absorbs the flavors from the braising liquid. I have slightly reduced the heat of the traditional dish to make it favorable to all. Debal curry goes well with French bread; leftovers the next day may taste even better. SERVES 4

1 chunk (6 ounces) bacon, cut into ½-inch-thick pieces

1 piece (1-inch) fresh ginger, peeled and julienned

10 cloves garlic, peeled and left whole

5 tablespoons Sambal Ulek (page 44 or store-bought); or 5 fresh red jalapeño chilies, seeded and sliced

1 teaspoon freshly ground black pepper

½ cup rice vinegar

2 pounds pork butt, cut into 2-inch pieces

Salt to taste

1. Heat a Dutch oven or other heavy pot over medium heat. Add the bacon and cook until the bacon bits are crispy and the fat has rendered, about 15 minutes.

2. Meanwhile, combine the ginger, garlic, sambal or jalapeños, black pepper, and vinegar in a food processor and blend to a smooth paste. Add the chili paste to the pot and mix well to combine with the bacon fat.

3. Add the pork and give it a good stir. Cover, lower the heat to medium-low, and cook until the pork is fork tender and most of the oils have separated onto the surface, about 1 hour. Season with salt to taste.

GRILLED SKIRT STEAK RENDANG

This twist on the all-American skirt steak delivers a wallop of flavor from the Malaysian rendang marinade. The rendang is rubbed all over the steak, then the steak is grilled until medium and juicy. You could serve the meat fajita-style, wrapped in tortillas with a side of sautéed onions, or simply enjoy it on top of your favorite salad. SERVES 6

3 tablespoons extra-virgin olive oil or coconut oil

5 shallots, chopped

1 tablespoon chili paste or Sambal Ulek (page 44 or store-bought)

2 stalks fresh lemongrass, outer leaves discarded, bottom 6 inches thinly sliced

1 piece (3-inch) fresh ginger, peeled and sliced

6 cloves garlic, peeled

5 macadamia nuts

1 tablespoon ground coriander

½ teaspoon ground turmeric

Salt to taste

½ cup coconut milk

2 pounds skirt steak, cut into 4-inch pieces

1. To prepare the rendang spice paste, heat the oil in a small pan and add the shallots, chili paste, lemongrass, ginger, garlic, and macadamia nuts. Stir-fry over medium heat for about 5 minutes. Add the coriander, turmeric, and salt and continue to stir-fry for about 1 minute, then remove from the heat.

2. Process the spice paste with the coconut milk in a food processor until smooth to make the marinade. It will be aromatic and orange colored.

3. Place the steak in a large baking dish. Pour the marinade over the steak and turn to coat evenly. Cover with plastic wrap and refrigerate for about 3 hours.

4. Light a grill and let it heat to medium-hot. Once the grill is hot, lightly oil the grate. Grill the steak, turning occasionally, for 6 to 8 minutes for medium rare, or about 12 minutes for medium. Transfer the steak to a cutting board and let rest for 10 minutes, then slice across the grain and serve immediately.

BRAISED PORK BELLY WITH SOY GARLIC SAUCE

When I was in elementary school, my father would occasionally pick me up at the convent in his old Volvo. I knew for sure that on these days we were having dinner at Rocky's, a family-owned Chinese restaurant in the neighborhood. He would order his same favorite dish every time—*tau yew bak,* slow-cooked pork belly braised in fresh garlic and soy sauce and served with jasmine rice. Each bite, perfectly brown and juicy and cloaked in an intensely delectable sauce, was so tender it would melt in your mouth. Although this recipe has only a few ingredients, the beauty of Asian pantry sauces such as soy sauce and oyster sauce lies in their ability to create abundant and varied flavors. Better still, you can easily double the recipe to feed many.

Pork belly is actually a tough cut of meat, so it must be allowed to cook undisturbed for a long time, at least an hour, in order to tenderize. During this time the sliced garlic and sauce become one with the meat. Every time I sit down to savor this dish, memories of my father and family enjoying a meal together at Rocky's flood my mind. SERVES 4

3 pounds pork belly, skin removed

¼ cup oyster sauce

3 tablespoons dark soy sauce

2 tablespoons soy sauce

1 teaspoon sesame oil

10 cloves garlic, peeled and left whole

1. Rinse the pork belly under cold water. Pat dry with a paper towel, then cut into 1½-inch pieces.

2. Place a Dutch oven or other heavy pot over medium-low heat. Put in the pork belly, then add the oyster sauce, dark soy sauce, soy sauce, sesame oil, and garlic. Cover and cook for about 1½ hours. The pork is done when it is fork tender. As the pork belly cooks it will lose some of its fat and shrink.

3. Remove the lid, raise the heat to medium, and bring to a quick simmer. Cook, spooning the sauces over the meat, until the meat is browned and glazed, about 5 minutes. Serve the pork belly and the reduced sauce immediately.

CHICKEN KORMA IN ALMOND CREAM

For a Malaysian Christian family, the glorious Chicken Korma sitting on the Christmas table is like a whole roasted ham on the American table. The festive dish, an aromatic stew of chicken, lamb, or mutton braised in a creamy almond sauce and eaten with rice pilaf, has celebration written all over it. Cardamom, ginger, cinnamon, star anise, and cloves elevate the flavor of the meat. The other key ingredient here is korma powder, a premade spice blend much loved even by local cooks. I often use Baba's brand, which is available online.

SERVES 4

¼ cup clarified butter (ghee) or virgin coconut oil

1 cinnamon stick (4 inches)

2 whole star anise

3 whole cloves

3 green cardamom pods, crushed

1 large onion, roughly chopped

2 fresh green jalapeño chilies, seeded and sliced lengthwise

¼ cup Ginger, Garlic, and Cilantro Paste (page 53)

1 cup whole almonds

1½ pounds chicken thighs and drumsticks

3 medium tomatoes, cut in half

2 medium red potatoes, peeled and halved

¼ cup store-bought korma powder or ground coriander

1 teaspoon ground turmeric

3 cups coconut milk

1 cup water

1 teaspoon salt, or to taste

¼ cup plain yogurt

1. Heat the clarified butter or oil in a large heavy pot over medium heat. Add the cinnamon, star anise, cloves, cardamom, onion, jalapeños, and ginger-garlic paste. Cook, stirring, until the onion is soft and fragrant, about 10 minutes.

2. Place the almonds in a blender and blend to a very smooth paste with the consistency of applesauce, adding a little water at a time. Add the almond paste to the pot and mix well to combine.

3. Now add the chicken, tomatoes, potatoes, korma powder, turmeric, coconut milk, and water and stir well. Cook, uncovered, stirring occasionally, until the meat is tender, about 40 minutes. Season with salt to taste.

4. Stir in the yogurt. Remove from the heat and let sit for 3 minutes before serving warm.

BEEF RENDANG

Rendang is the signature dish and comfort food of Malaysia: Think of it as akin to the American pot roast but featuring the Malaysian flavors of fresh lemongrass, galangal, ginger, shallots, cumin, cinnamon, turmeric, and chilies. There is one other difference in the technique: The searing of meat happens at the end of cooking, once all the liquid has evaporated, allowing the meat to brown in its own fat. Although beef rendang is a rich dish, in Malaysian cooking, seasonings such as turmeric, cinnamon, fresh garlic, and ginger are used for their anti-inflammatory benefits and to improve the digestion of meat. Rendang is delicious when paired with any sambal and Fragrant Coconut Rice (page 160). SERVES 6

SPICE PASTE

- 6 shallots, peeled and quartered
- 2 fresh red chilies, chopped
- 4 stalks fresh lemongrass, outer layer discarded, bottom 6 inches thinly sliced; or 5 tablespoons frozen lemongrass
- 1 piece (3 inches) unpeeled fresh galangal, chopped
- 1 piece (2 inches) fresh ginger, peeled and chopped
- 6 cloves garlic, peeled and left whole
- 1 tablespoon chili or cayenne powder
- ½ teaspoon ground turmeric
- ½ teaspoon ground cumin
- ¼ cup Tamarind Water (page 54)

BEEF

- ¼ cup peanut or coconut oil
- 2 cinnamon sticks (3 inches each)
- 3 whole star anise
- 3 pounds beef chuck, cut into 2-inch cubes
- 1 tablespoon sugar
- 2 cups coconut milk

- 1 cup toasted grated coconut or toasted desiccated coconut (kerisik; see page 263)
- Salt to taste

1. Prepare the spice paste: Place the shallots, chilies, lemongrass, galangal, ginger, garlic, chili powder, turmeric, cumin, and tamarind water in a food processor and blend into a smooth paste. If needed to facilitate blending, add a little water in small increments while the motor is running. You will end up with a fragrant, bright-orange spice paste.

2. Braise the beef: Heat the oil in a large Dutch oven or other large heavy pot over medium heat. Add the cinnamon and star anise and cook until fragrant, about 1 minute. Add the spice paste and mix well to combine. Add the beef, sugar, and coconut milk and mix well. Cover and cook over low heat until the meat is tender, about 1 hour 15 minutes, stirring occasionally to prevent the spices from sticking and scorching.

3. After about an hour and 15 minutes, you will have a lot of liquid in the pot. Uncover the pot, mix in the grated coconut, and continue cooking until most of the liquid is reduced, the oil has separated onto the surface, and the meat is fork tender, about 30 minutes. The sauce will appear thicker and darker brown at this point. As the meat starts to brown, it is key to stir occasionally to prevent the meat from sticking and burning.

4. Add salt to taste and mix well. Turn off the heat. Allow the meat to rest for a few minutes before serving.

HOW TO PREPARE TOASTED COCONUT (KERISIK) | *Kerisik* is toasted grated fresh coconut that adds texture and brings a smoky aroma and buttery flavor to meat dishes. In rendang, kerisik is added at the end to help thicken the sauce and give the dish a lovely brown color. To make kerisik, start with frozen unsweetened grated or shredded coconut, which comes in a 6- by 6-inch (16-ounce) package, imported from Thailand or the Philippines and sold at most Asian supermarkets.

1. Thaw the frozen coconut by placing the package in a bowl of hot water for about 30 minutes.

2. Place the thawed grated coconut in a dry wok over medium heat and toast, stirring occasionally to ensure the base does not burn, until it goes from white to brown, about 30 minutes. Once the coconut appears dry, brown, and fragrant, remove from the heat.

3. Pulse the coconut in a food processor into a rough powder. Alternatively, the traditional method is to pound the toasted coconut in small batches using a mortar and pestle to release the fragrant oils.

4. Store the toasted coconut in an airtight container. Toasted coconut can last up to 4 months in the pantry, 6 months in the refrigerator, and more than 1 year in the freezer.

SPICES AND HEALTH

Many people are by now familiar with antioxidants, compounds in food that are thought to assist the body in coping with chronic illnesses. For most Americans, this means fruits like blueberries, plums, oranges, and kiwis and greens like kale. What I want to share with you is that numerous spices, especially turmeric, ginger, cinnamon, and cumin, are also rich sources of antioxidants. These spices are so pervasive that we take them for granted. But studies indicate that a diet rich in whole foods and spices is the key to preventing disease. If you're looking to round out your healthy lifestyle, you will want to stock up on the following spices, which can both transform bland ingredients into flavorful dishes and restore and maintain your health and vitality.

TURMERIC

If I had to choose a single spice to rely upon for the well-being it provides, it would be the golden gift from mother earth, flavorful turmeric. Turmeric is a rhizome (an underground stem) with a light beige skin and knobby appearance. Underneath its skin is a bright orange-yellow flesh, somewhat earthy and slightly bitter in taste.

In the kitchens throughout Southeast Asia, local cooks love to season their curries and braised dishes with a dash of ground turmeric for its savory flavor and to add beautiful golden color. And because food is medicine in a Southeast Asian diet, most cooks are aware of turmeric's many health benefits.

The active compound in turmeric, curcumin, has powerful antioxidant and anti-inflammatory properties. Turmeric is thought by experts to strengthen the heart by lowering "bad" cholesterol levels, thus aiding in the prevention of heart disease, strokes, and heart attacks. It helps control blood sugar levels, and may reduce the risk of type 2 diabetes if eaten on a regular basis; may have anticancer effects; and might even counter addictions to alcohol and sugar. According to the American Cancer Society, tests have shown that curcumin can kill or slow cancer cells in laboratory dishes, reduce the development of several forms of cancer, and shrink tumors in lab animals.

In Malaysian homes, turmeric is simmered with milk until the aromatic compounds are infused, then drunk to help fight free radicals that damage skin, helping to preserve the skin's glow and elasticity.

GINGER

There is an ancient Indian proverb, "Every good quality is contained in ginger." Often called a root, ginger, like turmeric, is actually a rhizome that is believed to be native to Southeast Asia. For ages it has been treasured for its culinary and medicinal properties in most Asian cultures and continues to play a vital part in Ayurveda medicine.

Used extensively in Asian cooking, ginger

comes from the family that includes both galangal and turmeric and is lemony, pungent, flowery, and woodsy in flavor. In Malaysian cooking, it is often partnered with garlic to cut the richness of fatty dishes. One of my favorite ways to enjoy ginger is to add 1 inch of fresh ginger to my daily juicing routine; it is especially delicious with carrots, celery, and apples. When traveling, I bring with me a packet of candied ginger to help with nausea; candied ginger is also delicious as an after-dinner digestive aide. And of course it is a key ingredient for creating delicious stir-fries, braised dishes, and curries. It is also wonderful in meat marinades, since its principal enzyme, zingibain, digests protein, which tenderizes the meat; zingibain also has antibacterial, anti-inflammatory, and anti-oxidant properties. Many Asians drink ginger tea to warm the stomach, soothe a sore throat, relieve joint pain, stimulate appetite, improve circulation, or balance hormonal flow. It is also excellent for cold and flu relief. One study reported that ginger inhibits blood-thickening, which could help treat heart disease.

I also use ground ginger as a body scrub to improve circulation and to detoxify the body.

CINNAMON

When Europeans first discovered cinnamon, it quickly became one of the most sought after spices, which led to a series of spice wars throughout Southeast Asia. The inner bark of a tropical evergreen tree, it is sweet and spicy in aroma and flavor, loved for its culinary and medicinal values.

Studies have shown cinnamon to help control and reduce blood sugar levels, making it potentially useful in reducing the risk of type 2 diabetes. It can also accelerate the breakdown of fats from food sources that for some people may be difficult to digest. Eugenol, one of the essential oils in cinnamon, is known to increase the production of digestive enzymes necessary for preventing indigestion.

I can clearly remember how my father stored cinnamon in small glass bottles in his medicine cabinet. In mid-afternoon, he would brew several quills of cinnamon with Ceylon tea leaves to a make a delicious thirst quencher for the hot afternoon. He believed adding cinnamon to his tea would help relieve his muscle aches from a cold and help maintain his cardiovascular health.

CHILI PEPPERS

Before the 17th century, chili peppers were unknown outside South and Central America. We can thank the Spanish and Portuguese for spreading chilies throughout the world, especially in Asia. Before then, Asian cooks mainly relied on locally grown black pepper and ginger to provide heat in their cooking.

Southeast Asians use chilies in all forms— ground, fresh, and dried chilies reconstituted in water—daily in their cooking. The "heat" of chilies is widely considered therapeutic: Chilies are believed to raise the body heat, and the increased perspiration helps trigger the body's natural cooling systems and boost the over-all metabolic rate. Additionally, it is broadly believed that consuming food laden with chilies can help with weight loss and provide farm workers with more energy to work in the fields. Food that is "hot" is introduced to children slowly, usually around the age of four. By the time children are school-age, they are expected to eat food as hot as that of their parents.

Chilies get their characteristic heat from an oleoresin called *capsaicin,* which is found in the interior seeds and membrane, where a wealth of antioxidants and vitamins A and C are also found.

Although chilies have a reputation for aggravating stomach ulcers, studies have shown that they might actually prevent them or reduce the risk. One study from India found that capsaicin actually inhibits acid secretion because it stimulates gastric mucosal blood flow, which helps in the prevention and healing of ulcers. Population surveys in Singapore, which has an ethnically diverse population, have shown that gastric ulcers are three times more common among Chinese adults, who consume far less spicy food, than in Malaysians and Indians, who depend on chilies in their cooking.

CUMIN

In most Southeast Asian, Mediterranean, Indian, and Middle Eastern cuisines, cumin is used in curry powder, and to make satays, kebabs, lentil stews, and a variety of vegetable dishes. Somewhat peppery and savory in flavor, cumin has a distinctive yellow-green-brown color.

The tiny and humble cumin seeds are full of iron, manganese, copper, calcium, magnesium, phosphorus, zinc, and dietary fiber. Cumin seeds are also rich in beta-carotene, lutein, and zeaxanthin. As with so many spice seeds, cumin has aromatic oils that activate the salivary glands. Other compounds in cumin are widely believed to aid in the other steps of the digestion process. One study suggested that cumin seeds may have anticancer effects, particularly in the prevention of colon cancer.

Some of the seeds in the same family have mildly hypnotic effects, which is why so many are used in after-meal breath mints, as they contribute to a sense of relaxation.

BUTTER CHICKEN MASALA

When I first came to the United States, I often sought out butter chicken masala at Indian restaurants, only to be disappointed and unhappy each time, experiencing indigestion and extreme thirst from too much sodium. But there is nothing better than making it at home using quality spices and ingredients. The spice blend—cloves, cinnamon, and star anise—is alive and vibrant, rendering a naturally rich sunset-like color to the delicate cream sauce.

SERVES 4

1½ to 2 pounds boneless chicken thighs, cut into 1-inch slices across the grain

½ tablespoon ground chilies or cayenne pepper

½ teaspoon ground turmeric

Juice from ½ lime

¼ cup butter (ghee) or regular butter

2 cinnamon sticks (4 inches each)

3 whole cloves

1 whole star anise

1 teaspoon cumin seeds

4 bay leaves

3 small yellow onions, sliced

2 tablespoons Ginger, Garlic, and Cilantro Paste (page 53)

3 large tomatoes, chopped

½ cup water

1 teaspoon salt, or to taste

½ cup cream or half-and-half

1. Place the chicken pieces in a glass bowl, add the chili powder, turmeric, and lime juice, and mix well. Set aside to marinate for about 30 minutes.

2. Heat the butter in a medium saucepan over medium heat. Add the cinnamon, cloves, star anise, and cumin and cook until fragrant, about 1 minute. Add the bay leaves, onions, ginger-garlic paste, and tomatoes and sauté until the onions are light brown and the tomatoes are soft, 10 to 15 minutes.

3. Reduce the heat to low. Remove the cinnamon sticks and set aside on a plate. Carefully transfer the onion-spice mixture to a blender. Allow the hot spices to cool for 1 to 2 minutes. Blend, adding the water to achieve a smooth puree. You will end up with a sunset-colored paste.

4. Transfer the blended spice mixture back to the same pan and add the marinated chicken and the reserved cinnamon sticks. Cook over low heat until the chicken is cooked through and the meat appears white, 15 to 20 minutes.

5. Add the salt and cream and mix well to combine. Cook the chicken in the masala mixture until the oils separate onto the surface, about 10 minutes. Taste and add more salt if needed. Serve warm.

CASHEW CHICKEN

Cashew chicken couldn't be any easier to enjoy with a plate of piping hot rice on a busy weeknight. The key factor here is the roasted chili paste—a sweet, tangy, and slightly hot sauce that provides complexity. Roasted chili paste comes in a glass bottle in the sauce aisle at Asian grocery stores. I prefer the ones from Thailand labeled "Chili Paste in Soybean Oil" since they are made with all-natural seasonings such as shallots, garlic, and chilies and taste more sweet and tangy than spicy. You can also make your own chili paste.

One good way to learn to balance flavors is to combine the oyster sauce, roasted chili paste, and fish sauce in a small bowl before beginning to cook, then dip your finger, taste, and adjust according to your preference. If you want the dish spicy, add more dried chilies to the wok at the beginning. If on the other hand you'd like the dish sweeter, add more roasted chili paste and oyster sauce. For a saltier finish, add more fish sauce. You could use almonds or peanuts instead of cashews to vary the crunch. Every time I serve this dish, my family and friends tell me that they leave the dinner table feeling nourished, satisfied, and invigorated. Must be the magic of chilies! SERVES 4

5 tablespoons peanut oil or virgin coconut oil

8 cloves garlic, minced

⅓ cup dried red chilies de arbol

1½ pounds boneless skinless chicken breast, cut into ¾-inch pieces

2 tablespoons oyster sauce

1 tablespoon Southeast Asian Roasted Chili Paste (page 59, or use store-bought)

1 tablespoon fish sauce, or to taste

1 cup roasted unsalted cashews

4 green onions (white and green parts), cut into 1-inch pieces

1. Heat a wok or a large deep skillet over medium heat for about 40 seconds and then add the oil. When the surface shimmers slightly, add the garlic and chilies and cook, stirring constantly, until light golden, 4 to 5 minutes.

2. Add the chicken to the side of the wok and let sear undisturbed for about 1 minute. Now, move the chicken back and forth in the wok and continue to cook this way until the meat is no longer pink on the outside and fully cooked on the inside, about 7 minutes.

3. Add the oyster sauce, chili paste, fish sauce, and cashews and cook for about 3 minutes.

4. Raise the heat to high, toss in the green onions, and mix once just for about 3 seconds. Serve immediately.

PORK SPARERIBS IN MALAYSIAN BBQ SAUCE

This is a quick and easy barbecue dish that you could either roast in the oven during cold winter months or cook over a hot charcoal grill for a traditional smoky taste in the summer. My family's spice secret to a well-seasoned barbecue is correctly pairing the best spices to complement the meat: Here, garlic, paprika, pepper, salt, and mustard deeply flavor the pork, while a mix of ketchup, Worcestershire sauce, and molasses forms the sweet-sour base. If you like the meat saltier, add more salt or use soy sauce. I like to serve these ribs with Malaysian Potato Salad (page 108). SERVES 6

½ cup ketchup

¼ cup Worcestershire sauce

2 tablespoons garlic powder

2 teaspoons Dijon mustard

½ cup liquid palm sugar (see page 315–316) or molasses

1 teaspoon paprika

1 tablespoon salt, or to taste

1 teaspoon freshly ground black pepper

4 pounds St. Louis–style pork spareribs

¼ cup extra-virgin olive oil or coconut oil

1. Prepare the barbecue sauce: Combine the ketchup, Worcestershire sauce, garlic powder, mustard, palm sugar, paprika, salt, and pepper in a food processor and blend into a smooth paste. Taste and add more salt if needed. The marinade should taste well-balanced and sweet, sour, spicy, and salty.

2. Put the spareribs in a glass bowl and pour the marinade over. Mix well, allowing the marinade to cover the meat completely. Cover and refrigerate to marinate for at least 3 hours, or preferably overnight.

3. When ready to cook, preheat the oven to 350°F and line a baking sheet with parchment paper or foil and set a rack on top. (Or heat a grill to medium-high.)

4. If cooking in the oven, arrange the spareribs bone side down on the rack. If cooking on the grill, place the ribs meat side down on the hot side of the grill. Drizzle the oil over the spareribs but keep some for basting. If grilling, cook for about 5 minutes, until grill marks appear. Turn 90 degrees and cook for another 4 minutes. Then flip the ribs, move them to the cool side of the grill, and close the lid.

5. Bake or grill the ribs, turning them occasionally and basting with oil once or twice during cooking, until brown and smoky, 1½ to 2 hours. Transfer to a cutting board and let rest for 10 minutes so that they will be tender and juicy. To serve, cut the spareribs into individual ribs and arrange on a platter.

PORK SPARERIBS IN CINNAMON-NUTMEG SAUCE

This dish has a long cultural history, originating from the Peranakans, also known as Babas and Nyonyas (descendants of early Chinese settlers who intermarried with local Malays in Malacca). This braised stew makes a lovely Sunday brunch and should be served with piping hot rice and a bowl of Sambal Ulek (page 44). The foundation of onions and fermented soybean paste provides depth of flavor and an element of saltiness and complexity. The fermented bean paste, which you can buy at most Asian grocery stores or online, comes in a bottle labeled "Thai Soy Bean Paste." It is made from the solids left over after soy sauce is extracted from soybeans. Alternatively, you may use common Japanese miso but the dish will be not as complex. SERVES 4 TO 6

1 large red onion or 8 shallots, chopped

8 cloves garlic, peeled and left whole

1 tablespoon ground coriander

2 tablespoons Thai soybean paste or Japanese miso

2¼ cups water

¼ cup virgin coconut oil or peanut oil

2 cinnamon sticks (2 inches each)

2 whole star anise

4 whole cloves

2 pounds pork spareribs, cut into 2-inch pieces

3 tablespoons kicap manis (sweet soy sauce; see page 16)

2 teaspoons freshly ground nutmeg

1. Prepare the spice paste by placing the onion, garlic, coriander, soybean paste, and ¼ cup of the water in a food processor and blending into a smooth paste. Set aside.

2. Heat the oil in a Dutch oven or other large, heavy pot over medium heat. When the oil is hot, add the cinnamon, star anise, and cloves and cook until fragrant, about 2 minutes.

3. Gently add the spice paste to prevent splattering and cook, stirring to prevent it from sticking to the bottom of the pot. The onions have a natural tendency to burn on the bottom of the pan, so keep scraping as you stir the paste. Cook until some oils have separated onto the surface and the paste is golden brown and fragrant, about 15 minutes.

4. Add the ribs to the pot and mix well, then add the kicap manis and the remaining 2 cups water. Mix to combine the ingredients. Reduce the heat to low and cook, uncovered, until the meat is completely cooked through, about 40 minutes.

5. Sprinkle in the nutmeg and mix well. Simmer until the meat is tender and the sauce has thickened, about 10 minutes longer. Serve warm.

GRILLED LAMB CHOPS WITH ROSEMARY-GARLIC PESTO

I am crazy about lamb loin chops with just the right amount of fat on the bones, especially when paired with fresh herbs. Since I am blessed with plenty of fragrant rosemary plants and the forest-green leaves of bay bushes in my backyard garden, I am always finding ways to cook with them, which also helps to downsize them before they take over the garden. Blending the rosemary, garlic, and bay leaves with olive oil into a pesto enables the herbs to stick to the meat and penetrate it for a lot more flavor—and also prevents the rosemary from burning. Finally, since the chops have already been marinating in the pesto oil, you don't need to add more oil when grilling them. SERVES 6

½ cup extra-virgin olive oil

3 tablespoons Worcestershire sauce

Leaves from 5 sprigs fresh rosemary

4 fresh bay leaves

8 cloves garlic, peeled and left whole

1 teaspoon salt, or to taste

1 teaspoon freshly ground black pepper

12 lamb loin chops, each 1¼ inches thick

1 lemon, cut into wedges

1. Prepare the marinade by combining the olive oil, Worcestershire, rosemary, bay leaves, garlic, salt, and pepper in a food processor and blending into a rough marinade.

2. Put the lamb chops into a non-metal bowl and pour the marinade over the meat; mix well, making sure the marinade covers both meat and bones. Cover and refrigerate to marinate for about 3 hours.

3. When ready to cook, heat the grill to medium-high heat or heat a cast iron pan over high heat until it is hot but not smoking. In batches if necessary, carefully place the lamb chops on the grill or in the pan and cook until well browned on the bottom, about 3 minutes. Turn the chops and cook until brown, another 3 to 4 minutes for medium. Transfer to a cooking rack to rest while you cook the remaining lamb chops.

4. Once the last chops are cooked, allow them to rest for 2 minutes before serving. Arrange them on a serving platter and garnish with lemon wedges.

TURMERIC FRIED CHICKEN

Authentic Malaysian *ayam goreng*, or fried chicken, eaten at least once a week at our home, is typically made with a simple combination of turmeric, ground chilies, salt, and pepper. The turmeric also enhances that appealing golden-brown color you want in perfect fried chicken. I usually start with a whole chicken and cut it into 12 pieces, since small pieces are more flavorful than large because they get coated with more spice. SERVES 4

1 whole chicken (4 pounds), cut into 12 pieces

1½ teaspoons ground turmeric

1 teaspoon ground chilies

2 to 3 teaspoons salt

½ teaspoon freshly ground pepper

Canola oil for deep frying

Sweet Soy and Shallot Sambal, for serving (optional)

1. Put the chicken pieces in a large bowl and sprinkle with the turmeric, ground chilies, salt, and pepper. Rub the chicken thoroughly with the spices. Cover and refrigerate for at least 3 hours, or preferably overnight.

2. Heat 4 inches of oil in large wok or a deep pot over medium-high heat.

3. When the oil is hot (you can test the oil with a chopstick, if the oil bubbles around the stick that means the oil is ready), add the chicken, a few pieces at a time, without overcrowding the wok. Cook until the chicken is thoroughly cooked through and golden brown, 12 to 15 minutes, turning the chicken after about 5 minutes. Drain on a paper towel–lined plate or rack and repeat with the remaining chicken pieces, taking care to bring the oil back to temperature before each batch. Serve hot, with sambal on the side if you like.

ROAST CHICKEN WITH FRAGRANT LEMONGRASS

Over the centuries, the Malay Peninsula has hosted many Javanese vessels trading at the southern ports. Inevitably, traditional Javanese cooking styles have become part of Malaysian cuisine, especially in the southern regions of the country. What I love most about this dish is the lemongrass aromas that release from the roast when it comes time to carve the chicken. The carved chicken is then served with a rustic tomato–kicap manis sauce. SERVES 6

CHICKEN

- 1 whole chicken (4½ to 5 pounds)
- 6 stalks lemongrass, outer layer discarded, stalks smashed and cut into 4-inch pieces
- 10 makrut lime leaves
- 4 shallots, peeled and cut in half
- 5 cloves garlic, smashed
- 1 teaspoon salt
- 1 teaspoon freshly ground black pepper
- 1 tablespoon kicap manis (sweet soy sauce; see page 16)
- 1 tablespoon peanut oil or extra-virgin olive oil

SAUCE

- 1½ cups crushed tomatoes
- 3 to 5 fresh Thai bird's-eye chilies, stemmed
- 3 cloves garlic, peeled
- 1 to 2 tablespoons kicap manis (sweet soy sauce; see page 16)

1. Preheat the oven to 375°F. Place the chicken on a cutting board and, using a sharp knife, remove the clumps of fat under the neck.

2. Put the chicken on a baking sheet, then stuff the cavity with the lemongrass, lime leaves, shallots, and garlic, pushing the aromatics deep into the chicken. Close the cavity with a 5-inch bamboo skewer. With your hands, rub salt and pepper all over the chicken, then very gently rub in the kicap manis and oil.

3. Transfer the chicken to a roasting pan. Roast for about 1 hour 30 minutes, basting occasionally with drippings from the pan during the first hour. The chicken is done when its juices run clear when you prick a thigh with a fork. Transfer the chicken to a serving platter, reserving the pan juices, and let rest for about 10 minutes for the juices to settle down before carving.

4. While the chicken is resting, prepare the sauce: Combine the chicken juices, tomatoes, chilies, garlic, and kicap manis in a food processor and blend until smooth.

5. Heat a small saucepan over medium heat. Add the blended ingredients, bring to a boil, and cook until the sauce takes on a deep reddish-brown color and becomes slightly thickened, about 5 minutes.

6. Carve the chicken, arrange the pieces on a platter, and pour the sauce over them.

LENTIL, PORK, AND SQUASH DALCHA

My mother has a saying: "When life gets too complicated, just make dalcha." There are many variations of this comforting one-pot stew, including the chicken dalcha on page 250; here is another twist to the traditional home-style dish. You can add any sort of vegetable that you fancy. Opo squash is delicate and pairs well with pork and lentils; but you could use zucchini for a mild taste, or you might like to try butternut squash or pumpkin for a sweeter note. When it comes to the meat, be sure to use a cut of meat with good marbling. The fat rendered from the pork adds to the flavor, and the marbling delivers meat that is fork tender. SERVES 4

½ cup split yellow lentils (*toor dal*), or yellow split peas

4 tablespoons clarified butter (ghee) or coconut oil

1 medium red onion, minced

3 cloves garlic, minced

3 to 4 dried red chilies, broken in half

½ teaspoon cumin seeds

1 piece (1 inch) fresh ginger, peeled and minced

2 pounds pork butt, cut into 1½-inch pieces

1 opo squash, peeled and diced

4 cups chicken broth

¼ teaspoon ground turmeric

1 teaspoon freshly ground black pepper

1 to 2 teaspoons salt

1. Wash the lentils by gently rubbing them with your fingers in a bowl under cold running water until the water runs clear. (The running water allows debris, such as tiny stones or outer skin, to float to the top instead of sinking to the bottom with the lentils.) Drain the lentils.

2. Heat the butter or oil in a Dutch oven or other heavy pot over medium heat. When hot, add the onion, garlic, chilies, cumin, and ginger and stir until the onion is soft and brown, about 5 minutes.

3. Add the pork, lentils, squash, broth, turmeric, and pepper and give everything a good stir. Cover, reduce the heat to medium-low, and cook until the pork is fork tender and the lentils are broken down, about 1 hour. Skim off any foam that may appear on the surface during cooking.

4. Taste and add the salt as needed. Serve immediately.

LAMB MASALA

Mutton paratal is a prominent item on Malaysian menus especially among the Indian community. At Indian restaurants throughout the country, it is served on a cleaned fresh banana leaf with saffron pilaf and vegetables. When diners are satisfied with the meal, the banana leaf is folded in half toward the chest to express gratitude to the cook. This lamb gets its wallop of flavor from a masala mix that includes cinnamon, cardamom, star anise, cloves, onions, chili powder (such as Baba's chili powder), and turmeric, a blend that forms the basis of many Indian dishes. SERVES 4

6 tablespoons canola or peanut oil

2 cinnamon sticks (2 inches each)

5 green cardamom pods, crushed

1 whole star anise

4 whole cloves

2 small red onions, roughly chopped

1 fresh green chili, sliced lengthwise and seeded

2 tablespoons Ginger, Garlic, and Cilantro Paste (page 53)

Leaves from 2 sprigs fresh curry leaf

3 medium tomatoes, quartered

2 pounds lamb shoulder, chopped into 3-inch pieces

¼ teaspoon ground turmeric

2 tablespoons chili powder or ground cayenne

1 teaspoon salt, or to taste

¼ cup plain yogurt

1. Heat the oil in a large heavy pot or Dutch oven over medium heat. Add the cinnamon, cardamom, star anise, and cloves and cook until fragrant, about 1 minute. Add the onions, fresh chili, ginger-garlic paste, and curry leaves. Cook, stirring, until the onions are soft, about 10 minutes.

2. Add the tomatoes, lamb, turmeric, and chili powder and give it a good stir. Cover, reduce the heat to low, and simmer, stirring occasionally, until the meat is tender, about 30 minutes.

3. Season with salt to taste. Add the yogurt and stir until well blended. Uncover, raise the heat to medium, and cook until the mixture is thickened, about 15 minutes. Serve hot.

CHICKEN OPOR IN SPICED COCONUT MILK

In the backyard of my childhood home, close to the kitchen, we grew herbs and spices for our daily use. I still recall the beautiful experience of going out to the garden at sunrise to cut some soft green lemongrass or pluck a cream-colored galangal from the earth to make a delicate *opor ayam,* chicken in coconut milk. In making an opor, the cumin and coriander seeds, white peppercorns, candlenuts, and galangal form a creamy, thick flavoring paste that complements the poultry and coconut milk. The chicken is gently simmered in the spiced coconut milk, then finished off with coconut cream. The end result is an exquisite dish for anyone who loves the flavor of aromatics without the spiciness of chilies. SERVES 4

- 2 teaspoons cumin seeds
- 1 teaspoon coriander seeds
- 1 teaspoon white peppercorns
- ½ yellow onion, chopped
- 6 cloves garlic, sliced
- 3 candlenuts or macadamia nuts
- 1 piece (2 inches) unpeeled fresh galangal, thinly sliced
- 3 cups coconut milk
- 2 stalks lemongrass, outer layer discarded, cut into 4-inch pieces and smashed
- 2 fresh or dried bay leaves
- 1 whole chicken (2½ to 3 pounds), cut into 12 pieces
- 1 cup water
- 1 teaspoon salt, or to taste
- 1 to 2 tablespoons liquid palm sugar (optional, see pages 315–316)
- ½ cup coconut cream

1. Start with the spice paste by combining the cumin seeds, coriander seeds, and peppercorns in a mortar and using the pestle to grind into a smooth powder. Transfer to a food processor or blender and add the onion, garlic, candlenuts, and galangal. Blend into a very smooth paste with the consistency of applesauce, adding a little water at a time to facilitate the blending process.

2. Heat a deep skillet or Dutch oven over medium heat. Add the spice paste, coconut milk, lemongrass, and bay leaves and mix well. Simmer until the fragrant oil has separated onto the surface, about 15 minutes, stirring occasionally to prevent the spices and coconut milk from scorching. The coconut milk will have slightly thickened and have a soft light green color that comes naturally from the lemongrass.

3. Add the chicken to the pot and mix well into the coconut mixture. Add the water and continue to simmer gently, stirring occasionally, until the meat is completely cooked and tender, about 40 minutes.

4. Add the salt and the palm sugar (if using). Finally, add the coconut cream, mix well, and bring to a soft boil. Taste and add more salt if needed. Serve warm.

MALAYSIAN CHICKEN CURRY

Even after 20 years of living in the United States and enjoying a variety of international foods, this chicken curry is still one of those dishes that I must come back to at least a few times a month. In Malaysia, there are many cooking styles when it comes to curries. For instance, if you dine in the home of an Indian family, the curry is enriched with spices and aromatics. In a Chinese home it will be seasoned with sweetened coconut milk, while Malay cooks prefer to make their curry with chilies. This recipe balances the three cooking styles, making the curry light yet intensely flavorful and aromatic. Pay close attention as you cook the spice paste, since this is one of your foundational flavors. You never want to leave the spices unattended in hot oil since they can easily burn and turn bitter. Cooks in Malaysia will use store-bought Baba's meat curry powder or Baba's chili powder to achieve an appealing reddish gravy. You can purchase these online. SERVES 6

2 pounds bone-in chicken thighs or breasts

5 tablespoons extra-virgin olive oil

Leaves from 2 sprigs curry leaf

2 cinnamon sticks (3 inches each)

1 whole star anise

¼ teaspoon whole cloves

3 green cardamom pods, crushed

1 large red onion, chopped

2 tablespoons Ginger, Garlic, and Cilantro Paste (page 53)

1 medium potato, peeled and quartered

2 tomatoes, quartered

½ to 1 tablespoon hot meat and chicken curry powder

1 teaspoon ground turmeric

1½ teaspoons salt, or to taste

⅓ cup coconut milk

1. Cut chicken thighs in half, or the breasts into 5 pieces each. Set aside.

2. Heat the oil in a large pot over medium heat. When the oil is hot, add the curry leaves (make sure the curry leaves are dry or they will splatter in the oil), cinnamon, star anise, cloves, and cardamom. Stir and cook until fragrant, about 2 minutes.

3. Add the onion and cook until translucent and light brown, about 7 minutes. Add the ginger-garlic paste, stir, and cook for about 1 minute.

4. Add the chicken, potato, tomatoes, curry powder, and turmeric and mix well. Cover, turn the heat to medium-low, and cook, stirring occasionally, until the potatoes and chicken are tender, about 35 minutes. If you prefer a thicker sauce, do not cover the pot.

5. Add the salt and coconut milk, stirring to mix thoroughly. Cook, uncovered, until a little oil appears on the surface, about 10 minutes. Serve warm.

KOPI TIAM PORK TENDERLOIN IN BLACK PEPPER SAUCE

Hainan cuisine made its way to British Malaya in the late 1800s through cooks from the Chinese province who ventured to the colony in search of greener pastures. Working in expatriate homes, camps, and for wealthy Europeans, they soon mastered the culinary skills to make familiar European roasts, soups, and bread. Over time, the inevitable fusion of European and Chinese came to be known as Hainanese cuisine. You may still find some of these cooks, although advanced in age, working in Western-style steakhouse establishments, such as the 1921 Coliseum Café & Grill Room in Kuala Lumpur, churning out excellent dishes to satisfy Malaysian tastes. Among the more popular Hainanese recipes is chicken in a thick black pepper gravy, a specialty of many well-known restaurants. Today, *kopi tiam*, or old brick coffee shops, serve this specialty and at lunchtime they are packed with a crowd outside the door waiting for an open seat. Here I have replaced the more traditional chicken with pork tenderloin. SERVES 4

¼ cup clarified butter (ghee) or peanut oil

1 small onion, sliced

1½ pounds pork tenderloin, sliced 2 inches thick across the grain

½ cup chicken stock

2 tablespoons oyster sauce

1 tablespoon ketchup

1 tablespoon rice vinegar

1 tablespoon Worcestershire sauce

1 teaspoon garlic powder

½ teaspoon salt, or to taste

1 teaspoon freshly ground black pepper

1. Heat the butter or oil in a medium cast iron pan over medium heat. Add the onion and sauté until golden, about 2 minutes.

2. Add the pork and allow it to sear undisturbed until brown on the bottom, about 4 minutes. Flip and cook until golden brown on the other side, about 4 minutes more.

3. Add the stock, oyster sauce, ketchup, vinegar, Worcestershire sauce, garlic powder, salt, and pepper and mix well. Bring to a simmer and cook until reduced, about 15 minutes. Taste the sauce and add more salt if needed, but remember that Asian sauces develop their saltiness over time, particularly when the sauce is warm. Serve warm.

Kopi Tiam Pork Tenderloin served with rice and Stir-Fried Bok Choy with Bacon and Garlic (page 135)

PAN-ROASTED CHICKEN WITH SPICED ROSEMARY

The pine-like fragrance and tea-like flavor of rosemary pairs up with delicate coriander and fennel for an intriguing marinade for poultry. Then to give the dish a jolt, hot and smoky Sriracha sauce flatters the chicken like nothing else. When you work with rosemary, it is easy to strip the leaves off a stem by running your fingers along the stem from top to bottom. Although rosemary leaves can remain quite tough even when cooked, blending them with garlic powder and olive oil breaks that toughness and provides an incredible marinade for grilled meats. Just the thought of going out into the garden, crushing a few of those leaves between my fingers, and inhaling their aromatic scent promises the amazing flavors of this chicken. Serve with baked potatoes and Stir-Fried Asian Greens (page 131). SERVES 6

1 teaspoon ground fennel

1 teaspoon ground coriander

½ teaspoon garlic powder

1 teaspoon salt, or to taste

1 teaspoon freshly ground black pepper

Leaves from 4 sprigs fresh rosemary

5 fresh bay leaves

½ cup extra-virgin olive oil

2 tablespoons Sriracha sauce

2 pounds boneless skinless chicken thighs

3 tablespoons peanut oil

1 lemon, cut into wedges

1. Combine the fennel, coriander, garlic powder, salt, pepper, rosemary, bay leaves, olive oil, and Sriracha in a food processor and blend into a smooth paste to make a marinade.

2. Put the chicken in a bowl and pour the marinade over. Mix well, allowing the marinade to cover the chicken completely. Cover and refrigerate to marinate for about 3 hours.

3. When ready to cook, heat the peanut oil in a cast iron pan over medium heat. In batches, carefully place the chicken pieces into the pan, taking care not to overcrowd, as this would cool the oil. Cook until the chicken is seared and evenly brown, about 10 minutes, then flip and continue to cook until the other side is evenly brown, another 10 minutes. The chicken is cooked when its juices run clear. Repeat to cook all the chicken.

4. Transfer the chicken to a serving platter and garnish with lemon wedges.

GRILLED COCONUT-LEMONGRASS CHICKEN

AYAM BAKAR

This recipe is a guaranteed crowd-pleaser that is great for a dinner party or an afternoon barbecue since most of the work can be done in advance. Biting into *ayam bakar* reveals a touch of sweetness from honey balanced with coconut cream and a citrusy lemongrass aftertaste. Here the Asian sauces and the oils from the lemongrass lend a hand in tenderizing the meat while the garlic's role is to add complexity. Serve with a salad, rice, and Sweet Chili Dipping Sauce (page 45). SERVES 4

2 cups coconut cream

3 tablespoons honey

3 tablespoons oyster sauce

2 tablespoons fish sauce

3 tablespoons frozen grated lemongrass; or 2 stalks lemongrass, outer layer discarded, bottom 6 inches thinly sliced

6 cloves garlic, peeled and left whole

2 pounds boneless skinless chicken breasts

A handful of cilantro, chopped, for garnish

1. Combine the coconut cream, honey, oyster sauce, fish sauce, lemongrass, and garlic in a blender and process into a smooth paste.

2. Place the chicken in a large baking dish or glass bowl. Pour the marinade over the chicken and turn to coat evenly. Cover with plastic wrap and refrigerate overnight to marinate.

3. When ready to cook, prepare a charcoal or gas grill to medium heat, then lightly oil the grate. Grill the chicken, turning occasionally so it cooks up evenly, until the meat is no longer pink when sliced and the juices run clear, about 15 minutes. Transfer the meat to a plate and allow to rest for 10 minutes.

4. Transfer the chicken to a platter, garnish with cilantro, and serve warm.

CURRY KAPITAN

Here is the story behind this dish: When a British captain requested that a Nyonya cook in Penang make him dinner, the cook went out to the garden, gathered all the fresh aromatics, and came up with this dish. When the captain asked what was for dinner, she replied, "Curry, Kapitan!" (meaning "it's curry, Captain!") Her quick reply became the curry's name and it soon became a favorite among the British residents of Malaysia as well as the locals. Curry Kapitan epitomizes the marriage of Chinese and Malay cultures. Richer, thicker, and more vibrant than your usual chicken curry, its sauce features the citrus taste of fresh makrut lime leaves, lemongrass, and rose-scented galangal all cooked gently in creamy coconut cream. You can reduce the spiciness by adding more coconut cream, but remember that too much will dilute the rest of the flavors. Although toasted shrimp paste is an optional ingredient, it is a foundation of Nyonya cuisine, adding that vital umami quality so common in Malaysian cuisine. MAKES 6 SERVINGS

8 fresh makrut lime leaves, torn into quarters

1 piece (2 inches) unpeeled fresh galangal, thinly sliced

4 shallots, peeled and cut in half

3 stalks lemongrass, outer layer discarded, bottom 6 inches thinly sliced

3 fresh Thai red chilies, stemmed

½ teaspoon toasted shrimp paste (see page 116), optional

1½ cups water

¼ cup peanut oil

1½ pounds boneless skinless chicken thighs, cut into 2-inch pieces

1 daikon (about 6 inches long), peeled and cut into 1-inch rounds

1 cup coconut cream

1 teaspoon sugar

1 teaspoon salt, or to taste

1. Combine the lime leaves, galangal, shallots, lemongrass, chilies, and shrimp paste (if using) in a blender. Add 1 cup of the water and blend the ingredients into a fine paste.

2. Heat the oil in a wok or skillet over medium heat. Add the blended spice paste and sauté until aromatic and the oils have separated onto the surface, about 5 minutes.

3. Add the remaining ½ cup water, the chicken, daikon, coconut cream, sugar, and salt and mix well, ensuring each chicken piece is well coated with the spice paste. Cover the pan and cook until the chicken is tender and the gravy thickens, about 25 minutes. If the gravy gets too dry while cooking, add a bit more water.

4. Uncover the pan and give the curry a good stir. Taste and add more salt if needed. Serve immediately.

TAMARIND-GLAZED ROAST DUCK

You might be familiar with the delightful pairing of orange and duck. But in this recipe, you will find that adding the sour tang of tamarind is even better. The tamarind, when blended with palm sugar, lends a delicious sweet and tart flavor while tenderizing the duck to perfection; it also lends a deep caramel-like coloring to the duck. Gently piercing the fatty part of the duck helps the glaze penetrate, tenderizes the meat, and prevents the fat from burning. During cooking, you will hear sizzling noises coming from the oven, which means the fats are becoming crispy. Making this duck spreads happiness and a wonderful aroma all over the kitchen. Serve it whole on a platter because it looks so grand and glorious. SERVES 6

GLAZE

- 3 tablespoons tamarind pulp
- 1 cup boiling water
- 1 tablespoon cornstarch mixed with 1 tablespoon water
- ½ cup liquid palm sugar (see pages 315–316)

DUCK

- 1 whole duck (6 pounds), rinsed and dried thoroughly

  Salt and freshly ground black pepper
- 1 orange, cut in half

  Green lettuce leaf, to line the platter for serving
- 2 tablespoons butter

1. Preheat the oven to 400°F.

2. Make the glaze: Put the tamarind pulp in a bowl and add the water. Let stand for about 5 minutes to soften. When the water is cool enough to touch, squeeze the pulp to separate the seeds and pulp. Once most of the pulp has dissolved into the water, strain it into a bowl and discard the seeds. You should have 1 cup; if less, add more water as needed.

3. Combine the tamarind water, cornstarch mixture, and palm sugar in a small pot and bring to a soft boil, stirring constantly, until the mixture thickens into a gravy-like consistency. Set aside to cool. Taste; the glaze should be first tangy then sweet at the back of your palate. Set aside ¼ cup of the glaze to use later in the sauce.

4. While the tamarind glaze is cooling, prepare the duck: Place the duck, breast side up, on a rack set in a large roasting pan. Using a fork, gently pierce the skin where there is a lot of fat, this will help the meat to absorb the glaze and prevent the fat from burning during cooking. Season the cavity and outside liberally with salt and pepper. Squeeze the orange over the duck and tuck the squeezed orange inside the cavity, and then truss the duck with a string.

5. Roast the duck for 1 hour, basting generously with the tamarind glaze every 15 minutes. Reduce the oven temperature to 350°F, cover the duck with foil, and continue to roast until completely cooked, 35 to 40 minutes more.

6. Let the duck rest for about 10 minutes for the juices to settle down. Lift the duck and drain the liquids from the cavity into the roasting pan. Discard the orange inside the cavity and the trussing string.

7. Line a platter with lettuce and set the duck on top.

8. Prepare the sauce: First, tilt the roasting pan and spoon out as much fat as you possibly can. Pour the remaining juices into a small saucepan and bring to a soft boil over medium heat. Add the reserved ¼ cup tamarind glaze and taste for a balanced sweet, sour, and salty flavor. Add more palm sugar, salt, or pepper if needed. Add the butter, then turn off the heat and mix well to combine. Strain the gravy through a fine sieve into a bowl and serve alongside the duck.

Just 40 kilometers from Ipoh, the lush Cameron Highlands nestles on a 1,500-meter plateau stretching from Ringlet in the south, past Tanah Rata at its heart, to Brinchang and Tringkap in the north. The cool climate of the Highlands is home to several tea plantations, Tudor-style cottages, and fruit farms.

Picture yourself sitting in a typical double-storied shop house in a little rustic town like Tanah Rata. On the wooden signboard outside is a simple invitation, Kedai Teh Cameron (Cameron Tea Shop). Awaiting you are two well-dressed ladies doing the serving, a little dog ready to defend the premises, and a few holiday makers enjoying a brisk cup of *teh tarik,* or Malaysian pulled tea. The walls are plastered with glossy posters depicting white sticky rice with fresh mangoes and deep-fried savory snacks like banana bonbons and coconut ice cream.

One wall of the tea shop is completely covered by teak shelves that contain stacks of evaporated milk, Highlands tea, cans of sweetened cream corn and sweetened milk, boxes of rice flour, canned tropical fruits in syrup, small baskets of fresh strawberries, and cream from local farms. The waitress is wearing a John Lennon t-shirt with "Let It Be" stenciled across her chest. Wafting in the background is a radio station broadcasting news in Malay. One weary British traveler, sipping a cup of teh tarik, sighs and says, "I guess you could sit here for the rest of your life."

At 4 p.m. every day the scenes at the local cafes and hotels are transformed into a world of snacks and desserts. In residential homes throughout the country, it's time to put the kettle on for tea, a tradition left by the British who once colonized this country. However, unlike the British who formally sit down to tea with dainty tea cups, tea sandwiches, scones, and jams among other accoutrements, the locals imbue tea time with their multicultural sweets, a juxtaposition of Indian, Chinese, Malay, and Portuguese specialties. These sweets, featuring fresh and local Southeast Asian ingredients like sweet potatoes, tree-ripened bananas, jackfruit, pandan, corn, coconut, sticky rice, palm sugar, tapioca, and rice flour, are eaten in between meals or with tea—but rarely after dinner.

Malaysian snacks are less complicated than many other elaborate treats and often do not require any special equipment. Sweets or *kuih* (sweet cakes, pronounced *koo way*) are made fresh daily by local vendors selling from a makeshift wooden table under the banyan tree: Sweet Potato Doughnuts (page 318), Coconut Custard Crème Squares (page 300), and Banana Fritters (page 302). Savory snacks like Miniature Fried Rolls (page 244) and Curry Puffs (page 242) are also offered at local cafes or prepared at home. Whatever the selection may be, the snacks are always enjoyed with a cup of Malaysian-style teh tarik.

In this chapter, the sweets and snacks reflect a balance among comfort, adventure, and familiarity. My goal is to introduce you to new flavor combinations and something exotic from the street corners of Malaysia.

Just as every culture has their version of sweet fried dough, in Malaysia fresh tropical fruits are dipped in batter and then deep-fried until crispy

and golden. If you visit an Asian supermarket, you will find a variety of bananas, sweet potatoes, and taro root. Some of these are naturally sweet, while others may be savory. Explore them by using the methods I present in the Banana Fritters (page 302), Banana Bonbons (page 298), and Sweet Potato Doughnuts (page 318) recipes. You may enjoy them as they are, much as we do back home, or serve them with ice cream.

On the other hand, the creams and custards in this chapter take European-style desserts and give them a Malaysian twist by integrating Southeast Asian ingredients. Coconut cream, mango pulp, jackfruit, vanilla beans, and fragrant spices make the treats delicate and sensational. For instance, in Pandan Pots de Crème (page 303), the pandan leaves widely used in cooking throughout Southeast Asia give custard an eye-catching green color while their aromatic juice is infused into the cream. In my Crème Caramel (page 317), star anise and cinnamon are incorporated into the caramel syrup to make it complex and rich. The flavor and texture of tropical fruits canned in their own syrup blended with coconut cream balance well in custards like Jackfruit Clafoutis (page 309). Custards that contain tropical fruits are best served warm and eaten the same day as they won't keep well in the refrigerator.

When I was growing up, there was always some sort of simple agar agar in the refrigerator to snack on after school, the perfect snack under the hot and humid climate. These were light, refreshing, and creamy and mostly made with fresh fruits like mangoes, lychees, or papayas, and served with whipped cream. Years later when I became a chef at the Four Seasons resorts, I learned many sophisticated names like Bavarois and panna cotta, which, surprisingly, tasted like the velvety fruit creations in my mother's refrigerator. This is the sort of dessert where I pay homage to my mother and my professional training.

Puddings (*bubur*) are a typical comfort snack for Malaysians akin to a parfait, served as a pick-me-up in the mid-afternoon. In Southeast Asia, they are made by cooking sweet potato, taro, and tapioca in coconut milk for a contrasting blend of sweetness and creaminess with a hint of saltiness that is absolutely divine. Sweet Potato and Tapioca Pudding (page 321) is an example; Sweet Corn Pudding with Coconut Cream Topping (page 310) is another. The canned cream of corn that you find at major supermarkets, often sold to be served as a vegetable, is regarded as dessert in Malaysia. It is added to peanut pancakes, used in making kuih, and is a perfect match for coconut. Sweet Sticky Rice with Mango (page 301) is also a type of pudding, with the rice cooked in sweetened coconut cream.

Finally, there are two types of kuih. Despite the emergence of European-style cakes served at British-style high tea at major hotels, most Malaysians would rather enjoy a local style of cake known as *Nyonya kuih,* which are colorful bite-sized cakes, sometimes multi-layered, that have a glutinous texture. These intricate cakes are popular tea time snacks served mainly at local Baba-Nyonya coffee shops. However, making traditional kuih is arduous, and they do require plenty of patience and skill; layered cakes are steamed one layer at a time to ensure perfection. Often Nyonya girls are trained by their grandmothers in the art of making kuih from a very young age, and always using the *agak agak* (estimate) method of measuring ingredients.

Instead, I have opted to share similar but simpler recipes that use pantry ingredients available in the United States: My favorites are Pandan–Coconut Custard Cake (page 326) and Coconut Custard Crème Squares (page 300). Apart from traditional kuih, cakes served with tea are mostly moist, light, and fluffy, similar to sponge cake or angel food cake, like the Pandan Chiffon Cake on page 305. Local cooks add tropical flavorings to the batter or fruits such as mangoes, pineapples, and bananas to the base, similar to upside down cakes, as in Coconut-Banana Sponge Cake (page 311). These tropical cakes are usually served in small quantities and used to complement the other offerings with tea; one rarely eats these cakes to the point of feeling full.

I have to confess, I have such love for desserts that I cannot imagine a day without something sweet, but not cloying, to cross my palate. A few bites is all it takes to make life more enjoyable. I hope you have as much fun with the sweets in this chapter as I had creating them for you. Many of my students and friends tell me these desserts present exciting new flavor adventures that linger in their minds long after they eat. My wish is that you will experience the same.

VANILLA THINS

When I was working at the Four Seasons resort in Bali, I would make these cookies for our hotel guests. We would wrap them beautifully and have them placed in the rooms as a thank-you gift from the kitchen staff. Delicate and buttery tasting, the vanilla cookies are perfect with a hot cup of Earl Grey tea or espresso. In Indonesia, you will find bundles of vanilla beans, or *vanilli* in Indonesian, sold at markets all over the island. The beans are then fermented and preserved in their own alcohol. Although vanilla beans have found their way into so many cookies and desserts the world over, the Spice Islands of Indonesia are still among the biggest producers of vanilla beans. MAKES 32 COOKIES

7 ounces (14 tablespoons) butter at room temperature

2 cups plus 2 tablespoons all-purpose flour

⅔ cup confectioners' sugar

Pinch of salt

2 vanilla beans

¼ cup almond milk or whole milk

1 teaspoon vanilla extract

1. Combine the butter, flour, sugar, and salt in a mixing bowl and mix with your hands until the ingredients are crumbly.

2. Using a paring knife, split the vanilla beans in half lengthwise. Holding down one end of the bean on the cutting board, scrape out the seeds with the back of the knife, then add them to the butter mixture. Add the almond milk and vanilla extract and mix well until the mixture becomes a soft dough.

3. Remove the dough and roll it into an 8-inch-long log. Wrap the dough in plastic wrap and allow it to rest overnight in the refrigerator until firm.

4. Preheat the oven to 320°F.

5. Cut the cookie dough into ¼-inch slices and place the cookies on a baking sheet ½ inch apart. Bake for about 15 minutes. Allow to cool completely on a wire rack.

BANANA BONBONS

KODOK PISANG

These bonbons are magic: When people ask me what is my favorite childhood dessert, the answer is these and now you can make the same treat in your kitchen. The bonbons repurpose overripe bananas into hot, golden fritters. Unlike the fritters on page 302, where the bananas are quartered, battered, and fried, these bananas are mashed into a thick batter and then deep-fried. They are so irresistible that they are quickly snapped up right out of the hot wok, rarely making it to the table. MAKES 12 FRITTERS

4 very ripe bananas, or 6 to 8 baby bananas

¼ cup sugar

½ teaspoon vanilla extract

⅓ cup plus 3 tablespoons all-purpose flour

¼ teaspoon baking powder

¼ teaspoon salt

About 1½ cups canola oil, for frying

1. Peel the bananas and place in a medium glass bowl. Add the sugar and vanilla and mix until the bananas are completely broken down into a smooth mixture.

2. Mix the flour, baking powder, and salt in a separate bowl, then add to the bananas. Mix well until all the ingredients are incorporated.

3. Heat about 2 inches of oil in a small wok over medium heat. To test if the oil is ready for frying, add a pinch of the batter; it should sizzle immediately. Now, drop a tablespoon full of the banana mixture into the hot oil. As the mixture puffs up, use 2 metal spoons to form it into a ball (it does not need to be perfectly round). Continue to drop the batter by the tablespoonful and form into balls. Be sure not to overcrowd the oil or the temperature will drop and the fritters will become soggy. Fry until golden underneath, then use a slotted spoon to gently flip and continue to cook until evenly golden, a total of 5 minutes. For sweeter, darker brown fritters, cook for an additional 2 minutes per side.

4. Remove with a slotted spoon and transfer to a plated lined with paper towels. Serve immediately.

COCONUT CUSTARD CRÈME SQUARES

HAUPIA

This creamy, delicate cake is presented at every high tea function at top-notch hotels throughout Malaysia. When I moved to Hawaii many years ago, I was exceptionally happy to discover that *haupia* was a must-have at every luau. In both Malaysia and Hawaii, coconut trees are abundant and the taste of coconut cream is a favorite among islanders as it delivers a luscious touch to desserts. The Malaysian version of haupia differs in that it carries the fragrance of pandan, although you can omit it.

This is one of the easiest desserts you can make, with just four ingredients plus the optional pandan leaves. However, the taste is determined by the quality of the coconut cream; it should be as pure as possible without additives. If you love coconut as much as I do, it's worth picking up the coconut cream at an Asian grocery store, since those brands are not sweetened and are pure, 100-percent coconut cream. The pandan leaves lend an herbal, vanilla-like aroma and flavor. You will find this leaf at the Asian grocery store either in the produce or freezer section. MAKES 24 PIECES

2 cups coconut cream

1 fresh or frozen pandan leaf, cut in half (optional)

½ cup sugar

Pinch of salt

⅔ cup cornstarch

1 cup water

1. Combine the coconut cream, pandan leaf (if using), sugar, and salt in a medium saucepan and cook over medium heat, stirring occasionally, until the sugar is completely melted and the cream comes to a boil, about 15 minutes. Remove the pandan leaf and discard.

2. Mix the cornstarch and water in a measuring cup until smooth. Add the cornstarch mixture to the coconut cream and cook, stirring constantly with a whisk, until the mixture thickens to a yogurt-like consistency, about 5 minutes. Remove from the heat to prevent overcooking.

3. Transfer the coconut mixture to 13- by 9-inch glass dish and smooth the top with a spatula. Cover with plastic wrap, making sure the plastic touches the custard to prevent air and bubbles from forming. Set aside to cool at room temperature for 10 minutes, then refrigerate to set for at least 4 hours.

4. After chilling, cut into 2 inch squares and serve cold. Leftover squares can be kept covered in the refrigerator for 3 days.

SWEET STICKY RICE WITH MANGO

Sticky rice is enjoyed for breakfast, but when sweetened it becomes a dessert that you will find throughout Southeast Asia. Sold along countryside roads, it is often wrapped in a banana leaf and served with some sweetened shredded coconut. In homes and restaurants, sweetened sticky rice is served with slices of fresh fruit on top. When mangos are in season, the match of the honey-like fruit with sticky rice is perfect.

   To make this dessert correctly, you will need sticky rice (also called glutinous white rice), which you can find at most Asian grocery stores and in some supermarkets. The rice must be soaked overnight so the grains will soften. Then, as the rice steams, it soaks up the wonderful sweet and slightly salty coconut sauce so that each grain of rice is infused with flavor.

SERVES 6

2 cups white glutinous rice, washed and soaked in 2 cups water overnight

1½ cups coconut cream

½ cup water

½ cup sugar

½ teaspoon salt

1 teaspoon toasted white sesame seeds

1 very ripe mango, peeled and sliced

1. Drain the rice and place in a 9-inch round cake pan. Place the pan in a bamboo steamer basket. Bring 3 inches of water to boil in a wok and set the steamer basket over it. Cover and steam for 25 minutes, until the rice is cooked and no longer appears grainy. (Alternatively, line the steamer insert of a pasta pot with cheesecloth and add the rice. Bring 3 inches of water to a boil in the pasta pot. Place the insert into the pot, cover, and steam the rice until shiny and tender, 35 to 40 minutes.)

2. Combine the coconut cream, water, sugar, and salt in a saucepan and bring to a soft boil over medium-high heat, stirring to prevent the coconut cream from burning.

3. Pour the coconut milk mixture over the rice and mix well to combine, then flatten the rice using a wooden spoon and continue to steam until the rice becomes one with the coconut mixture and is set, about 10 minutes more.

4. To serve, spoon the warm sticky rice into individual ramekins, sprinkle with sesame seeds, then add a few slices of mango on the side.

BANANA FRITTERS

GORENG PISANG

"Goreng pisang, goreng pisang!" the young lad sings as he carries a shopping basket filled with banana fritters while roaming the back streets of our neighborhood. His mother has made the fritters, an all-time favorite, using a variety of bananas available in the neighborhood. We anticipate his arrival every afternoon. His call also means it's time to put the kettle on for tea. Using rice flour in the batter to coat the fritters helps keep them crispy. I have used regular bananas in this recipe, but do try it with Asian or Ecuadorian baby bananas if you come across them. Either way, the little crispy, golden treats hot off the frying pan are perfect with vanilla and coconut ice cream, or just eat them plain with a cup of tea. SERVES 4 TO 6

4 ripe bananas, or 6 or 8 baby bananas
¼ cup all-purpose flour
⅔ cup rice flour
¼ cup cornstarch
¼ teaspoon salt
½ teaspoon baking soda
⅓ cup plus 2 tablespoons cold water
1 large egg
About 1½ cups canola oil, for frying

1. Peel the bananas, slice in half lengthwise, then slice horizontally to create 4 pieces. If using baby bananas, slice them lengthwise only.

2. Combine the all-purpose flour, ⅓ cup of the rice flour, the cornstarch, and salt in a mixing bowl and stir well.

3. In a small bowl, combine the baking soda with the water and mix well. Pour into the bowl with the flour mixture. Then crack in the egg and stir well to create a smooth batter without lumps.

4. Sprinkle the remaining ⅓ cup rice flour on a plate and set next to the batter.

5. Carefully dip the banana pieces first in the batter, then gently turn them in the rice flour.

6. Heat 1 inch of oil in a small skillet or wok over medium heat. To test if the oil is hot enough, add a pinch of batter; it should sizzle. Working in batches to avoid overcrowding the pan, carefully set the bananas in the hot oil. Fry, turning once, until the batter puffs up slightly and turns light to medium golden-brown, about 2 minutes per side. Remove and drain on a paper towel–lined plate. Serve immediately.

PANDAN POTS DE CRÈME

Back when I worked at the Four Seasons resort in Bali, Indonesia, I spent a lot of time making pandan pots de crème, the fusion of a French classic with Southeast Asian flavors, using the abundance of fresh pandan leaves from our organic garden. Making these custards was one of my tasks for the lunch and dinner buffet; after a while, I could have made the dessert in my sleep.

The pandan is an integral part of Malaysian and Indonesian desserts. As my Balinese friends would say, "The kitchen gods are always watching, so we must respect each ingredient, including the pandan, for without our earth's bounty we would not be able to enjoy such delicious flavors." Pandan leaves impart herbal and vanilla-like flavors; this recipe uses pure pandan juice, which is extracted from the fresh leaves. This lends a subtle matcha green tea–like flavor and distinctive fragrance. This dessert is a cousin to flan, and much loved in Malaysia for high tea. SERVES 6

8 pandan leaves, washed and cut into 1-inch pieces

1 cup water

1¼ cups whole milk

½ cup heavy cream

1 large egg

3 large egg yolks

⅓ cup granulated sugar

1. Preheat the oven to 300°F.

2. Put the pandan leaves and water in a blender and blend into a liquid. The leaves will still appear chunky, but try to blend as much as you can to liquefy them. Strain the pandan juice through a fine-mesh sieve into a saucepan, using your hands to squeeze out as much juice as you can from the leaves. Add the milk and cream and bring just to a boil.

3. In a glass bowl, whisk the egg, egg yolks, and sugar until light and fluffy.

4. Gradually pour the hot milk mixture over the eggs, stirring constantly. Skim off the surface to remove any foam. Ladle the mixture into six 4-ounce ramekins and place in a baking pan. Pour hot water into the baking pan to reach halfway up the sides of the ramekins.

5. Bake until the custard is firm to the touch, about 30 minutes. Remove the ramekins from the baking pan and let the custards cool on a wire rack. Serve warm or cover and refrigerate for at least 4 hours and serve cold.

PANDAN CHIFFON CAKE

Pandan, a tropical plant with long palm-like leaves, infuses this cake with a distinctive herbal and matcha tea–like flavor. It also gives the cake a beautiful soft light green color. Like all chiffon cakes, it is made light by folding beaten egg whites into the batter, with oil and egg yolks helping to keep it super moist. To get the pandan flavoring, I pulverize the leaves, then squeeze them through a sieve to extract the fresh green juice. You will find fresh and frozen pandan leaves in most Asian supermarkets (if you buy frozen, be sure to thaw before using). However, if you cannot find the leaves, use an additional 2 teaspoons pandan extract (also available in most Asian groceries). The extract, however, will create a darker shade of green and will not have the delicate herbal flavor from the juice. Because coconut milk is substituted for dairy, this cake is suitable for people with milk or lactose allergies; but if you are not lactose-intolerant, it is delicious served with whipped cream. SERVES 8 TO 10

6 pandan leaves, washed and roughly chopped

½ cup water, or more as needed

6 large eggs, separated, plus 3 large egg whites

1 cup sugar

½ cup vegetable oil

¾ cup coconut milk

2 teaspoons pandan extract

1¾ cups cake flour

2 teaspoons baking powder

¼ teaspoon salt

½ teaspoon cream of tartar

1. Adjust the oven rack to the middle position and preheat the oven to 350°F. Line the bottom of a 10-inch angel-food cake pan with parchment paper.

2. Place the chopped pandan leaves and water in a food processor. Blend until the leaves are pulverized, about 1 minute (add an extra tablespoon water if the mixture is too thick to blend). Strain the mixture though a fine-mesh sieve or cheesecloth, squeezing tightly to extract as much juice as possible. You should have at least 3 tablespoons juice.

3. In large bowl, whisk the 6 egg yolks with ½ cup of the sugar until very light, about 1 minute. Whisk in the oil until combined. Whisk in 3 tablespoons pandan juice, the coconut milk, and pandan extract until combined.

4. Sift the flour, baking powder, and salt into a medium bowl. Gently add the flour mixture to the pandan mixture and whisk until smooth.

5. In the bowl of a stand mixer fitted with the whisk attachment, beat the 9 egg whites on medium-low speed until frothy. Add the cream of tartar, raise the speed to medium, and continue to beat until the meringue begins to look opaque. Raise the speed to medium-high and slowly add the remaining ½ cup sugar. Continue to beat until the meringue reaches stiff but not dry peaks.

6. Fold one-third of the meringue into pandan batter until combined. Carefully fold in the remaining meringue in two stages until just combined, being careful to not deflate the meringue.

7. Pour the batter into the tube pan and bake until the cake is golden on top, set, and a long skewer inserted into the center comes out clean, about 45 minutes. Let cool completely in the pan, about 2 hours. Invert onto a serving plate to serve.

BANANA SPICE BREAD

When I was growing up, we had many varieties of banana trees in our backyard. Despite the abundance of fresh tree-ripened bananas, I rarely ate them just for snacking. My mother would send my brother and me off to school with a ripe banana in our lunch boxes every day and we would eat everything except the banana. My mother would make such a fuss about it. But after a week, my brother and I would have enough overripened blackened bananas for my mother to make this delicious banana bread, which of course was our very intention! Her recipe, featuring sweet chunks of rich dark palm sugar and hints of nutmeg and clove in each bite, is light and moist. Palm sugar comes in block form when you first purchase it (see pages 315–316 for more information). I use a sharp knife to slice it into very fine slices. You can also microwave it for easier slicing. These slices of palm sugar lend a delicious depth, sweetness, and richness, but you can certainly use dark brown sugar as an alternative.

SERVES 12

1¾ cups all-purpose flour

⅓ cup granulated sugar

1 teaspoon baking powder

½ teaspoon baking soda

½ teaspoon salt

½ teaspoon freshly grated nutmeg

¼ teaspoon ground cinnamon

¼ teaspoon ground cloves

5 large overripe bananas, peeled and cut in half; plus optional 1 banana, peeled and thinly sliced

8 ounces (2 sticks) butter, melted

2 large eggs

6 ounces palm sugar, grated or finely sliced; or ¾ cup packed dark brown sugar

1 teaspoon vanilla extract

⅓ cup whole milk

1. Preheat the oven to 350°F. Line a 9-inch square pan with parchment paper.

2. Combine the flour, granulated sugar, baking powder, baking soda, salt, cinnamon, nutmeg, and cloves in a large bowl and mix well.

3. Place the halved bananas in a large bowl and mash with a potato masher until soft and broken down. Add the melted butter, eggs, palm sugar, and vanilla and continue to mash until the mixture is very smooth and liquidy. Pour in the milk and mix well to combine.

4. Sift the dry ingredients into the banana mixture and stir well until combined with no lumps.

5. Pour the batter into the lined pan. If you like, arrange the additional sliced banana neatly in the center in one straight line on top of the batter. Bake until a wooden skewer inserted in the center comes out clean, about 60 minutes. Let the banana bread cool in the pan for 15 minutes before slicing. Serve warm.

MANGO-RASPBERRY BAVAROIS

Who could have predicted that Bavarian cream would taste like this when made with Asian ingredients? Whenever I serve it to my friends, it never fails to impress. It has a texture somewhere between a mousse and a panna cotta, and the combination of raspberries with pure mango nectar is divine! Making it is easy but success lies in the ingredients: I use pure Alphonso mango pulp, which comes in a can and is sold at most Indian grocery stores, for an intense mango taste. Mango pulp is also what most Indian restaurants use to make the famous yogurt drink lassi.

The successful preparation of this dish depends on two things. First, use easy-to-dissolve powdered gelatin rather than the clear strips of agar agar, which are more difficult to measure. Second, make sure the cream is properly whipped, until it is light, smooth, and airy. The lighter the cream, the more delicate the dessert. You might also try variations of other sweetened tropical fruit pulp such as guava nectar, hibiscus conserve, or passion fruit nectar, which are available online or at Asian and Mexican grocers. I would advise you to make a double batch, because this Bavarois will be quickly gone. SERVES 6

1¼ cups whole milk

1½ cups canned Alphonso mango pulp

2 tablespoons sugar

1 large egg

3 large egg yolks

1 cup fresh raspberries

2 teaspoons powdered gelatin

1 cup heavy cream

1. Combine the milk, mango pulp, and sugar in a saucepan and bring just to a boil, stirring.

2. Meanwhile, combine the egg and egg yolks in a glass bowl and whisk until light and fluffy.

3. Gradually pour the hot mango-milk mixture over the eggs, stirring constantly. Pour the mixture back into the saucepan and return just to a boil. Add the raspberries and stir well to combine. Remove from the heat.

4. Sprinkle the gelatin over the hot mango mixture and mix once. Let sit until the gelatin expands for a minute. Let cool without stirring.

5. Meanwhile, whip the cream until light and firm.

6. Fold the whipped cream into the cooled mango mixture. Ladle into six 4-ounce ramekins. Cover and refrigerate for at least 5 hours to set before serving.

JACKFRUIT CLAFOUTIS

Clafoutis is a French dessert traditionally made with black cherries. I have given it a tropical twist by using coconut cream and sweet canned jackfruit. In the United States, you can sometimes find fresh jackfruits sold alongside other tropical fruits, but the canned version is better for the clafoutis because it is easier to cook with and sweeter—perfect for desserts. You can find cans of jackfruit with other baking items in Asian supermarkets. Jackfruit, indigenous to Southeast Asia, is the largest tree fruit in the world. Some, like the ones in my yard in Malaysia, can weigh as much as 100 pounds. The treasure lies when you cut into the large outer shell to obtain many small, pale yellow fruits with a sweet custard-like taste. In this recipe, the pieces of jackfruit are surrounded by a coconut-cream batter enhanced with a dash of rum. The jackfruit becomes even sweeter and more tender after baking. SERVES 4

1 cup heavy cream

½ cup coconut cream

1 vanilla bean

3 large eggs

¼ cup plus 2 tablespoons sugar

½ cup all-purpose flour

1 tablespoon rum

1 can (20 ounces) jackfruit in syrup, fruit sliced into 1-inch pieces, 3 tablespoons of the jackfruit syrup reserved

1. Preheat the oven to 350°F.

2. Combine the heavy cream and coconut cream in a saucepan. Split the vanilla bean in half lengthwise, then scrape out the seeds with the tip of a knife and add both seeds and bean pod to the cream mixture. Bring the mixture to just a boil over low heat.

3. Meanwhile, in a glass bowl, mix together the eggs, sugar, and flour and whisk until light and fluffy.

4. Once the cream comes just to a boil, remove the vanilla bean pods. Add the rum. Gradually pour the hot cream into the egg mixture, stirring constantly. Add the jackfruit and the reserved jackfruit syrup and mix well.

5. Pour the mixture into a 9-inch pie pan. Bake until golden on the top, about 40 minutes. Serve warm.

SWEET CORN PUDDING WITH COCONUT CREAM TOPPING

This famous dessert originates from the *babas* (men) and *nyonyas* (women) of Malacca, who are descendants of inter-marriages between Chinese traders and Malay women. Even now, whenever I visit my friend's home in Malacca, I excitedly wait for the *Baba kuih man,* "Baba cake man," to pass the house every afternoon, lugging his old black and red lacquered basket laden with Nyonya desserts under the scorching sun. His specialty is corn pudding topped with cream and artistically wrapped in banana leaf. (In Malaysia, corn is considered a dessert ingredient rather than a vegetable.) I have created this simple recipe from memory, using sweet creamed corn. Enjoy it with a cup of black coffee. SERVES 6

SWEET CORN PUDDING

- 1 can (14 ounces) creamed sweet corn
- ¼ cup rice flour
- ½ cup sugar
- 1¼ cups water

COCONUT CREAM TOPPING

- 1½ cups coconut cream
- ½ cup water
- 2 tablespoons rice flour
- 1½ tablespoons sugar
- 1 teaspoon salt

1. Make the sweet corn pudding: Combine all the ingredients in a wok over medium heat. Cook, stirring to prevent the mixture from burning on the bottom of the wok, until the mixture thickens, about 20 minutes. The mixture should have a smooth consistency, with pieces of corn in it.

2. Spoon the mixture into 6 small bowls or 6-ounce ramekins, filling them only halfway and leaving space for the coconut cream topping. Set aside.

3. Make the cream topping: Wash the same wok and return it to the stove over medium heat. Combine all the topping ingredients in the wok and cook, stirring constantly, until thickened, about 15 minutes. The coconut cream mixture should be fragrant, slightly sweet, and thick in consistency, and it should easily coat the back of a spoon.

4. Spoon the coconut cream mixture to top the pudding in the bowls or ramekins. I recommend serving the pudding warm. If you prefer cold pudding, refrigerate for at least 4 hours and then serve cold.

COCONUT-BANANA SPONGE CAKE

Baby bananas, which you may occasionally find at supermarkets, are is sweeter than average, it is good for baking into breads or cakes, like this sponge cake. What is really nice and distinctive about the cake is that, unlike banana bread and some other banana cakes, the bananas are in a layer on top of the cake rather than mixed into the batter. There is no butter in the light-textured cake; the lightness is created by folding egg whites into the batter. Because of bananas' natural sweetness, children love this cake and every time I make it, there are hardly any leftovers. SERVES 6

6 baby bananas or 2 large bananas, peeled and thinly sliced on the diagonal

3 tablespoons dark brown sugar

3 large eggs, separated

⅓ cup ice water

¾ cup plus 2 tablespoons granulated sugar

½ teaspoon coconut extract

¾ cup plus 2 tablespoons sifted cake flour

½ teaspoon baking powder

⅛ teaspoon (a pinch) salt

½ teaspoon cream of tartar

1. Preheat the oven to 350°F. Generously butter the bottom of a 9-inch round cake pan. Cut a circle of waxed paper, place it on the bottom of the pan, and butter the waxed paper again. (This will help to caramelize the bananas as the cake bakes.)

2. Arrange the banana slices on the bottom of the cake pan, then sprinkle the brown sugar over them.

3. Beat the egg yolks in a large mixing bowl until thick and lemon-colored. Gradually add the ice water, beating constantly until the mixture is pale and foamy. Gradually add the granulated sugar and beat until completely dissolved. Blend in the coconut extract.

4. Sift together the flour, baking powder, and salt in a medium bowl. Resift the flour over the yolk mixture in two additions, folding gently until completely incorporated.

5. In a clean mixing bowl with clean beaters, beat the egg whites with the cream of tartar until stiff but not dry. Gently fold the whites into the yolk mixture. Carefully pour the batter over the bananas in the cake pan and smooth the top.

6. Bake until the cake springs back when lightly touched, about 25 minutes; do not overbake!

7. Let the cake cool in the pan for about 10 minutes. Turn out onto a rack, banana-side up, and carefully remove the waxed paper. Transfer the cake to a plate for serving. Any leftover cake can be covered and kept in the refrigerator for 2 to 3 days.

CHOCOLATE-CINNAMON CHEESECAKE

I like to have friends over for tea in the garden in the cool summer afternoon, especially when the roses are fully in bloom. We drink Earl Grey tea by the potful and enjoy it with cake. Most of my friends expect a Malaysian-inspired dessert to make the tea party complete. Of course, I am happy to do so whenever the occasion calls for it. My best-kept secret, however, is this cheesecake. It is my late mother-in-law's old-fashioned German cheesecake recipe, and I've been making it for ages. But, of course, I give it a twist by swirling in a cinnamon-chocolate topping, the way chocolate is served in Malaysia. I also make the crust using my favorite childhood digestive biscuit. A quintessential British cookie that is also widely available in the U.S., digestive "biscuits" are round with a crumbly texture and sweet nutty taste. They were originally made in factories as a portable snack in Britain to provide workers travelling on the railway a complement to their tea. In this recipe, adding cornstarch to the filling prevents the cheesecake from cracking and also makes it easier to cut it into clean slices. Even with many other choices on the table for tea, the cheesecake never fails to inspire plenty of second helpings and is the first to go. SERVES 8 TO 10

CRUST

12 digestive biscuits or 9 sheets (1 pack) graham crackers

3 tablespoons butter, melted

FILLING

1 pound ricotta cheese

1 pound (two 8-ounce packages) cream cheese

1½ cups sugar

4 eggs, slightly beaten

⅓ cup cornstarch

2 tablespoons lemon juice

1½ teaspoons vanilla extract

½ cup (1 stick) butter, melted

2 cups sour cream

6 ounces good-quality chocolate

1 teaspoon ground cinnamon

1. Adjust the oven rack to the middle position and preheat the oven to 325°F. Wrap a 10-inch springform pan with aluminum foil to prevent water from seeping in during baking. Grease the pan. Put a kettle on to boil.

2. Make the crust: Process the digestive biscuits into crumbs in a food processor. You should have 1¾ cups crumbs. Stir in the melted butter. Mix well, then press the mixture onto the bottom of the springform pan.

3. Make the filling: In a large mixing bowl, beat the ricotta, cream cheese, sugar, and eggs on medium-high speed until combined and

smooth, about 3 minutes. Reduce the speed to low and add the cornstarch, lemon juice, vanilla, and butter and mix until well blended. Now add the sour cream and continue to mix for 1 to 2 minutes more. Pour the mixture on top of the crust.

4. Melt the chocolate in a double boiler (a small pot or bowl set over a saucepan of simmering water). Once the chocolate is melted, add the cinnamon and mix well to combine. Using a teaspoon, drizzle the melted chocolate in a thin stream over the cheesecake filling. Using the handle of the teaspoon, swirl the two mixtures to create a marbled effect.

5. Place the cheesecake into the center of a roasting pan. Carefully pour enough boiling water from the kettle into the pan to reach halfway up the side of the springform pan. Be careful not to splash water on the cheesecake batter. Bake for about 1 hour 20 minutes. The cake is done when it pulls away from the sides of the pan and, when you tap the side of the springform pan with a spoon, the center jiggles slightly. Remove the cake to a wire rack to cool completely. Refrigerate uncovered for at least 4 hours before removing the cake from the pan and serving.

PALM SUGAR

The taste of palm sugar is velvety smooth and well-balanced, with notes of light caramel and floral honey blossom combined. Known as *gula melaka* in Malaysia, *gula jawa* in Indonesia, and *jaggery* in Sri Lanka, palm sugar has many roles in cooking, quite apart from its sweetness. Even the spiciest chili dish will lose some of its intensity with the addition of palm sugar, and it is a useful balancing agent in Southeast Asian salad dressings because of its capacity to complement a multitude of flavors.

Manufacturing palm sugar is still very much a cottage industry throughout Southeast Asia. The palm tree (*Arenga pinnata*) and the atta palm (*Nypa fruticans*) are the two species of palms grown specifically for their sweet sap. Sap extraction usually starts when the tree is quite young, perhaps three or four years, and is a process similar to the harvesting of maple syrup. The sugar palm farmer usually empties a gallon-size container once a day, though it could be up to twice a day during the most productive phase.

The sap needs to be collected before the flower opens. In order to prevent the blossoming, the flower is closed with a strong fiber. The flow of the sap is then brought out by tapping the flower stalk with a stick, which causes enough cell damage to bring the sap to that stalk. After a few weeks, the tip of the stalk is cut, and a bucket is hung below to collect the sap.

Every day, the farmer has to climb the tree with great agility to recut the surface so the sap can ooze out unhampered. In the tropical heat, the whitish sap starts to ferment within a few hours, so processing has to begin right away. The sap is first strained, then boiled for four to five hours in a huge wok until the liquid thickens. To test whether the sap has boiled long enough, a drop of the sap is placed into water. If it solidifies, it is ready. The syrup, which should now be thick and golden, is poured into another wok and stirred with a wooden paddle until it starts to caramelize. Finally, the cooked palm sugar is poured into small molds or vertical bamboo canes, which are then lifted out of the sugar once it has hardened.

There are so many wonderful ways to use palm sugar, but before you begin, let's go shopping. You will notice that palm sugar sold mostly in Asian supermarkets and online in the United States comes hardened in either large 2-pound jars, as a 17-ounce block, or in plastic packets of several small discs packed together.

Palm sugar is very hard in its solid form and difficult to shave or cut even with the sharpest knife. Instead, I prefer to dissolve palm sugar in water until it melts into a syrup. This syrup is also an effective way of storing palm sugar. In recipes throughout the book I refer to this as **liquid palm sugar** (it's also known as melted palm sugar).

Here's how to liquefy palm sugar:

Place the entire 17-ounce block of palm sugar in a small pot with 1 cup water and bring to a boil over medium heat without stirring. After about 20 minutes, the sugar should be completely melted. Do not stir the sugar while it is boiling or it will harden again when cooled. When the palm sugar is completely melted, you will see large bubbles appearing on the surface and the sugar will appear thicker. Let it cool before pouring it into a glass jar. I store mine in a ceramic jar. Place the cooled melted sugar in the refrigerator. Once refrigerated, the sugar will have a consistency of a syrup similar to maple syrup and will keep for up to 3 months, or 6 months in the freezer.

Palm sugar is added to salads to balance the dressing, especially to cut vinegars; to soups, curries, and stir-fry dishes; to desserts and cakes; and is delicious in coffee.

Palm sugar is natural and not highly processed like brown sugar. Muscovado or dark brown sugar is an acceptable substitute although it will not have the smooth body, delicateness, and floral aroma.

Palm sugar has been promoted as a healthful alternative to refined cane sugar. There are definitely benefits to palm sugar, including the presence of minerals and fiber and a lower glycemic index (indicating that sugars from palm sugar are absorbed into the bloodstream more slowly). However, palm sugar is still sugar and you shouldn't overdo it with any sugar.

Palm sugar is not to be confused with coconut palm sugar, which seems to be gaining popularity in the market. Manufacturers of coconut palm sugar boast of its low glycemic index, claiming it is a better choice for people with diabetes than regular sugar. Coconut sugar comes from the buds of coconut tree flowers, while palm sugar is made from the sap of the sugar palm tree.

CRÈME CARAMEL WITH STAR ANISE AND CINNAMON

One of the most beloved dishes of the Portuguese colonists in Malacca is this crème caramel. At Little Lisbon square in Malacca, spices are combined with palm sugar instead of regular white granulated sugar, resulting in a caramel with a dark, rich, complex flavor with subtle hints of star anise and cinnamon infused into each bite. You might also want to try adding fragrant spices such as cardamom, cloves, ginger, or pepper to the caramel. Or add new essences to the custard such as jasmine, coconut, or passion fruit extract. SERVES 4

CARAMEL

- ½ cup water
- 8 ounces palm sugar, chopped; or 1 cup packed dark brown sugar
- 3 whole star anise
- 2 cinnamon sticks

CUSTARD

- 3 cups whole milk
- 2 vanilla beans
- 1 large egg
- 5 large egg yolks
- ¼ cup granulated sugar

1. Make the caramel: Combine the water, palm sugar, star anise, and cinnamon in a medium heavy-bottomed saucepan over medium heat. Allow the sugar to simmer until completely melted, stirring occasionally. Discard the star anise and cinnamon.

2. Immediately pour about 2 tablespoons of caramel sugar into each of four 6-ounce rame-kins. Tilt each ramekin to coat the bottom. Place the ramekins in a baking pan.

3. Preheat the oven to 350°F and put a kettle on to boil.

4. Make the custard: Put the milk in a medium saucepan. Using a paring knife, split the vanilla beans in half lengthwise, scrape out the seeds, then add both seeds and bean pod to the milk. Bring the milk just to a boil and then reduce the heat to low.

5. Whisk the egg, egg yolks, and granulated sugar in a large bowl until light and frothy. Pour the hot milk mixture slowly into the eggs, whisking constantly.

6. Strain the custard through a fine-mesh strainer into a large measuring cup. Very gently (to prevent the caramel from moving) pour the mixture into the caramel-coated ramekins. Pour enough boiling water into the baking pan to reach halfway up the sides of the ramekins.

7. Bake for about 40 minutes, until the custards are firm to the touch. Let the custards cool in the baking pan. Serve warm or refrigerate for at least 4 hours and serve cold. Before serving, run a small knife around the edge of each custard and invert onto a plate.

SWEET POTATO DOUGHNUTS WITH PALM SUGAR CARAMEL
KUIH KERIA

For me, one of the most exciting culinary experiences is visiting a residential market or road-side vendor around 4 p.m., when these delightful Malaysian pastries are served as a teatime or mid-afternoon snack. Resembling mini-doughnuts, they are much easier to make at home than a traditional wheat-based doughnut because they are not yeasted. The charming snacks are basically pureed sweet potatoes that are mixed with flour, then formed by hand into plump rings and fried until golden brown. Their subtle sweetness is enhanced when dipped in a glaze of palm sugar caramel but you could just eat the doughnuts plain if you like. The doughnuts are best eaten on the same day. You can make them gluten-free by replacing the all-purpose flour with rice flour. MAKES 12 DOUGHNUTS

DOUGHNUTS

About 1 pound yellow- or orange-fleshed sweet potatoes, scrubbed clean

1 cup plus 2 tablespoons all-purpose flour

½ teaspoon baking powder

About 2 cups canola oil, for frying

CARAMEL

8 ounces palm sugar, chopped

½ cup water

1. Make the doughnuts: Place the sweet potatoes in a pan and cover generously with water. Boil over medium heat until tender, about 20 minutes; a bamboo skewer inserted into the thickest part of a potato should go through without resistance. Remove the sweet potatoes from the water and let cool.

2. When the sweet potatoes are cool enough to handle, peel off the skins. Pick out any tough fibers and discard. Use a potato masher to mash until smooth and free of lumps.

3. Combine the flour and baking powder in a large bowl and mix well. Add the mashed sweet potatoes and knead into a smooth dough. Dust some flour on your hands to prevent the dough from sticking and take a small piece of dough (about the size of a lime) and roll it into a smooth ball in your palms. Flatten the ball slightly and make a hole in the center with your finger or a floured wooden spoon handle. Using your fingers, lightly pat the outer edges and the edges around the hole to form a smooth round doughnut. Repeat with the rest of the dough, placing the doughnuts on a clean cloth on a cutting board or tray until ready to fry.

4. Heat about 2 inches oil in a small wok or pan over medium heat. Carefully place three doughnuts at a time into the wok, reduce the heat to medium-low, and fry until golden underneath, then flip and continue to fry until golden brown, about 7 minutes total. Drain on a paper towel–lined plate. Repeat until all the doughnuts are cooked. Let the doughnuts cool completely (or else they won't coat well).

5. Make the caramel: Bring the palm sugar and water to a rapid boil in a small wok or saucepan over medium heat until the sugar is completely melted, about 10 minutes. Then continue to simmer until the sugar thickens to a caramel-like consistency, about 5 minutes.

6. Dip the cooled doughnuts into the palm syrup, tossing them quickly to coat before the sugar hardens. Serve immediately.

GOLDEN MILK

This healing golden milk is my must-have breakfast treat for health and vitality. The milk is infused with turmeric spice, which creates a vibrant, golden-orange color. The turmeric and cinnamon infuse their savory, sweet, and ginger-like flavor that is simply comforting. Turmeric, the root of the *Curcuma longa* plant, has so many amazing health properties, particularly fighting against oxidation and inflammation, and potentially protecting against heart disease and cancer (see page 266 for more on turmeric's health benefits).

SERVES 2

2 cups unsweetened almond milk or whole milk

1 teaspoon ground turmeric

½ teaspoon ground cinnamon

1 teaspoon raw honey, or to taste

1. In a small pot, bring the milk to a soft boil without allowing it to boil over.

2. Whisk the turmeric and cinnamon into the milk and simmer for about 2 minutes in order for the turmeric to be properly combined with the milk. Remove from the heat, add the honey, and whisk until frothy. Pour into mugs and drink hot or warm.

SWEET POTATO AND TAPIOCA PUDDING

BUBUR CHA CHA

This porridge, called *bubur* and made of sweet potatoes and tiny pearl tapioca in warm coconut milk, is enjoyed as a sweet breakfast back home, but is also a soothing dessert after a spicy meal. When the coconut cream is combined with the sweet potatoes simmering in water, it thins out the cream into a milk-like consistency and the flavors blend beautifully. I like to use a combination of Japanese yams and regular sweet potatoes, and sometimes even taro or dark orange yams when I find them in stores. Each variety brings out a different sort of sweetness and texture, making the pudding constantly variable. SERVES 4 TO 6

1 small Japanese yam, peeled and cut into ½-inch cubes, rinsed well

1 small sweet potato, peeled and cut into ½-inch cubes, rinsed well

3 pandan leaves, washed and tied into a knot

3 cups water

1 cup coconut cream

½ cup sugar

Pinch of salt

¼ cup pearl tapioca

1 ripe banana, peeled and sliced into half-inch rounds

1. Place the yam and sweet potato in a medium saucepan with the pandan leaves and water and bring to a boil. Reduce the heat to medium and cook until the yam and sweet potato are tender, about 20 minutes.

2. Combine the coconut cream, sugar, and salt in a bowl and mix well, then pour the mixture into the pan and give it a good stir. Reduce the heat to low and simmer for about 10 minutes.

3. Gently wash the tapioca in a sieve under slow-running water and then add to the pot. Now add the sliced banana and simmer until the tapioca is clear and transparent, about 10 minutes. Mix well, raise the heat, and bring to a boil. Remove from the heat and serve hot or refrigerate for at least 4 hours and serve cold.

MANGO-CARDAMOM KULFI

Somewhere between a sorbet and an ice cream, *kulfi* is an Indian-inspired dessert that is typically served as a nice way to cool off the palate after a meal of hot curry. For this recipe, you will need to use canned Alphonso mango pulp, which you can find at Indian groceries and online. Most cans of mango pulp are already sweetened, so you need very little added sugar. For that reason, I use palm sugar, as it has a more subtle flavor than white granulated sugar. Kulfi tastes best when allowed to sit for about 5 minutes right from the freezer before serving; this allows the flavors to be concentrated and softens the texture a little. You can also use this recipe to make ice cream in an ice cream maker. SERVES 6

¼ cup palm sugar

1½ cups canned Alphonso mango pulp

½ cup coconut cream

4 cardamom pods

1 cup heavy cream

1. Coarsely chop the palm sugar and microwave for 40 seconds just to soften it.

2. Combine the softened palm sugar, mango pulp, and coconut cream in a blender and process until smooth. Pour the contents into a large glass bowl.

3. Place the cardamom pods in a mortar and smash several times to reveal the black seeds. Discard the green outer pods, leaving the black seeds in the mortar, then grind the seeds to powder.

4. Whip the cream until it forms stiff peaks. Fold the whipped cream into the mango mixture. Sprinkle in the ground cardamom and mix well.

5. Pour the mixture into a metal loaf pan (or, for individual servings, pour into small ceramic bowls). Cover tightly with foil and freeze until set, at least 6 hours, or up to 24 hours. Remove the kulfi from the freezer about 5 minutes before serving to soften it.

Clockwise from top left: Lychee-Strawberry Sorbet (page 325), Mango-Cardamom Kulfi, and Coconut and Nutmeg Kulfi (page 324)

COCONUT AND NUTMEG KULFI

As you stroll along the old bustling Chowrasta market in Penang, you will find rows upon rows of sundry nutmeg and mace products, as well as the dishes laced with these spices, including nutmeg pickles, dried sweet nutmeg candy, and nutmeg juice, which is a refreshing antidote to heat and humidity. Native to the Banda Islands in present-day Indonesia, nutmeg trees were cultivated in Penang in the late 18th century by the British East India Company as a way to expand their lucrative spice trade and compete with the Dutch, who had conquered Indonesia. This kulfi, a frozen dessert similar to ice cream, is one of my favorite ways to feature the tingling addition of nutmeg; be sure to use freshly grated whole nutmeg. SERVES 6

2 cups coconut cream

⅔ cup sweetened condensed milk

½ cup coconut milk

¼ cup sugar

6 pandan leaves, washed and tied into a knot

⅓ cup unsweetened shredded coconut

1 teaspoon freshly grated nutmeg

1. Combine the coconut cream, condensed milk, coconut milk, sugar, pandan leaves, and coconut in a saucepan over medium heat, stir well, and bring just to a soft boil.

2. Turn off the heat, add the nutmeg, and mix well. Allow the mixture to steep until it reaches room temperature. Remove the pandan leaves and discard.

3. Pour the mixture into a metal loaf pan (or, for individual servings, pour into small ceramic bowls). Cover tightly with foil and freeze until set, at least 6 hours, or up to 24 hours. Remove the kulfi from the freezer about 5 minutes before serving, just to soften it.

LYCHEE-STRAWBERRY SORBET

In Malaysia, lychee lemonades are a very popular drink accompanying dinner at restaurants, and I had that drink in mind when I created this sorbet. Fresh lychee fruit is one of my favorite summer flavors, but lychees can be difficult to find the rest of the year, and fresh ones can be extremely costly in the United States. So I use canned lychees, which are readily available, and combine them with strawberries, mint, and lemon in a blender to create a simply refreshing, fruity, and fun sorbet. Canned lychees come with a syrup, which makes them ideal for sorbet and means you do not need any extra sugar. I always have this sorbet in my freezer as it delightfully complements any main course in this book. SERVES 6

1 can (20 ounces) lychee in syrup, undrained
1½ cups fresh mint leaves (from 1 bunch)
4 strawberries
Juice of 1 lemon

Place all the ingredients in a blender and process on the highest speed until smooth and liquid. Pour into a plastic freezer container or loaf pan, cover, and place in the freezer. Stir with a whisk after 2 hours to break up the ice crystals for a smooth texture. Freeze overnight, covered with foil. Alternatively, churn the mixture in an ice cream maker following the manufacturer's instructions. Keep in the freezer until ready to serve. Let sit at room temperature for about 5 minutes before serving.

PANDAN–COCONUT CUSTARD CAKE

At mid-afternoon, women throughout Malaysia gather around the sweets vendor to purchase a few pieces of *kuih bakar pandan*, which features a thin golden crust with sprinkles of sesame seeds and a delicate custard inside replete with the fragrance of pandan, for a snack with Earl Grey tea. The trick is to find a reputable vendor who has been making this cake for ages and will not be stingy about using quality ingredients. Here is my perfect no-fail recipe for a cake worthy of challenging the best street vendor in Malaysia. MAKES 9 SQUARES

8 pandan leaves, washed and cut into ½-inch pieces

1 cup water

3 eggs

¾ cup plus 1 tablespoon sugar

¼ teaspoon salt

1¼ cups coconut cream

½ cup plus 3 tablespoons all-purpose flour

2 drops pandan extract

3 tablespoons butter

1 tablespoon sesame seeds

1. Preheat the oven to 350°F.

2. Put the pandan leaves and water in a blender and blend until liquid. The leaves will still appear chunky during blending; turn off the blender and push the leaves down using a spatula every so often to pulverize the leaves. Strain the pandan juice through a sieve or use your hands to squeeze out as much juice as you can from the leaves. Set the juice aside and discard the leaves.

3. Using an electric mixer, beat the eggs, sugar, and salt in a bowl on high speed until light and frothy. Add the coconut cream and continue to beat until well combined, about 1 minute. Reduce the speed of the mixer to low and slowly add the flour until the batter is well combined and smooth, 3 to 5 minutes.

4. Add the pandan juice and the pandan extract and beat for another minute, until the liquid is well combined into the batter.

5. Put the butter in a 6-inch square cake pan and heat it in the preheated oven for 1 to 2 minutes, until the butter is completely melted. Immediately remove the pan from the oven and swirl the butter to coat all corners and sides of the pan. You can use a pastry brush, working quickly, to brush the sides of the pan while the butter is still hot and melted. This step is necessary to provide the delicious brown crust. Pour the batter into the hot pan and sprinkle with the sesame seeds.

6. Bake for 30 minutes. Increase the oven temperature setting to 400°F and continue to bake until the cake is golden brown and crusty, about 15 minutes more. Test by inserting a toothpick in the center; it should come out clean. Allow the cake to cool completely before cutting into squares.

ACKNOWLEDGMENTS

I want to express my heartfelt gratitude to all who have helped me along the way.

To my literary agent, Joy Tutela, thank you for your fire, energy, and loyalty. We have travelled together on this journey for over a decade, and I thank you for believing in me.

To my editor, Stephanie Fletcher, thank you for your patience and understanding. Your advice, interest, and direction have brought out the best. You have made me a better writer.

To Adam Kowit for the title of this cookbook and for your enthusiasm in making this cookbook possible.

To all the people I have met who have come to love this cuisine through our experiences cooking and eating together, you have also been my teachers. Thank you for your curiosity and questions, allowing me to refine my efforts and share my passion with you.

I am constantly inspired by great writers and personal coaches whose words have influenced me, built and kept me going in my life through the wisdom of their words. In particular, my gratitude goes to John C. Maxwell for your leadership, to Neil Pasricha for reminding me to believe in happiness, and to Dr. Wayne W. Dyer for teaching me to value my inner creativity.

To ace photographer Penny De Los Santos, who came to Seattle to capture the food that I love and helped make this book beautiful. The meticulous eyes of her team members Karen Shinto and Anne Treanor Miska and their love helped style the dishes to become objects of art.

I'd also like to thank photographer David Hagerman for your stunning contribution, capturing the little towns in Malaysia through your evocative travel photos.

To Mufleh, thank you for your guidance.

To freelance proofreader Cliff Sloane, thank you for guiding my path to writing. Your contribution and knowledge has been invaluable to this book.

To Datuk Dr. Wong Lai Sum, former CEO of MATRADE (Malaysian External Trade Development Corporation). You certainly empowered me to share this cuisine with the people of the United States of America.

To Dr. Ted Clark, my partner, for encouraging me, supporting me from the very beginning of this project. Thank you for your unconditional love.

To my sons, Anton and Zachary, for appreciating and loving my cooking.

Above all, I give thanks to God for His endless gifts and allowing me to start and end my day with Him.

REFERENCES

Aggarwal, Bharat and Deborah Yost. *Healing Spices*. New York: Sterling Publications, 2011.

"Cinnamon." Accessed 01/13/2016. www.holisticonline.com/herbal-med/_Herbs/h196.htm

Drury, H.C. *The Useful Plants of India*. London: Allen, 1978.

Enig, Mary. *Know Your Fats: The Complete Premier for Understanding the Nutrition of Fats, Oils and Cholesterol*. Silver Spring, MD: Bethesda Press, 2000.

Fundukian, Laurie, ed. *The Gale Encyclopedia of Alternative Medicine, 3rd ed*. Detroit: Gale, 2009.

Hidaka, H., T. Ishiko and T. Furunashi. "Curcumin inhibits interleukin 8 production and enhances interleukin 8 receptor expression on the cell surface: impact on human pancreatic carcinoma cell growth by autocrine regulation." *Cancer* 96(6):1206–14, 2002.

Hirasa, Kenji and Mitsuo Takemasa, *Spice Science and Technology*. Tokyo: Marcel Dekker Inc., 1998.

Madar, Z., R. Abel and S. Samish. "Glucose-lowering effect of fenugreek in non-insulin dependent diabetics." *European Journal of Clinical Nutrition* 42:51–54, 1988.

Mallavarapu, G.R. and S. Ramesh. "Composition of essential oils of nutmeg and mace." *Journal of Medicinal and Aromatic Plant Sciences,* 20:746–8, 1998.

Meilink-Roelofsz, M.A.P. *Asian Trade and European Influence in the Indonesian Archipelago between 1500 and about 1630*. The Hague: Martinus Nijhoff, 1962.

Nagabhushan, M. and S.V. Bhide. "Curcumin as an inhibitor of cancer." *Journal of the American College of Nutrition* 11(2):192–8, 1992.

Olatunde, Oluwatosin, and Godwin. "Influence of chloramphenicol on rat hepatic microsomal components and biomarkers of oxidative stress: Protective role of antioxidants." *Pharmacological Toxicology* 91:129–134, 2002.

Peter, K.V., ed. *Handbook of Herbs and Spices*. London: Woodhead Press, 1998.

Pizzorno, Joseph Jr., and Michael Murray. *Textbook of Natural Medicine Second Edition*. St. Louis, MO: Elsevier Churchill and Livingstone, 2006.

Radhakrishna, P., A. Srivastava and T. Hassanein. "Induction of apoptosis in human lung cancer cells by curcumin." *Cancer Letters* 208: 163–170, 2004.

Shah, B.H., Z. Nawaz and S.A. Pertani. "Inhibitory effect of curcumin, a food spice from turmeric, on platelet- activating factor- and arachidonic acid-mediated platelet aggregation through inhibition of thromboxane formation and Ca2+ signa." *Biochemical Pharmacology* 58(7):1167–72, 1999.

Sharma, R.D., A. Sarkar and D.K. Hazra. "Use of fenugreek seed powder in the management of non-insulin dependent diabetes mellitus." *Nutritional Research* 16:1331–1339, 1996.

Sharma, R.D., T.C. Raghuram and N.S. Rao. "Effect of fenugreek seeds on blood glucose and serum lipids in type I diabetes." *European Journal of Clinical Nutrition* 44:301–306, 1990.

St-Onge, M.P. and P.J. Jones, "Physiological effects of medium-chain triglycerides: potential agents in the prevention of obesity." *Journal of Nutrition* 132(3):329–332, 2002.

Surh, Y.J., E. Lee and J.M. Lee. "Chemoprotective properties of some pungent ingredients present in red pepper and ginger." *Mutation Research* 402:259–267, 1998.

Thomson, M., K.K. Al-Qattan and S.M. Al-Sawan. "The use of ginger (Zingiber officinale Rosc.) as a potential anti-inflammatory and antithrombotic agent." *Journal of Natural Medicine* 67:457–478, 2002.

Toda, Miyase, and Arichi. "Natural antioxidants. Antioxidative components isolated from rhizome of Curcuma Longa L Chen." *Chemical and Pharmacological Bulletin* (Tokyo) 33:172–178, 1985.

"Trigonella foenum-graecum L" in Simon, J., A. Chadwick and L. Cracker. *Herbs: An Indexed Bibliography 1971-1980.* Hamden, CT: Archon Books, 1984.

Yeung, Him-Che. *Handbook of Chinese Herbs and Formulas.* Los Angeles: Institute of Chinese Medicine, 1985.

INDEX

Date Due